Binding, Finishing, and Mailing

Binding, Finishing, and Mailing: The Final Word

Second Edition

by
T.J. Tedesco, Dave Clossey, and Jean-Marie Hershey

with
- Marty Anson • Ken Boone • Fred Daubert
- Chris Eckhart • Barry Franklin • Dave Gischel
- Sue Hein • Brian Hills • Tony Hoholik
- Jeff Klein • Kris Koch • Sylvia Konkel
- Chuck Manthey • Gary Markovits • Jack Rickard
- Bruce Sanderson • Bill Seidl • Frank Shear
- John Snyder • Bob Windler

PIA/GATF*Press*
PITTSBURGH

PIA/GATF*Press*
Printing Industries of America/
  Graphic Arts Technical Foundation
200 Deer Run Road
Sewickley, PA 15143-2600
Phone: 412-741-6860
Fax: 412-741-2311
Email: AWoodall@piagatf.org
Internet: www.gain.net

Order to:
Online: www.gain.net
Mail: PIA/GATF Orders
200 Deer Run Road
Sewickley, PA 15143
Phone (U.S. and Canada): 866-855-4283
Phone (all other countries): 301-393-8624
Fax: 301-393-2555

Contents

This book is dedicated to

Peter "Cappy" Capodilupo,
English Teacher and Football Coach,
Newton North High School

...for contributions he doesn't know he made.

Foreword

The graphic arts industry has experienced tremendous change in the last quarter century. While the prepress and press areas have received the majority of the attention from the trade media, the bindery and finishing areas have gone largely unnoticed.

Despite the critical importance of the final stage in the printing process, bindery operations have remained the least understood and most underutilized aspect of printing.

What an irony it is that while the printed word remains the single greatest form of communication, the lack of clear communications has adversely affected the production process in the graphic arts industry.

But, as Bob Dylan said, "the times they are a-changing." Printers and customers are beginning to look at the versatility in the bindery and finishing areas and are relying more and more on the expertise offered by trade binders. They have the technical knowledge, equipment, and personnel required for the more complex jobs and can often produce results more quickly and efficiently than the larger printers who offer in-line finishing as part of their bindery process.

This publication, *Binding, Finishing, and Mailing: The Final Word, Second Edition,* is a valuable information resource about this important segment of the production process. It provides practical and concise information about binding and finishing.

Many of the contributors to this book are active members of the Binding Industries Association (BIA), which serves the binding and loose-leaf manufacturing industries. A special industry group of Printing Industries of America/Graphic Arts Technical Foundation, BIA is dedicated to educating its members and communicating the value and capabilities of the industry it represents. With close to two hundred members worldwide, BIA conducts an annual spring conference, and a fall program in conjunction with Graph Expo, in addition to publishing studies, surveys, special reports, newsletters, and other publications. BIA can be reached at 100 Daingerfield Road, Alexandria, VA 22314; 703-519-8137; bparrott@piagatf.org; website: www.gain.net, click on Special Interest Groups.

Beth Parrott
Program Manager
Binding Industries Association

Preface

Binding, Finishing, and Mailing: The Final Word will take readers through a comprehensive exploration of the world of binding, finishing, and mail preparation. Most major postpress processes will be discussed on two levels. First, each process will be examined within the context of the entire industry so graphic arts professionals can make useful recommendations to their customers. Viewed as part of a greater whole, each process will fit in the bigger picture of the graphic arts industry. Second, the minutiae of each, such as communication, layouts, and manufacturing performance expectations, will be explained so readers can more effectively manage their postpress projects.

This book will be helpful to people performing a variety of functions at graphic arts companies.

- Owners and top managers need information about industry trends and a broad overview of postpress services. Binding and finishing processes play major roles in a company's ability to compete in today's unforgiving graphic arts environment. Company leaders should first read this book themselves and then distribute copies throughout their organization.

- Customer service representatives, sales professionals, estimators, and production managers should embrace the concept of continual training for maximum job performance. Growth-oriented companies recognize that the training process never stops. This book explains binding and finishing processes in a way that should be accessible to lower-level professionals with virtually any graphic arts background. Binding and finishing knowledge is an under-represented skill set, and those with a good command of these processes stand apart from the crowd. A major goal of this book is to help people advance their graphic arts careers.

- Graphic designers and printing professionals need to know what's possible in the exciting arena of binding and finishing. When they don't, this lack of knowledge limits their job effectiveness and professional growth. Designers and printers should appreciate the down-to-earth descriptions of binding and finishing processes without being lost in overly technical descriptions. In short, they should discover new tools to help them create more effective designs.

- Bindery production employees need to know the right questions to ask. This book will help all bindery workers, either trade, in-house, or in-plant, know what is "normal" in the postpress industry. Even the most specialized bindery worker will benefit from learning how their skill set fits into an overall graphic arts framework.

T.J. Tedesco

Acknowledgments

Binding, Finishing, and Mailing: The Final Word, Second Edition wouldn't have been possible without the help, wisdom, and contributions from some very gifted people. The authors extend special thanks to the following individuals for their technical expertise, business experience, and willingness to share:

- Marty Anson, President, Bindagraphics, Inc., 2701 Wilmarco Ave., Baltimore, MD 21223. Marty can be reached at 800-326-0300 or marty@bindagraphics.com.

- Ken Boone, President (retired), Direct Marketing Associates, Baltimore, MD. Ken can be reached at 443-772-0922 or kboone@adipress.com.

- Fred Daubert, President, The Riverside Group, 655 Driving Park Ave., Rochester, NY 14613. Fred can be reached at 800-777-2463 or fredd@riversidegroup.com.

- Chris Eckhart, Co-Owner, Eckhart & Company, 4011 W. 54th St., Indianapolis, IN 46241. Chris can be reached at 800-443-3791 or chriseckhart@eckhartandco.com.

- Barry Franklin, General Manager, Vulcan Information Packaging, 1 Looseleaf Lane, Vincent, AL 35178. Barry can be reached at 800-633-4526 x230 or BFranklin@vip.EBSCO.com.

- Dave Gischel, Vice President, Victor Graphics, 1211 Bernard Dr., Baltimore, MD 21223. Dave can be reached at 410-233-8300 or dgischel@victorgraphics.com.

- Sue Hein, President, Rapid Bind, Inc. P.O. Box 42493, Portland, OR 97242-0493. Sue can be reached at 800-372-8715 or sue@rapidbind.com.

- Brian Hills, President, Nationwide Laminating, 8494 Terminal Rd, Lorton, VA 22079-1424. Brian can be reached at 800-322-5701 or brian@ nationwidelaminating.com.

- Tony Hoholik, Vice President Sales & Marketing, The John Roberts Company, 9687 East River Rd., Minneapolis, MN 55433. Tony can be reached at 800-551-1534 or thoholik@johnroberts.com.

- Jeff Klein, President, Spiral of Ohio, Inc., 5344 Bragg Rd., Cleveland, OH 44127. Jeff can be reached at 800-444-8826 or jklein@spiralohio.com.

- Kris Koch, President, Allied Bindery, 32451 N. Avis Dr., Madison Heights, MI 48071. Kris can be reached at 800-833-0151 or kris@alliedbindery.com.

- Sylvia Konkel, Vice President, Marketing, EU Services, 649 N. Horners Lane, Rockville, MD 20850. Sylvia can be reached at 800-230-3362 or SKonkel@euservices.com.

- Chuck Manthey, President, Sentinel Printing Company, 250 N. Hwy 10, St. Cloud, MN 56304. Chuck can be reached at 800-450-6434 or cmanthey@ sentinelprinting.com.

- Gary Markovits, President, E&M Bindery, 11 Peekay Dr., Clifton, NJ 07014. Gary can be reached at 800-736-2463 or gary@embindery.com.
- Joe Piazza, General Manager, Action Bindery, 6432 Warren Dr., Norcross, GA 30093. Joe can be reached at 888-337-2463 or joep@actionbindery.com.
- Jack Rickard, President, Rickard Bindery, 325 N. Ashland Ave., Chicago, IL 60607-1001. Jack can be reached at 800-747-1389 or jrickard@rickardbindery.com.
- Bruce Sanderson, Co-Owner, Springfield Printing Corporation, P.O. Box 19, Precision Dr., North Springfield, VT 05150. Bruce can be reached at 800-437-9244 or bruce@springfieldprinting.com.
- Bill Seidl, President, Seidl's Bindery, Inc., 8035 Blankenship, Houston, TX 77055. Bill can be reached at 800-380-3815 or bill@seidlsbindery.com.
- Frank Shear, President, Seaboard Bindery, 10 Linscott Rd., Woburn, MA 01801. Frank can be reached at 781-932-3908 or frank@seaboardbindery.com.
- Brenda Slacum, formerly Vice President, Freedom Finishing Solutions, Linthicum, MD 21090.
- John Snyder, President, HBP, P.O. Box 190, Hagerstown, MD 21741. John can be reached at 800-638-3508 or johns@hbp.com.
- Mike Welsch, President, Muscle Bound Bindery, 701 Plymouth Ave., Minneapolis, MN 55411. Mike can be reached at 612-522-4406 or mikew@mbbindery.com.
- Bob Windler, President, Diecrafters, Inc., 1349 South 55th Court, Cicero, IL 60804-1211. Bob can be reached at 708-656-3336 or BWindler@diecrafters.com.

*   *   *

In addition, significant contributions were received from:
- Mark Beard, President, Finishbinders, Inc., 1900 Delaware Ave., Des Moines, IA 50317. Mark can be reached at 888-788-7314 or mark@finishbinders.com.
- Jerry Bridges, National Sales Manager, Vulcan Information Packaging, 1 Looseleaf Lane, Vincent, AL 35178. Jerry can be reached at JBridges@Vulcan-Online.com.
- Mike Conlon, General Manager, Meredith Print Advantage, 1716 Locust St., Des Moines, IA 50309-3023. Mike can be reached at 515-284-3000 or Mike.Conlon@meredith.com.
- Jim Egan, Sales Manager, Rickard Bindery, 325 N. Ashland Ave., Chicago, IL 60607-1001. Jim can be reached at jegan@rickardbindery.com.
- Russ Haines, Vice President, Rapid Bind, Inc., P.O. Box 42493, Portland, OR 97242-0493. Russ can be reached at russ@rapidbind.com.
- John Helline, COO, Spiral of Ohio, Inc., 5344 Bragg Rd., Cleveland, OH 44127. John can be reached at jhelline@spiralohio.com.
- Gary Junge, Estimating Manager, Rickard Bindery, 325 N. Ashland Ave., Chicago, IL 60607-1001. Gary can be reached at gjunge@rickardbindery.com.

- John Leonard, Vice President, SMR/Tytrek, 201 Carlaw Ave., Toronto, ON, CANADA M4M 2S3. John can be reached at 416-461-9271 or jleonard@smrtytrek.com.
- Jeff Marr, Vice President, Colter-Peterson, 75 West Century Rd., Paramus, NJ 07652. Jeff can be reached at 800-932-0780 or jeff@colter-peterson.com.
- Ed Miller, President, K&W Finishing, Inc., 1207 Bernard Dr., Baltimore, MD 21223. Ed can be reached at 888-243-5266.
- Jerry Nocar, President, Advantage Book Binding, Inc., 85 Dover Rd., Glen Burnie, MD 21060-6507. Jerry can be reached at 800-762-0008 or jerry@advantagebookbinding.com.
- Peter Pape, Owner, The Riverside Group, 655 Driving Park Ave., Rochester, NY 14613. Peter can be reached at ppape@riversidegroup.com.
- Peggy Rhodes, Manager, Sperry Graphic, Inc., 4 Horne Dr., Folcroft, PA 19032. Peggy can be reached at 610-534-8585 or prhoades@sperrygraphic.com.
- Kevin Rickard, Vice President, Rickard Bindery, 325 N. Ashland Ave., Chicago, IL 60607-1001. Kevin can be reached at krickard@rickardbindery.com.
- Tom Ross, President, Ross Gage, Inc., 2323 N. Illinois St., Indianapolis, IN 46208. Tom can be reached at 317-283-2323 or tomross@rossgage.com.
- Rod Rothermel, President, Buchan Industries, Clifton Heights, PA. Rod can be reached at rodroth@aol.com.
- Joe Sferlazza, former Owner, S & F Graphic Finishers, Inc. Joe can be reached at 718-948-0647.
- Jim Shear, Vice President, Seaboard Bindery, 10 Linscott Rd., Woburn, MA 01801. Jim can be reached at jim@seaboardbindery.com.
- Art Simpson, President, EU Services, 649 N. Horners Lane, Rockville, MD 20850. Art can be reached at ASimpson@euservices.com.
- Charlie Smith, President, Smith Litho, 1029 E. Gude Dr., Rockville, MD 20850. Charlie can be reached at 800-622-2577 or CSmith@smith-litho.com.

*　　*　　*

Also, thanks go to the following people: Joe Anderson, John Beall, Lorraine Beard, Frank Cancro, Tim Carr, Ed Doyle, Dave Dunnett, Marty Durant, Bill Eckhart, Brent Eckhart, Norm Engelberg, Carmen Falibene, Jim Freisinger, John Goché, Bruce Heston, Reese Hicks, Mike Hill, Adam Jacobowitz, Mark Lee, Rick Maida, Bill Main, Tony Manna, T.J. Manning, Matthew McBride, Ria Merry, Tom Pflueger, Debbie Redditt, Mark Sanderson, Harold Shear, Bob Tier, Rob Tunney, Bill Ulrich, Adam Van Wye, Terry Woods, and Kathi Young.

If we've forgotten to mention anyone here, the oversight was unintentional.

All of these remarkable individuals are recognized leaders in their business niches and together have centuries of postpress knowledge.

*　　*　　*

Finally, appreciation needs to be extended to several publishing companies and individual publications for all their guidance, patience, and support throughout the years.

- *Advents* is a leading direct mail publication serving the Mid-Atlantic direct mail community and can be reached at 7702 Leesburg Pike, Tyson's Corner, VA 22043-2612, 703-590-9996. Special thanks go to Nancy Scott, Editor.

- *American Printer* is a leading publication serving the printing industry and is located at 29 N. Wacker Drive, Chicago, IL 60607, 312-726-2802. Special thanks go to Katherine O'Brien, Editorial Director.

- Cygnus Business Media, Inc., publishes *Print and Graphics, Printing Views, Southern Graphics, Printing Journal, Quick Printing,* and *Printing News.* Cygnus Business Media, Inc. is at 445 Broad Hollow Rd., Melville, NY 11747-4722, 800-447-4237. Special thanks go to David Lindsay, Editor-in-Chief.

- *DM News* is a leading publication serving the direct mail industry and is located at 100 Avenue of the Americas, New York, NY 10013, 212-925-7300. Thanks go to Scott Hovanyetz, Associate Editor.

- *Graphic Arts Monthly* is a leading publication serving the printing industry and is located at 345 Hudson St., New York, NY 10014, 212-519-7326. Thanks go to Roger Ynostroza, Editor-in-Chief.

- Innes Publishing Co. publishes *High Volume Printing, Instant & Small Commercial Printer,* and *In-Plant Printer.* Innes Publishing Co. can be reached at P.O. Box 7280, Libertyville, IL 60048, 847-816-7900. Special thanks go to Ray Roth, Editor-in-Chief, and Mary Ellin Innes, President.

- *Printing Impressions* is a leading publication serving the printing industry and is located at 401 N. Broad St., Philadelphia, PA 19108, 215-238-5300. Special thanks go to Mark Michelson, Editor-in-Chief.

Section I
Before Production

1 Postpress Knowledge Sells Printing

If you're in the graphic arts industry, you must earn your customers' trust and keep on earning it, job by job, day after day. Today's volatile and hyper-competitive business climate holds no guarantee of repeat business without complete customer satisfaction. Your postpress knowledge, presented in a proper way to your customers, can be a competitive advantage. This is what this book is all about.

What You Will Learn

- Why bindery, finishing, and mailing processes are important
- Add value to customers
- Information is everything

Buyers don't pass out opportunities to everyone who asks. Trust must be earned, an exemplary work history established. Those who possess and disburse useful information are more valuable than their less-inclined competitors.

Most credible printing professionals are knowledgeable about prepress and pressroom issues. Yet many of these same people don't know the basics of binding, finishing, and mailing, even though postpress operations frequently account for a significant percentage of a job's value. Yes, the ability to explain how ink is placed on paper is important, but how comfortable is a print buying prospect going to be when a print sales representative pitching for their business can't provide any significant guidance about the highly visible postpress aspects of a job?

Regardless of your job function within the graphic arts industry, it is worth your while to learn the basics of binding and finishing because this knowledge is an effective way to differentiate you and your company from the majority of your competitors. If you earn your livelihood from the postpress side of the business, your expertise will help you convert more prospects into customers, building loyalty every inch along the way.

Keep Information Flowing

In any industry, the most successful business people are those who ask the right questions. Good retail clothing sales clerks uncover unspoken needs, such as whether people buying dress shirts need matching neckwear. Successful salespeople in the automotive and real estate industries ask questions that flush out a prospect's needs, wants, and ability to pay. Similarly, competent graphic arts sales professionals inquire about a product's end use before submitting bids.

Sales professionals add value by offering solutions that fit the stated and unstated needs of print buyers. Salespeople who accept specifications without knowing the product's end use can't add value to the job planning process. Instead, they function merely as providers of commodity services. In this undifferentiated realm, jobs are awarded on price, rather than value. Value is a function of expertise, decision-making guidance, and the ability to produce what customers really need. Steven Covey says, "Begin with the end in mind." Let's follow his advice. Create value by starting with the end use and working backward. In short, let the tail wag the dog.

*　　*　　*

The Final Word...

Complete your graphic arts knowledge and learn about postpress functions. The people who come in contact with you will feel more comfortable and your industry "stock" will rise. Information is everything; give it freely, win trust, and increase business.

Contributors:

- *Chris Eckhart, Eckhart & Company, Indianapolis, Indiana*
  www.eckhartandco.com
- *Frank Shear, Seaboard Bindery, Woburn, Massachusetts*
  www.seaboardbindery.com
- *Bob Windler, Diecrafters, Inc., Chicago, Illinois*
  www.diecrafters.com

2 Mid-Decade Postpress Outlook

We've heard it all before: Printed products are bought and sold more and more on price. Low pricing has replaced quality and service as the chief motivator in many print purchasing decisions. We're a commodity. Let it suffice to say that the authors of this book don't agree. It is possible for finishers—and printers—to keep their margins at sustainable levels by adding compelling postpress sophistication.

What You Will Learn

- Demand is growing
- Equipment is available
- Outsourcing is efficient

Despite the increased pricing pressure and competition brought on from non-print forms of communication, there are plenty of money-making graphic arts projects available. The key is to explore outside your comfort zone. A project with an unusual size or shape, or one that requires a fair amount of finishing work, is often much more profitable than a simpler, less demanding one. Yes, these projects may require more effort to bring to life, but they are likely well worth it as measured on the bottom line.

Once considered a production afterthought, binding, finishing, and mailing operations have risen to the top of a short list of ways to achieve differentiation. Print is here to stay, but so are more stringent customer demands. Today's graphic arts landscape is often dictated by shorter runs, higher quality standards, and near-impossible turnaround times.

Let's consider the impact of the trend toward shorter production run lengths and their impact on the financial performance of postpress services companies. First, binderies that are able to change their machinery over from one job to the next faster than their competitors have a tangible competitive advantage, which can go a long way toward offsetting marketplace pricing pressure. Today's postpress services company must make every attempt to extract all production efficiencies, whether through retrofitted automation, new machinery, or better workflow design.

Second and less obvious is a potentially hidden benefit of shorter production lengths. Frequently, per-piece prices increase even as production volumes decline. Although not intuitively obvious, this is a trend which, if properly managed, can preserve bindery margins. Consider direct mail: With today's data mining techniques yielding better targeted and smaller mailing lists, direct mail designers are looking for more design effects that will allow their products to stand apart from crowded mail boxes— and most importantly, get opened. Better yet, they can afford it because smaller mailing lists mean less postage, which is a huge component of direct mail campaigns.

The bottom line for the postpress industry is that there is an opportunity to help their customers design "eye candy" using finishing techniques that increase a product's per-unit price and maintain production margins, even as the total finishing price is reduced.

How Has the Bindery Evolved?

A walk around the floor of any graphic arts trade show is instructive. Everywhere you turn, you'll see increasingly sophisticated examples of computer-driven automation. Productivity enhancements are multiplying at an astonishing rate.

A historical barrier to creative binding and finishing solutions has been longer-than-average job turnaround times. As postpress equipment gets faster, compressed schedules make unusual binding and finishing operations practical for a wider range of jobs. Until recently, much of our industry's major productivity and quality improvements have occurred in the prepress and pressroom arenas. However, bindery equipment manufacturers now understand that time- and labor-saving features, including automatic makereadies, smart pockets, and computerized on-the-fly adjustments, make good economic sense, especially for binderies and finishers with higher equipment utilization rates.

Today's big bindery lines—often comprised of multiple in-line bindery operations—are servomotor-driven and self-adjusting. Chains and drive shafts are beginning to disappear in favor of sprockets equipped with computer-driven, direct-drive servomotors.

Because fewer and fewer adjustments are being made manually, bindery operators can keep their wrenches in their pockets and their fingers on their keyboards. For example, late-model adhesive binding lines offer optical signature recognition sensors, automatic adjusting calipers, and programmable trimmers. While run speeds have increased somewhat, it is makeready speeds that have experienced the most dramatic improvements in productivity. It's now commonplace to program the next job while finishing the current run. In the 1980s, it would have taken an irate customer with a loaded shotgun to interrupt a long-run job. Thanks to improved automation, reduced makeready times, and a general willingness to meet the needs of demanding customers, today it's possible to simultaneously keep more adhesive binding customers happy than every before.

Similar advances are being made in saddle stitching, diecutting, case binding, mechanical binding, poly-bagging, and more. For example, when making pockets ready on an automated saddle stitching line, feeder adjustments and signature settings now move automatically. When it's time to set up the trimmer, size adjustments also are made automatically, enabling stitcher operators to remain hands-off and wrench-free. As a natural result of improvements in speed and automation, there has been a corresponding increase in quality consistency.

Flexible Specialization

The definition of a big inflexible bindery investment used to be an in-line purchase. But with flexible bindery components, in-line systems are both extremely productive on long-run jobs, yet flexible enough to handle short runs when necessary. Available now are folding systems that fold, apply remoistenable glue strips, punch/drill, start/stop perforate, and wrap, all in one tidy operation. But since they are comprised mostly of mobile components, they can be split up in a heartbeat. Today's blend of electronics and mechanics is very much like Java in the computer world, where everything can talk to everything else. Long-run efficiencies are being gained by stringing together equipment components in creative ways. Short-run efficiencies are being achieved with super-fast computer-assisted makereadies.

The Human Factor

From an occupational standpoint, all of this automation has been a boon to the typical bindery worker. People weren't designed to do the same things over and over. Repetitive motion disorders, back problems, and excessive sick days are less of a burden today than they used to be. Lifters, joggers, stackers, and conveyers are popping up all over progressive binderies, and we are seeing a corresponding reduction in injuries due to stooping, bending, and lifting. Safer operating environments lead to better productivity and more consistent quality.

Integrated Printing and Finishing JDF/CIP Workflows

Digital workflow standards are commonplace in technologically advanced commercial printing facilities. For printers with standardized workflows, such as the one offered by the CIP consortium at drupa 2000, there are numerous integration possibilities with the bindery, whether in-house or outsourced. Remarkable reductions in both production time and manufacturing costs, as well as a healthy increase in job yield, are achievable.

As of this writing, a wide array of CIP4-compatible finishing equipment is currently available. Binderies can be electronically linked to prepress and pressroom equipment, using the same files and specifications that drive these operations. So, as printing information is uploaded, the same can be true of folding, stitching, and other binding and finishing operations. This means that appropriately wired equipment can be automatically set up just before the job hits the bindery. Look for great progress in this exciting area in the very near future.

* * *

The Final Word...

Look at what technology has wrought: Labor costs go down but productivity goes up. Prices go down but capacity goes up. Quality improves. Today's competitive binderies now offer great quality and on-time delivery at fair prices. In addition, good binderies are becoming relationship oriented, placing the customer at the center of their decision-making processes. This will continue to drive the demand for bindery services and development of fast, efficient, automated responses to demand. In our estimation, the forecast for bindery service demand is optimistic. Binding and finishing growth means more competition, falling prices, shorter lead times, and ultimately a prolonged demand for bindery services.

Contributors:

- *Mark Beard, Finishbinders, Inc., Des Moines, Iowa*
  www.finishbinders.com

- *Barry Franklin, Vulcan Information Packaging, Vincent, Alabama*
  www.Vulcan-Online.com.

- *Jeff Klein, Spiral of Ohio, Inc., Cleveland, Ohio*
  www.spiralohio.com

- *Jack Rickard, Rickard Bindery, Chicago, Illinois*
  www.rickardbindery.com

- *Frank Shear, Seaboard Bindery, Woburn, Massachusetts*
  www.seaboardbindery.com

- *Charlie Smith, Smith Litho, Rockville, Maryland*
  www.smith-litho.com

3 Designers, Printers, and Finishers Should Talk

Over the years, the graphic arts industry has seen an influx of graphic designers who have spent their educational years so entrenched in computers that they have never learned how to incorporate traditional finishing techniques into their work. The "gulf" between designers and finishers still needs to be bridged.

What You Will Learn

- Close the "communication gap"
- The value of sharing information
- Create educational opportunities

Although the quality of most printing, including digital, has dramatically improved, there is still nothing like high-quality finishing techniques to complement even the most beautifully printed materials. Unfortunately, many designers immersed in the bits and bytes of computer-obsessed professional lives understand very little about enhancing their designs with finishing excellence.

The world of foil stamping, embossing, diecutting, UV coating, laminating, folding, binding, gluing, and other postpress processes is truly diverse. Creative use of these can greatly improve the effectiveness of a graphic arts project's impact. Each process can make the difference between merely good and truly great results. However, all require proper planning and coordination to ensure that the intended effect actually can be achieved on time and within budgetary constraints.

Cross-Purposes

When things go wrong, it's plain that binders and finishers are so removed from the design process that meaningful communication rarely takes place. If designers had the opportunity to come to the bindery, see techniques in motion and talk to a knowledgeable bindery representative, a lot of time, money, and miserable headaches could be saved. Every finisher who has been around for a while has dozens, if not hundreds, of these types of examples. For the good of the graphic arts industry, this communication "gap" between designer and finisher should be targeted for oblivion.

Narrowing the Communication Gap

How do we tighten this gap between designers and finishers? There is no easy answer, but there is room for progress on both sides. Designers, for example, should take advantage of educational opportunities offered at community colleges, associations, trade show seminars, and education-oriented postpress services companies.

To this last point, some enlightened trade finishing, binding, and mailing service providers offer valuable courses geared toward print designers as well as customer service representatives, estimators, and sales representatives. In many such hands-on educational environments, class attendees can walk from the classroom into the plant and observe theoretical concepts being transformed into reality right on the plant floor.

Designers who regularly design for print and who have encountered some frustration in the process should consider asking the leading finishing company in their area if they would offer training opportunities at a nominal fee, or even sponsor a design contest for graphic arts students. Such opportunities encourage the design community to take advantage of the rich diversity of the finishing industry. The logic is simple and irresistible: two-way communication improves the industry.

*   *   *

The Final Word...

It seems incredible, but some print professionals will freely admit that they don't recommend certain finishing techniques because they don't understand the relevant processes. This blasé attitude cheats the customer of options, while the print provider loses precious value-added sales opportunities. Every designer and printer should accumulate useful finishing knowledge. How can you plan properly if you don't even know what you're planning? Remember: information is the currency of progressive customer relationship management.

Contributors:

- *Marty Anson, Bindagraphics, Inc., Baltimore, Maryland*
  www.bindagraphics.com
- *Dave Gischel, Victor Graphics, Baltimore, Maryland*
  www.victorgraphics.com
- *Tony Hoholik, The John Roberts Company, Minneapolis, Minnesota*
  www.johnroberts.com
- *Bruce Sanderson, Springfield Printing Corporation, Springfield, Vermont*
  www.springfieldprinting.com
- *Bob Windler, Diecrafters, Inc., Chicago, Illinois*
  www.diecrafters.com

4 Project Planning Starts at the Finish

It happens more often than it should: A beautifully printed piece arrives on the shop floor, ready for postpress conversion. The purchase order calls for nothing out of the ordinary, with no handwork, lengthy makeready, missing components, or any other difficulty. A piece of cake? No, because the look the designer had in mind is going to be difficult—if not impossible—to achieve with the finishing option they've chosen. In the end, the finisher is left scrambling for a viable solution to get the job done properly and on time.

What You Will Learn

- Success starts with a plan
- Proceed only after the product's intended use is understood
- Pressroom considerations may not always come first

Printers and designers have a multitude of postpress finishing and binding techniques from which to choose. Before making the final choice for your product, consider its intended use, cost, and longevity. Disasters can be avoided easily if everyone involved in the production of a piece remembers one thing: Planning starts at the finish.

It's fruitless to come up with a great design that can't make its way from the computer screen to the client's hand. By encouraging your customers to consult with you, the finisher, during the design phase of the production process, they can be sure that the great ideas taking shape in their heads can be produced accurately and efficiently.

For jobs to flow easily from one production step to the next, everyone involved must agree on solutions that fit within time and budget constraints. When printers plan jobs, it's common for them to place too much emphasis on finding the most cost-efficient way to get it on press, without regard to what happens in the bindery. Saving pennies in the pressroom often results in higher bindery costs, which can raise the overall cost of the entire project.

Ask the Right Questions

Taking job specifications and returning quotes doesn't require much selling skill; in fact, nearly anyone with listening skills can do it. Graphic arts professionals—printers and binders alike—need to ask lots of questions about a product's end use before they submit bids. The best reps formulate irresistible selling propositions based on the product's end use, a practice that never fails to add value to the process. In order to do this, however, the rep needs to know as much about the end of the process as the beginning.

Bindery professionals should think of themselves as being in the business of education as much as the business of manufacturing—and with good reason. On-time deliveries and "reasonable" product quality alone won't satisfy customer demands anymore. To remain competitive, we all must become excellent communicators.

What's the End Use?

This is one of the first questions that designers, printers, and finishers should ask when planning a project. The design should focus around the end use. Ask yourself, "How is this piece going to be used?" Then, picture the final project in your mind. See who is using it and how it's being handled. Determine whether it needs to be fancy and eye-catching or simple and functional. For example, cookbooks are much more user-friendly if they can lie on a countertop, making lay-flat binding methods (i.e., mechanical or lay-flat adhesive) appropriate.

Planning with the end use of a piece in mind allows designers and finishers to focus only on processes that meet their creative and productivity requirements. Another important consideration when deciding which materials and methods to use is the intended useful life of a product. There are dozens of factors that need to be considered about a project before ink is laid to paper. Something as basic as the choice of stock should not be made independent of subsequent finishing processes. A particular paper may yield a brighter image but can cause production delays, poor product performance, and budget overruns at the bindery.

When glue adhesion is involved, test different types of paper coatings (inks, varnishes, aqueous coatings, UV coatings, and film lamination) to ensure that they work as intended. Some coatings interact poorly with some glues, and sometimes the whole process feels like black magic. But the right time to become aware of potential problems is before the production run. Quality finishers can steer you away from ink and coating combinations that may not produce the best long-term results, or at least perform tests in advance.

Planning with the end use in mind also helps determine the proper use of diecuts, tabs, foldouts, and more. For example, a product catalog that doubles as a promotional piece may be enhanced with creative diecut covers. Tabs will help organize the catalog to make it more user-friendly, while pockets inside the covers can hold additional materials.

Collaboration between designer, printer, and finisher during the design process can work wonders for the overall efficiency of the project. A quality finisher knows much more than just the proper binding solution for a particular job. They can recommend a proper stock weight, type of coating, or optimum page layout. By partnering with a finisher you trust, every step of a job's production can be streamlined, saving both time and money.

A design is useless if it doesn't fit into the budgets of everyone involved. A design that looks great on the computer screen may cost a bundle when put into actual production. For a bindery, that means the budgets of both the printer and print buyer must be met. Once a job is printed, though, frequently it's too late at that point to figure out how to get it bound on budget. Other factors are at play when determining the total cost of a project, and they vary based on what type of piece you're producing. Designers and finishers should ask each other plenty of questions regarding the feasibility of a particular plan.

For complex projects, a pre-production sample (*a k a* dummy) will help you make sure that you've planned the job right. This pre-production sample should be made from the specified paper and have exactly the right page count and dimensions.

These are some of the many considerations that must be made when planning a project. But they illustrate the depth of thinking that is required for a graphic arts project to go smoothly. Even the slightest forgotten detail can cause significant delays and cost overruns. However, by securing the details of a production process from design to delivery, you stand a much better chance of avoiding production problems.

✳   ✳   ✳

The Final Word…

To ensure success in the bindery, consider the technical requirements, marketing considerations, and associated costs during the design and budgeting stages of your project. By starting your project planning with the end in mind, you will be sure that there are no surprises as it makes its way through every step of the production process. A quality finisher can be a valuable partner, offering important job planning suggestions. Simply asking questions and providing every detail of a piece will save you and your customer both time and money, while giving all involved the peace of mind that the project is in good hands.

Contributors:

- *Jim Egan, Rickard Bindery, Chicago, Illinois*
  www.rickardbindery.com

- *Russ Haines, Rapid Bind, Inc., Portland, Oregon*
  www.rapidbind.com

- *Tony Hoholik, The John Roberts Company, Minneapolis, Minnesota*
  www.johnroberts.com

- *Chuck Manthey, Sentinel Printing Company, St. Cloud, Minnesota*
  www.sentinelprinting.com

- *Bob Windler, Diecrafters, Inc., Chicago, Illinois*
  www.diecrafters.com

5 Planning Impositions

Proper impositions can make the difference between winning or losing jobs, making or losing money, and having unhappy or delighted customers. Communication between printing and binding people, whether it's inter- or intra-company, is vitally important.

· What You Will Learn

- Job factors to consider
- Determining sheet size
- Unusual size imposition

Most shops have standard impositions for books with common trim sizes. These were created long ago and are widely used as standard operating procedures. The real need to understand imposition minutia occurs when dealing with unusual trim sizes, multiple-up impositions, and ink problems. If the bindery has uncommon folder capabilities (e.g., sections, plates, split guides, and spot gluing), these can be used for a more efficient imposition, thereby saving paper and press time, as well as bindery and finishing expense.

A Definition

Imposition is the positioning of the pages on the press sheet so that when the sheet is printed and folded the pages fall in the desired order, in the correct orientation (i.e., right-side up), and with the correct margins.

The individual who has accumulated the knowledge and experience to understand each of the subjects below is just as important as your top salesperson! There are more than thirty ways to fold a 16-page signature on a buckle folder. When determining which ones are right for your particular project, consider these factors:

- Press sheet size
- Number of pages or size of project
- Length of run
- Weight of stock
- Crossovers and alignment across folds
- Trim size and trim allowances (plus lip if saddle stitched)
- Mechanical capabilities of folding machines

- Paper grain
- Type of binding
- Ink problems (e.g., printed elements demanding different ink requirements that fall in-line in the press sheet or have ghosting potential)
- Printing, folding, and binding capabilities
- Cost to operate the equipment plus plates, paper, and so forth

In addition, there are numerous ways of positioning the pages on a sheet. For example, three primary types of imposition are used for printing on both sides of a sheet: sheet-wise, work-and-turn, and work-and-tumble.

Determining the Imposition for a Job

A signature is a sheet of paper that, when folded and cut, forms a section of a book, magazine, or pamphlet. As a unit, signatures contain from 4 to 96 pages. The most common sizes are 4-, 8-, 16-, and 32-page signatures. Fitting the page to the sheet requires calculating how many pages can be imposed on a given paper size. For example, assume you have a project with the following measurements:

A—Paper size: 25×38 in. (796.3×965.2 mm)

B—Two-page spread size: 12×9 in. (304.8×228.6 mm)

C—Spread size with trimming allowances: 12½×9¼ in. (317.5×235 mm)

How can this project best be imposed on the sheet? To calculate the answer, divide C into A. In this example, eight double-spreads (16 pages to a side or 32 pages to a sheet) can be imposed.

It is relatively easy to determine what press sheet size is needed for standard trim sizes. The accompanying chart shows the most common trim sizes and standard sheet sizes that fit most economically.

When dealing with an uncommon trim size, determine your maximum press sheet size and divide this by the length and width of your two-page spread, including trims. Take the maximum number out and multiply it by two. This equals the number of pages to a side. Again, multiply it by two and you will get the number of pages to a sheet. Eliminate any unneeded paper from your maximum press sheet and you have your desired press sheet size. If your schedule and number of pounds permit, you can get a make-order (i.e., custom paper size) and save a lot of money.

Unusual layouts sometimes yield great savings. For example, one of our clients once recommended imposing a book as 18-page signatures, rather than as standard 16-page signatures, on a making-size (nonstandard) sheet for a large-quantity job. A lot of production cost was eliminated in both the pressroom and in folding. If you don't have time to purchase a make-order, the closest standard sheet size will have to do. The more you go through imposition exercises, the better and faster you'll become.

Final trim sizes		Standard sheet sizes
5½×8½ in.	fits into	17½×23 in.
		23×35 in.
		19×25 in.
6×9 in.	fits into	25×38 in.
		38×50 in.
7×10 in.	fits into	23×29 in.
		17½×23 in.
8½×11 in.	fits into	23×35 in.
		35×45 in.
		19×25 in.
9×12 in.	fits into	25×38 in.
		38×50 in.

Common product trim sizes and standard paper sizes with economical fits.

*   *   *

The Final Word...

Just because you can print it, doesn't mean you can fold it. Consult your folding department or trade shop first. Remember that the signature you plan must be compatible with other bindery equipment.

Contributor:

- *Marty Anson, Bindagraphics, Inc., Baltimore, Maryland*
  www.bindagraphics.com

6 Smart Marks

In today's competitive graphic arts environment, jobs must be done right the first time, on time. Properly marked-up proofs and film that are understood by everyone are essential to making the lives of everyone involved in production easier.

What You Will Learn

- Marks: a hidden language
- Center and collating marks
- Important visuals

In the graphic arts industry, communication shouldn't always be verbal. Some of our best communication takes the form of small marks made on film during prepress, which later appear on the press sheet and provide essential information up and down the production chain. In essence, these marks form a "code" that ensures everyone in the production process knows and agrees on what the job will entail.

Although no formal, standardized set of marks exists, there is general agreement about the most frequently utilized marks and their functions. By and large, the most important thing is that all parties have a common understanding of the code, not that every printer and finisher makes exactly the same marks. The goal is to generate fewer errors and thereby promote more efficient production.

Center marks, tick marks, register marks—whatever you want to call them— are critical postpress finishing guides. Unfortunately, the proliferation of pre-register devices in use means that a lot of printers have abandoned certain practices that binders and finishers have long relied on. For example, side guide marks are absent in many cases, making a determination of which side is which a feat of detection. Even if a tag is in the load of paper indicating "side guide," without a visual mark running down the whole load, bindery operators still need to ensure that the tag is on the correct side.

Each side of a press sheet is identified by a name (e.g., gripper edge, side guide, trailing edge, and off-guide). Binders and finishers need to be able to identify the side guide and gripper edges before they can perform many postpress operations. After the sides have been identified, the next step is to ensure that the press sheets are in registration with each other. If there were side guide or gripper problems in printing, then any critical downstream operation will be adversely affected. It's at this point that center marks come into play.

A center mark is a one-point rule that bleeds off three sides of a press sheet, as shown in the accompanying illustration. The center mark indicates whether the presswork was in registration from sheet to sheet. A lift of paper, jogged to its proper guides, will ideally show the center mark as a straight line running down the lift. If the line is not straight, you will have inconsistent sheet-to-sheet registration, creating a quality decision.

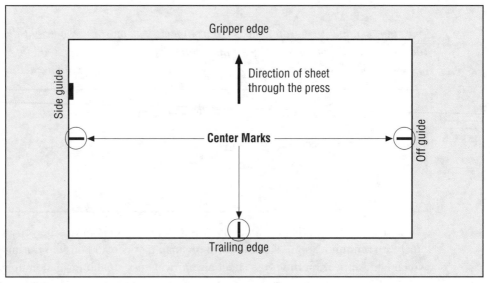

Center marks.

There can be other printed aids on a press sheet, including fold marks, final trim marks, version or volume number notes, and collating marks, to name a few. Collating marks, also known as plugs, are short lines about $\frac{3}{32}$ in. (2.4 mm) thick and printed on the spine of each signature in a stair-step fashion, as shown in the accompanying illustration. These plugs give the binder an immediate visual reference showing whether signatures have been collated in proper order.

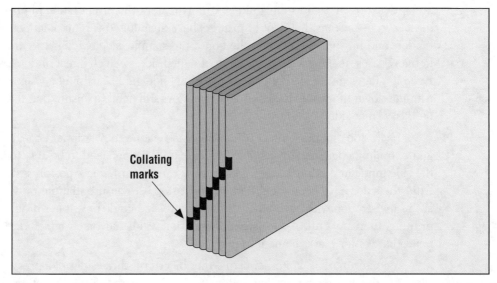

Collating marks, or "plugs."

In addition to all the printed marks, every job should ideally come with a rule-up, which is a press sheet on which rules have been drawn from the marks to show trim, final size, perforations, scoring, folding, and so forth. A folding dummy is another important visual aid. Often the dummy is a proof that's been folded and marked to look like the finished piece, or it may be a folded blank sheet that was originally created for planning and estimating purposes. Whatever the folding dummy, make sure you mark the rotation of folds so if someone unfolds the piece, he or she can refold it correctly.

*   *   *

The Final Word...

A good rule of thumb is "communicate until the finishing is finished." Hopefully, you'll find that all these marks, as well as the rule-up and folding dummy, are essential means of communication and will prove their worth with the successful completion of your postpress projects.

Contributor:

- *Marty Anson, Bindagraphics, Inc., Baltimore, Maryland*
  www.bindagraphics.com

7 Preflight in the Bindery

In printing, the term preflight *is generally used to refer to the process of immediately examining electronic files upon their receipt to check for any potential problems that could hinder production. While preflighting files is second nature to printers today, unfortunately the preflighting concept still isn't within many binding, finishing, and mailing companies.*

What You Will Learn

- What is preflight?
- Benefits of preflight
- Implementation of preflight

For years, most printers have received electronic artwork rather than in traditional mechanical form. Since designers have varied training and virtually no universal guidelines, there are no guarantees that their files contain all the necessary information to successfully print their jobs. Important elements are often missing or the files themselves may be incorrectly prepared. Some of these principles hold true in the postpress arena as well.

Save Time and Money

Although the binding and finishing industries do not have the same electronic formatting difficulties as printing, the preflight concept can be adapted to achieve similar benefits. With so little slack in most job schedules, proper preflight techniques help binderies identify missing components and catch layout mistakes in time to meet the deadline with good product quality. Binderies that sit on untouched jobs until the last minute risk looking foolish if they discover a problem at the eleventh hour. Unprofessional behavior such as this understandably makes printers' blood boil.

Postpress preflighting needn't be complicated. Binding and finishing companies should immediately check that every job is complete and ready for production upon its arrival and quickly alert customers when problems are found. Working together, printers and postpress companies can reach the right decision and either (1) move ahead with the job as it exists, (2) make adjustments to accommodate the difficulty, or (3) return the job.

Liftoff in the Bindery

The preflight leader has the responsibility to inspect each job as it arrives and search for layout issues as well as any other mistakes that may have occurred during planning and printing processes that could affect the quality of the final project or production rates. The preflighting department next should pull samples of every signature or component and create a sample product. This sample should closely resemble the actual finished product and incorporate as many of the required binding applications as practical. A rigorous checklist should be used.

The most common errors detected during preflighting operations include:

Page Layout Problems

- Pages stripped out of position causing type to be trimmed off
- No compensation for push-out (very important on text with indexes)
- Insufficient bleed allowances (less than 0.125 in.), especially on the face trims of covers when spine adjustments are necessary
- Bleeds masked to final trim line instead of fold line
- Misalignment of bleed indexes or indexes stripped in the wrong position
- Folios placed at random, sometimes falling outside face or foot trim
- Insufficient margins or no allowance for drill holes
- Image on first and last text page in hinge score areas. (0.25 in. on perfect bound and 0.5 in. on lay-flat adhesive binding)
- Insufficient margin for punch holes on mechanically bound products
- Tick marks left on work
- Color bars located too close to the image area
- Miscalculated spine thickness on lay-flat and perfect-bound books

Press and Folding Problems

- Wet ink, especially reflex blue and metallics; matte stock can be slow to dry
- Unvarnished sheets with heavy ink coverage
- Excessive spray powder on laminating jobs
- Sheet misregistration
- Offsetting from strapping or transit marking
- Web fold misregistration
- Drag marks from the press or folder
- Signature curl caused by poor packing.

Preflighting takes an average of twenty to thirty minutes per job and ideally should be performed within two hours of delivery. If the person doing the preflighting discovers a problem, the customer should be alerted immediately. Couriers and overnight shipping services should be used liberally. While preflighting involves obvious costs, it is significantly less expensive than the potential loss of production and goodwill.

If everyone working on a job sees the preflighted sample, then bindery operators will handle fewer unforeseen problems and achieve better productivity. Sharing
information really helps second and third shifts eliminate downtime because their
questions frequently stop production in the absence of anyone to answer them.

*   *   *

The Final Word...

Preflighting isn't just for printers. When binderies receive work and discover an error,
they must contact the customer immediately and search for a reasonable alternative.
Ours is a detail-oriented industry, and sometimes the only thing standing between
success and failure is the suggestion and implementation of a creative alternative.
Dumping problems back into the customer's lap without suggesting possible solutions
is, simply put, bad business.

Contributors:

- *Marty Anson, Bindagraphics, Inc., Baltimore, Maryland*
  www.bindagraphics.com

- *Fred Daubert, The Riverside Group, Rochester, New York*
  www.riversidegroup.com

- *Bruce Sanderson, Springfield Printing Corporation, Springfield, Vermont*
  www.springfieldprinting.com

- *Bill Seidl, Seidl's Bindery, Houston, Texas*
  www.seidlsbindery.com

8 Efficient Makereadies

Here's a riddle: If a complicated bindery job has a twelve-hour makeready and requires thirty-six hours of machine run time, how long will it take to produce it from the time stock arrives? Forty-eight hours on one machine? Are you sure? Good planning can reduce this time to forty hours or even less. Everyone wins when "impossible" schedules are met, but successful deadline compliance doesn't just happen by itself. Good planning coupled with competent plant management and communication is essential.

What You Will Learn

- Strive for a 90 percent setup solution
- The value of unsetting machines
- The impact of redundant machinery

When working on jobs needing super-fast turnaround times, good binderies ask for properly marked proofs, dummies, and makeready stock a day or two in advance. This enables job orders to be written, distributed to the plant, and understood so that setup mechanics can begin the makeready process. Then, when the job finally arrives, about 90 percent of the makeready is complete. All that remains is cutting the stock and fine-tuning the setup process. This "90 percent solution" can rescue a lot of customers from missed deadlines.

In addition, fast turnaround times depend on how effectively multiple-shift companies streamline the order-entry system. It's impossible for a setup mechanic to make ready a job without clear instructions about what must be done. Since it's difficult to get product-related questions answered during non-traditional business hours, good inter- and intra-company communications are essential for work scheduled around the clock. When jobs arrive late in the day, good binderies immediately call their customers to resolve any issues that have arisen during the preflight process. So that the makeready process can begin on time, job tickets are written and materials distributed to all appropriate departments. This process ensures a company's ability to work on rush jobs during their second and third shifts.

Unsetting Machines (Returning to Original Condition)

One key factor determining makeready speed is the starting condition of machines. Here are three possible scenarios:

- If the last job off a machine is similar to the next one being set up, and the machine hasn't been "unset," makeready speed for the new job should be lightning fast.
- If the last job off a machine is very different from the new one, and the machine hasn't been unset, makeready speed for the new job will be correspondingly slow.
- If the machine has already been unset, makeready speed for the new job will be as quoted.

Some companies unset all machines after every job, some never do until the next job is present, and others do a little of each. Choosing the right strategy for your company depends on how many redundant (overlapping) machines you have, the variety and scope of your typical projects, and the average requested turnaround times. In general, job-shop binderies with little machine duplication should unset machines after each use because most jobs require different setups. On the other hand, those with a lot of redundancy are better off not unsetting machines after finishing "common" jobs.

Routinely unsetting machines results in fewer lost parts, better maintenance, fewer glue problems, and so forth. Since unsetting machinery requires less skill than making jobs ready, labor costs are lower than when highly paid setup mechanics unset and reset jobs under tight deadline pressure. On the other hand, skipping unsetting when running similar jobs means that makeready times and production costs are reduced. When the details for the next job scheduled for a machine are already known, it's easy to make unsetting decisions. If it's different—as to size, paper thickness, and/or page count, for example—unsetting the machine makes sense. If it's similar, it may be best to leave it alone.

If a machine doesn't have any jobs scheduled for it in the near future, another decision must be made. For highly specialized machines, the next job may be days or even weeks down the road. For example, if the next scheduled job is in five days, and it is similar to the one just finished, it is tempting to leave the machine set up. If a rush job with different specifications unexpectedly arrives the next day, however, the machine will have to be unset and (expensively) made ready by setup mechanics. In this case, the unsetting strategy, or the lack thereof, has backfired.

For smaller binderies with little machine overlap, unsetting decisions are relatively easy. If jobs typically are similar, machines should remain set up. If not, they should be unset. For larger companies with a lot of machine duplication, unsetting decisions can be complicated. Companies are rewarded for good unset decisions by maintaining low operating costs and fast turnaround times. Companies that are able to make their unset decisions pay off will realize some net savings in labor costs per setup, but the real gain will be in their ability to satisfy so-called "impossible" customer demands.

*   *   *

The Final Word...

Prosperity and longevity in the postpress business depend on managing details well. Effective machinery setup and unsetting procedures are important for quick turnaround times, low production costs, and satisfied customers. Proven skill in these areas and striving for the "90 percent setup solution" can set up a company for lucrative repeat business.

Contributors:

- *Kris Koch, Allied Bindery, Madison Heights, Michigan*
  www.alliedbindery.com
- *Kevin Rickard, Rickard Bindery, Chicago, Illinois*
  www.rickardbindery.com

Section II
In the Bindery

9 Book and Booklet Binding Overview

Printers and designers have many binding options from which to choose. Before making the final choice for your product, consider its intended use, cost, and required longevity.

What You Will Learn

- Select the right binding method
- Book binding options
- Booklet binding options

There are many questions to answer before selecting a binding style. For example, does the product need to have a printed spine? Should it lie flat when opened? How durable must it be? Does it have to fit in someone's pocket? There are also marketing issues to consider. For example, does your product have competitors with a common binding type? If so, should yours imitate the competition for increased recognition or should a different binding style be chosen to distinguish yours from the crowd? The following is an overview of common binding options.

Saddle Stitching

Saddle stitching is technically one of the more simple binding methods. It is achieved by inserting one or more wires through the fold line of a product's spine. The number of pages that saddle stitching can accommodate depends upon the weight of the paper. Some heavy-duty equipment can stitch books as thick as ½ in. (12.7 mm), but a good rule of thumb is to keep books thinner than ¼ in. (6.4 mm). Brochures, booklets, newsletters, and magazines are all common saddle-stitching applications. This binding method offers a number of advantages, including:

- A saddle-stitched piece will lay flatter than a perfect-bound product.
- Saddle stitching generally offers quicker turnaround times than alternative methods.
- Since there's more available capacity for saddle stitching in most geographic markets, saddle stitching is usually available at a lower relative cost.

Trade binderies are often able to support unusual stitching requirements. Sophisticated equipment includes many pockets and additional capabilities such as

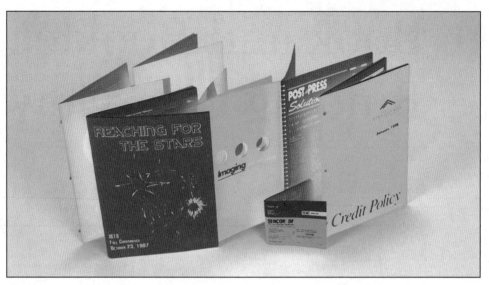

Examples of saddle-stitched publications.

card feeders, two-up trimmer attachments, in-line folders, wafer sealers, and inkjet printing.

Although saddle stitching has many advantages, the following are a few of its potential shortcomings:

- It requires working only with whole signatures in four-page multiples, whereas perfect or mechanical binding allows single leaves to be bound.
- It's not as durable as some other methods and may be inappropriate for pieces subject to heavy use.
- The spine forms a blunt point on which you cannot print.
- Thick, small-format books have a tendency to spring open.

Adhesive Binding

Perfect binding, a form of adhesive binding that uses glue to hold pages together, is an especially versatile binding method. Generally, books as thick as $2\frac{5}{8}$ in. (66.7 mm) can be perfect bound. Specialized machinery can accommodate thicker books. Signatures and single leaves are assembled into a book block by stacking one component upon another. The backbone is then roughened to expose the paper fiber, which is a better surface to hold the adhesive.

Examples of perfect-bound publications.

Hot-melt glue is applied to these edges, the cover is wrapped around the book block, and it proceeds through a three-knife cutter to trim the head, foot, and face.

Until a decade or so ago, perfect-bound products with coated text could not withstand heavy use without coming apart. Today's polyurethane reactive (PUR) glue formulations allow coated stock to be securely bound either alone or with uncoated stocks. PUR glue is so effective that it's now commonly used to bind high-quality catalogs that formerly had been sewn. Ideally, the grain of both the cover and text stock should run parallel to the spine.

Although there are many benefits to perfect binding, the following are some of its limitations:

- The cost is usually, but not always, higher than saddle stitching.
- Generally, the minimum thickness is ⅛ in. (3.2 mm) if the spine is to be printed, ⅟₁₆ in. (1.6 mm) if the spine is not printed.
- Perfect bound books do not lie flat when opened. This can prove frustrating for end users who need hands-free reading while referring to technical manuals, music books, cookbooks, or directories.

Lay-flat adhesive binding offers a solution to this last disadvantage. The cover of a perfect-bound book typically attaches to the spine across its full width. Because the spine is stiff, perfect-bound books don't lie flat when opened. With lay-flat adhesive binding, of which Otabind is the best example, the book can lie flat when opened. The accompanying illustration shows how this is accomplished.

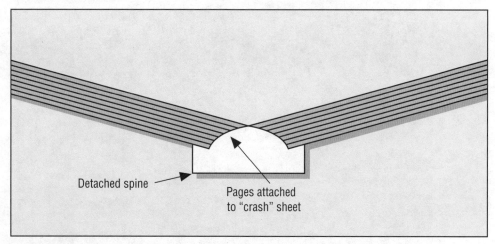

Lay-flat adhesive spine.

The Otabind lay-flat adhesive-binding process provides lay-flat adhesive bindings with strength and durability. Introduced to the United States from Europe, Otabind has proven to be a great alternative to both mechanical and perfect binding because it lies flat and information can be printed on the spine. With PUR glue, Otabind enables coated or uncoated sheets to be bound into a durable and flexible book that is truly user friendly.

An example of a book bound using the Otabind binding process.

Mechanical Binding

Mechanical binding entails clasping individual sheets together with plastic, small wire, or metal rings. Except for very short runs, mechanical binding is typically more expensive than saddle stitching and perfect binding. The mechanical-binding process requires two steps: gathering, then binding—and the latter has been highly automated.

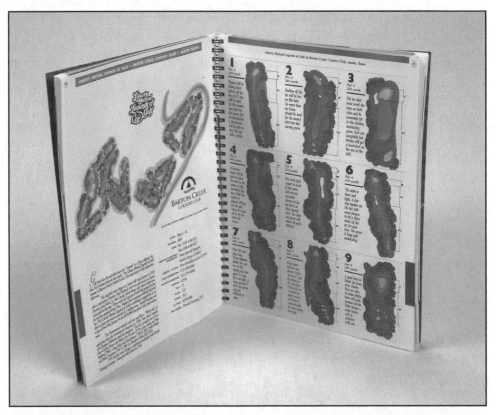

Wire-O® binding, in which double-looped wire with interlocking fingers run through holes punched in the binding edge.

Wire-O® (trademark of James Burn International) binding is double-looped wire with interlocking fingers that run through holes punched in the binding edge. Wire-O pages align more closely than spiral binding and also don't step up. Wire-O binding elements are sturdy and attractive and are popular for calendars, cookbooks, and similar publications. Wire color options are plentiful, and books can be bound in semi-concealed styles. Although there is no printable spine on ordinary Wire-O, it is possible to print on the spine of either semi- or fully concealed styles.

Semi-concealed Wire-O binding.

Spiral binding is often used for manuals and workbooks. It utilizes a single metal or plastic wire wound in a continuous spiral through holes in the binding edge of the sheets. Because there is no printable spine, this binding may not be appropriate for books to be displayed edgewise on bookstore or library shelves. Another disadvantage to spiral binding is that facing pages step up when opened, making critical crossovers impossible and creating an alignment nightmare for graphics that jump the gutter. Spiral binding, along with other mechanical binding options such as Wire-O® and plastic comb binding, requires a generous gutter margin. It is very important to make allowances for the gutter in your design.

An example of a publication spiral-bound using plastic coil.

Plastic comb binding, achieved by punching slots or holes through the binding edge and inserting formed plastic material, does not allow pages to be rotated 360°, but it does align without a step-up. With proper equipment, plastic comb elements can be inserted and removed at will, which is an advantage for reports and materials that need frequent updating. Combs are available in many colors, may have imprinted spines, and will accommodate up to 1¾ in. (44.4 mm) of paper bulk.

Case Binding

Case binding, the process that produces a hard-cover book, offers high durability and good looks but typically costs more than other binding methods. In case binding, the signatures are often, but not always, sewn. Although the machine used to sew books is more complex than a home sewing machine, the process of sewing pages together follows the same principles. After gathering and sewing signatures, the book block is trimmed and placed into a case consisting of binders' board covered with paper, cloth, plastic, or leather. The case is held to the signatures by glue running along the spine and between end sheets.

The indisputable advantage of a sewn book is its strength. Reference books and others with anticipated heavy use, archival function, or extra durability are often sewn. The end use of these products justifies the higher cost of this binding

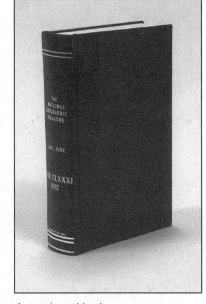

A case-bound book.

method. To cut costs, a perfect-bound book block may be inserted into a case; this method, however, eliminates the strength of sewing. Typical applications for perfect-bound case binding are for books being sold through retail distribution.

Ring Binding

Another binding option is the ring binder, which comes in both loose-leaf and screw-and-post styles.

Although bookbinding work occurs near the end of the production process, it shouldn't be an afterthought. Many designers and printers don't evaluate binding alternatives because they mistakenly believe one or another method is prohibitively expensive. In some instances, perfect binding may even be less costly than saddle stitching.

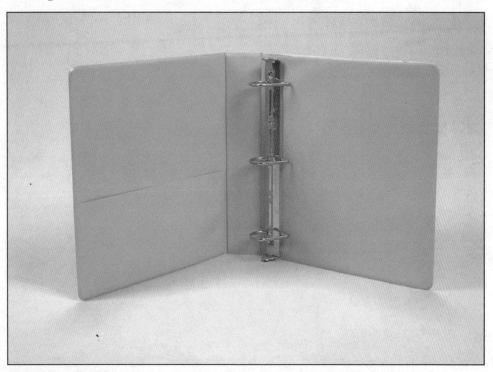

A three-ring binder.

*   *   *

The Final Word...

One of the roles of good trade binderies is to provide information about alternative binding styles. To ensure success in the bindery, consider the technical requirements, marketing considerations, and associated costs during the design and budgeting stages of your project.

Contributors:

- *Marty Anson, Bindagraphics, Inc., Baltimore, Maryland*
  www.bindagraphics.com

- *Chris Eckhart, Eckhart & Company, Indianapolis, Indiana*
  www.eckhartandco.com

- *Sue Hein, Rapid Bind, Inc., Portland, Oregon*
  www.rapidbind.com

- *Kris Koch, Allied Bindery, Madison Heights, Michigan*
  www.alliedbindery.com

- *Peter Pape, The Riverside Group, Rochester, New York*
  www.riversidegroup.com

- *Jack Rickard, Rickard Bindery, Chicago, Illinois*
  www.rickardbindery.com

- *Bill Seidl, Seidl's Bindery, Houston, Texas*
  www.seidlsbindery.com

- *Jim Shear, Seaboard Bindery, Woburn, Massachusetts*
  www.seaboardbindery.com

10 Cutting

Little things make a big difference in the bindery. Postpress success depends on good planning and attention to detail. When people hear about difficult Wire-O or perfect-binding jobs gone awry, behind-the-scenes processes like cutting often are to blame. No matter which portion of the job receives the most attention, every process is vital to smooth production, meeting deadlines, and making money. Don't be penny wise and pound foolish. Cutting isn't a stepchild; rather, it is vital to job success—or lack thereof.

What You Will Learn

- Cut and bind in the same location
- Combat "draw"
- Avoid chop cuts

Cutting affects every process that follows it, from folding through binding. On the one hand, a small mistake in cutting can cause problems for every subsequent process. On the other, cutting can correct potential problems. Since paper can either stretch or shrink during the printing process, the paper cutting operator may be the last person with a real opportunity to make corrective adjustments to eliminate or at least minimize the problem.

Some printers try to keep as much work as possible in-house. Without getting into the pros and cons of outsourcing, do yourself a favor: keep the cutting and binding portions of your jobs together. This will reduce unproductive finger pointing and increase vendor accountability. If printers cut jobs prior to outsourcing to other post-press operations, they have, by default, accepted at least partial responsibility for the overall quality of the project. If the cutting is off, it will affect folding, binding, and everything else that happens afterward. Also, by not cutting the sheets prior to transportation, any damage in transport such as dirt on the edges or damage due to strapping or mishandling can still be corrected by the bindery.

Unlike three-knife trimming, in which every side is uniformly cut on a finished product, precise flat-sheet trimming is more involved. Cutting that seems right during a production run may be problematic once the product is collated and binding begins. At this point, small cutting variations between lifts may be very noticeable and likely will undermine the high-quality appearance you want. Regardless of whether you're comfortable with outsourcing, at least let those who bind your books cut them, too.

Paper and Ink

In general, the harder the substrate, the more difficult it is to cut. Coated sheets with significant clay content have hard surfaces and require frequent knife changes—sometimes as often as twice a day. Recycled sheets can be difficult to cut because they contain a potpourri of paper fibers and miscellaneous waste. When cutting difficult stocks, it is hard to get clean, consistent cuts throughout whole production runs, no matter what precautions are taken. When problems arise, it is best to determine whether your paper is to blame. Do this by substituting a different sheet. If the problem disappears, then paper is the culprit. Take appropriate action.

If reflex blue or other slow-drying colors are present on a sheet, brace yourself for more problems, including the following Catch-22: Normal clamp pressure may produce excessive offsetting of ink. On the other hand, reducing clamp pressure to avoid this will increase the likelihood of knife draw problems. The time to combat reflex blue ink is before the job hits the bindery. Hint: Dry-trap-applied varnish usually works wonders.

Technical Tips

Logical layouts. When you lay out book jobs, think about how they're going to be converted in the bindery. For instance, if the volumes will be bound mechanically, you must do more than line up common trim lines. Make sure all pages flow in a logical sequence, such that your components will be in production-friendly order for downstream operations. This may seem obvious, but companies often have to re-skid poorly laid-out jobs after cutting.

Draw. The four main causes of "draw" problems are: wrong clamp pressure; a dull knife; wavy stock; and a too-thick lift of paper. Knives need relief as cuts are made or else sheets will be pulled. Full-sized lifts are fine for most porous stocks, but lift sizes should be reduced for cutting dense, heavily calendared paper with brittle clay fillers. To maintain high quality standards, lift thickness routinely needs to be reduced by 50 percent or more. Draw problems are especially noticeable on books with common images that bleed off pages, such as bars or lines. It is important that printers work with bindery professionals who understand these tradeoffs and are willing to make sure that all jobs are done right.

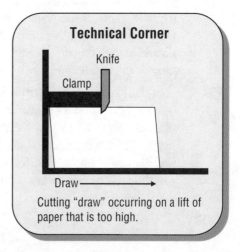

Technical Corner

Knife

Clamp

Draw ⟶

Cutting "draw" occurring on a lift of paper that is too high.

Trim allowance. Even if your images don't bleed, try to avoid single chop cuts. The inherent problem with chop cuts is that you get only one try. Once the cut has been made, there can be no more adjustments without reducing the final trim size. Cutting problems become magnified and affect folding accuracy and crossover image alignment. Whenever possible, allow at least ⅛-in. takeout trim margin.

Trim allowance for tabs. Trim allowance is especially important when planning tabs. Unless your job planners work with tabs every day, it is very difficult to get tab copy positioned accurately enough for a single chop cut. The bottom line is this: Even though chop cuts save a few strokes on the cutter, the risk of poor quality and outright error significantly outweigh the miniscule savings.

True printers' guide and gripper. As diecutting and foil-stamping experts know, easy identification of a press sheet's true guide and gripper saves time and reduces errors. The same holds true for cutting. Registration accuracy is much better if a sheet is converted in the same direction it is printed. Sometimes guide and gripper sides are obvious; sometimes, however, they are nearly impossible to identify.

Maps. Map quality depends as much on cutting precision as folding accuracy. When cutting maps, make sure you accurately preflight the job. Thick maps with overhanging covers and outside panels that fold on color breaks look terrible if cut improperly. Take extra care when working on maps with ten or more folds—their front panels can easily start looking a little short.

Gatefolds. Before beginning a gatefold job, cut a makeready lift, fold it, and make sure the gap in the center is the right size. If the gap is too tight, you can still make adjustments. If it is too large, and there are folds on color breaks, you're stuck. The bindery that skips this makeready step might as well be cutting with blinders on.

Mechanically bound books. When cutting flat sheets for downstream collation and mechanical binding, make sure they look as if they were cut on a three-knife trimmer. Unless you consistently cut all of your forms, books with common bleeding graphic elements will exhibit a lot of page position variation, resulting in an unattractive "sawtooth" jagged bleed.

Rotary scoring. When your job needs rotary scoring, score first, and then cut. Like die scoring, rotary scoring is more accurate when the true guide and gripper are still on the sheet.

Back-trimming padded book blocks. A cost-effective way to manufacture mechanically bound books is to collate, pad-bind, and three-knife-trim book blocks in-line and back-trim the spine offline. When making the final offline cut, it is important to use a double stroke that first removes the glue and then evens up the sheets.

In recent years, the need to reduce costs and improve efficiency has fueled cutting technology workflow process improvements. Binderies should consider maximizing operator productivity to remain competitive. Automated cutting systems are a must for high-volume postpress operations. While complete systems can be expensive for smaller shops. the addition of some basic equipment can dramatically improve productivity and quality.

*   *   *

The Final Word...

The best binding job can't disguise and won't compensate for a poor job of cutting. Good cutting is transparent, easing subsequent binding processes. The effects of poor cutting, on the other hand, can be glaring in light of subsequent postpress operations. Resist the temptation to save a little time and money at the cutting stage, where careful planning and precision execution can make or break a smooth-functioning production workflow.

Contributors:

- *Jeff Marr, Colter-Peterson, Paramus, New Jersey*
  www.colter-peterson.com

- *Kevin Rickard, Rickard Bindery, Chicago, Illinois*
  www.rickardbindery.com

- *Brenda Slacum, formerly of Freedom Finishing Solutions, Baltimore, Maryland*

11 Folding

Many printing projects featuring superb printing don't look good because of inaccurate folding. Folding makes a world of difference, especially if you coordinate with your customer early in the job preparation stage. Potential folding problems can be prevented if they are caught early.

What You Will Learn

- Job planning for folding
- Choosing paper
- Coatings and their impact

It Starts with the Layout

The intelligent use of binding and finishing not only makes pieces intended to persuade stand out in the marketplace, but it also makes informational printing more user-friendly. The best way to create eye-catching and/or super-effective graphic arts projects is to choose layouts in which the form complements the intended function.

Usually there are several ways to run any job. Simple layout changes can produce remarkable time and dollar savings. Panel size alterations and other minor design adjustments can make products look great, function better, and be more compatible with available folding machinery.

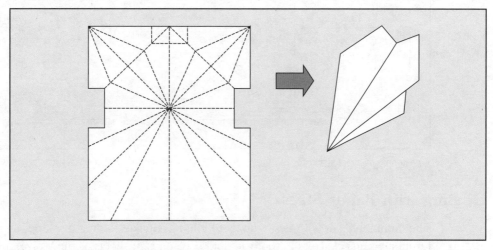

This paper airplane is a prime example of how multiple folds must be shingled to avoid excessive pushout. Eight folds (!) intersect at the nose of the plane, requiring channel scores that are spaced as much as 1 in. (25.4 mm) apart.

Layout is more important to folding than most other postpress functions. Binding styles have defined margins that must be met in order for the book to be properly bound. Folding layouts also can be tweaked for optimized production, or to permit the execution of an intricate diecut. Even slight variation in layout can mean the difference between smooth, automated production and costly, time-consuming handwork.

Many folding jobs should have small variations in panel sizes, but don't. While the shape of individual panels may look similar, they often need to be sized differently to allow for shingling, wraparound, washout (creep), and pushout. Paper is three-dimensional so don't ignore its thickness. Correctly designed panels will allow you to fold the product on the color breaks rather than alongside of them. In other words, what looks like sloppy bindery work may really just be poorly conceived design.

Always provide proofs, rule-up press sheets, bulking dummies, and a marked and sequenced folding sample (e.g., first fold A to A, second fold B to B, and so forth). Leave ⅛ in. (3.2 mm) between copy and intended trim position and another ⅛ in. for take-off trim. This allows for natural variation in both the printing and binding processes without risking product damage. Smaller margins are possible, but check first. Allow for washout when folding right-angle pieces or when one sheet of paper is slit to nest. Your paper thickness will determine how much washout peeks out. Contrasting colors will make washout more noticeable, but careful pre-planning can enhance a product's appearance.

For roll folds, the outer two panels should be the final finished size with each succeeding interior panel decreasing by ³⁄₃₂ in. (2.4 mm). The last panel should be ¹⁄₁₆ in. (1.6 mm) smaller than the preceding one. Failure to perform these steps can lead to bend-overs, bad color breaks, jams, waste, and increased spoilage.

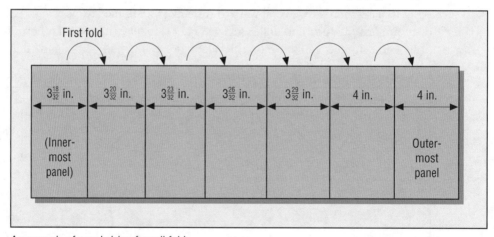

An example of panel sizing for roll folds.

Dealing with Paper Stress

The immutable laws of physics apply to folding. Buckle-folding machines apply different amounts of stress to the front and back ends of sheets as they travel through fold rollers and into the fold plates. Every fold has two sides: one heading into the

Table of Equivalent Basis Weights

These are approximate measurements only. There is a thickness variation from brand to brand and from finish to finish. It is always best to make a pre-production sample!

Caliper Thickness (Inches)

Offset Stocks	0.002	0.0025	0.003	0.0035	0.004	0.0045	0.005	0.0055	0.006	0.0065	0.007	0.0075	0.008	0.0085	0.009	0.0095	0.010	0.0105	0.011	0.0115	0.012
Newsprint	25#	28#	32#	35#																	
Text-Weight Offset (Smooth)			40#	45#	50#	60#	70#		80#	90#	100#		110#	120#							
Vellum Offset					50#		60#		70#		80#										
Bond	12#		13#	16#	20#	24#															
High Bulk											65#		70#	75#							
Tag												100#			125#				150#		
Cover-Weight Offset												50#					65#				
Bristol Index											90#				110#				140#		

Enamel Stocks	0.002	0.0025	0.003	0.0035	0.004	0.0045	0.005	0.0055	0.006	0.0065	0.007	0.0075	0.008	0.0085	0.009	0.0095	0.010	0.0105	0.011	0.0115	0.012
Text-Weight Gloss	50#		60#	70#	80#		100#														
Text-Weight Dull			50#	60#	70#	80#	100#														
Matte			50#	60#	70#	80#					105#										
Label (C1S)			55#	60#	70#																
Krome Kote (C1S)				55#	60#		70#														
Cover-Weight Gloss								60#				80#			100#						
Cover-Weight Dull								60#					80#				100#				
Cover-Weight C1S													0.008 in.				0.010 in.			0.012 in.	

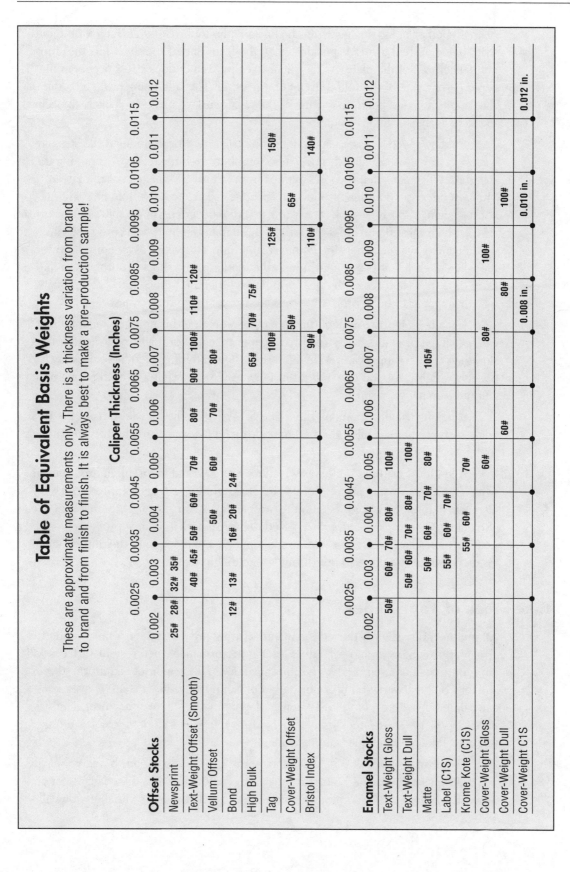

plate, the other being pushed from the back by the fold rollers. The side of the fold
that's being pushed forms a "buckle" when the front end of the sheet hits the stop
at the back end of the plate. As the sheet buckles, tremendous stress occurs in the
paper on one side of the fold, but not on the other. The side being pushed by the fold
rollers gets a severe bend: fracturing of the paper surface or fibers is likely to occur if
the stock is thicker than 10 points.

Folding speed stresses paper at a geometric rate. For example, if the stress on
a sheet is "5" when the speed is "5" (these numbers are only relative), doubling the
speed to "10" means that the stress jumps from "5" to "25" (instead of the linear
"10"). In this case, doubling production speed translates to a five-fold increase in
stress—enough to ruin a project. Assume you're in a car crossing a railroad track with
six-inch-high rails. If you cross the rails at three miles an hour, your tire raises up over
the rail and down the other side with a small bump. At five miles an hour, however,
the wheel feels like it is coming through the fender as the shock absorbers top out
from the explosive force of the tire springing off the rail. Suffice it to say that many
jobs that appear to be improperly set up are simply being run too fast.

If a job is ineptly planned, the paper stress created during right-angle folding
can be a huge problem. The structure of paper is such that it is stronger under tension than under compression. When poorly designed folding sequences cause two
panels to "fight," the top one under tension always wins, while the bottom one under
compression always wrinkles.

Cracking usually occurs on the first fold. Why? As the buckle starts in the right-
angle section, the first fold bends around a very tight corner, greatly stressing the first
fold.

A bindery customer once was wrestling with a wrinkling problem experienced
while folding a 16-panel poster. Four sequential right-angle folds had produced wrin-
kled paper (tension vs. compression). A two-parallel, two-right-angle folding sequence
also failed. The simple solution that solved this customer's wrinkling problem involved
nothing more than a different folding sequence that enabled both the outside and
inside panels of the piece to flex during the folding process.

Take Stock of Your Paper

All products vary slightly during the manufacturing process. Paper is no exception.
Irregularities do occur and will affect folding performance. Inconsistent surfaces will
contribute to decreased bindery performance. Even if a paper lot is uniform, there
still may be great variation in paper bulk. For example, 80-lb. uncoated cover stock
can caliper anywhere from 8 to 13 points, depending on the manufacturer. This is significant because 10-pt. stock usually folds well while paper 12 pt. or thicker requires
different folding techniques and machines.

Avoid running odd lots. Changing paper in the middle of your bindery job will
affect downstream folding, so be sure that your customer marks the change spot and
properly advises you. Generally, the thicker your stock, the more variables you will

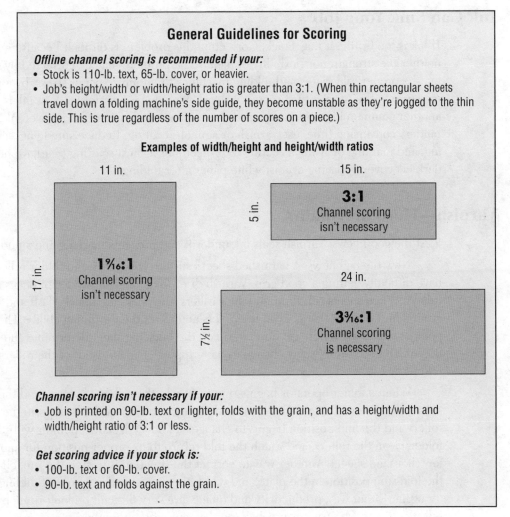

General Guidelines for Scoring

Offline channel scoring is recommended if your:
- Stock is 110-lb. text, 65-lb. cover, or heavier.
- Job's height/width or width/height ratio is greater than 3:1. (When thin rectangular sheets travel down a folding machine's side guide, they become unstable as they're jogged to the thin side. This is true regardless of the number of scores on a piece.)

Examples of width/height and height/width ratios

11 in.

15 in.

5 in.

3:1
Channel scoring
isn't necessary

17 in.

1⁹⁄₁₆:1
Channel scoring
isn't necessary

24 in.

7½ in.

3³⁄₁₆:1
Channel scoring
<u>is</u> necessary

Channel scoring isn't necessary if your:
- Job is printed on 90-lb. text or lighter, folds with the grain, and has a height/width and width/height ratio of 3:1 or less.

Get scoring advice if your stock is:
- 100-lb. text or 60-lb. cover.
- 90-lb. text and folds against the grain.

face. Pre-score your stock if it is 110-lb. text weight or heavier. Sometimes thicker stocks without critical color breaks can be wet-scored in-line or folder-scored, but always ask for an opinion before bypassing diecut scoring. When folding stock thicker than 10 pt., watch for ripple cracking on buckle folders. Stock will generally not ripple crack on a knife folder unless the stock is extremely thick, causing the sheet to fracture as it bends around the rollers.

Know your grain direction. Cracking can be reduced and the need for pre-scoring or in-line wet scoring can be eliminated if the first fold is made with the grain. If this is not possible, consider choosing a stock with short fibers and off-machine coating for better moisture control.

Paper fibers can break during folding, resulting in cracking. Often, choosing proper fold plates, machines, and production techniques eliminates some of the problems. The shock load on paper fibers increases geometrically with machine speed. Therefore, when fibers are breaking, slowing down your folder greatly reduces fiber stress and many times eliminates the problem.

Ink Can Sink Your Job

If ink is too brittle, it may crack. Correcting this problem is difficult because ink has neither the strength nor flexibility of paper. The problem may be corrected by choosing the proper fold plates and folding machines to minimize paper stress, by adding moisture to the surface (wet score), or by slowing down your folder. Wet ink is another common bindery problem. If there is a good chance of having wet ink at bindery conversion time, use varnish or aqueous coating. Reduce smudging, scratching, and marking by using a coating to protect jobs against scuffing that have heavy dark ink coverage laying against white paper after folding.

Varnish—Hero or Villain?

First the good news: Varnish seals ink under it and prevents marking and smudging.

Now the bad news: A varnished sheet's surface is slippery and folder rollers have difficulty getting a good grip. Varnish dries to an uneven surface of peaks and valleys. When sheets run through folder rollers, the peaks are knocked off and ground into powder that gets on the rollers and alters their gripping ability. The exact point at which the rollers get a solid grip on the buckling sheet determines the position of a fold. If there is any change in the gripping characteristics of the rollers, the fold moves.

When a folder operator begins running a job, the rollers are clean and the job runs well. However, after a few thousand pieces, varnish powder is deposited on the rollers and the fold position begins to change. A knowledgeable operator will stop the folder, clean the rollers, and watch the fold return to its proper position for another few thousand sheets. Another way to correct the situation is to stop the run, change the fold stop position in the plate, and watch the piece quickly go out of folding register again. Either way, productivity and quality are very difficult on long-run jobs with full (flood) varnish. A non-varnished job that runs at ten thousand pieces per hour might yield only six thousand or seven thousand if it were varnished.

More Tips

The following are a few important tips that can help your jobs move along more smoothly:

Allow your bindery to cut the job. You will substantially decrease transit problems and increase your yield.

When using slitters, always check for clean edges. Asking your folding machine operator about edge sharpness on multiple-up or folder trimming jobs is appropriate. For good product appearance, do not use rotary knives to trim final folded enamel stock thicker than 0.024 in. (0.61 mm) or offset thicker than 0.028 in. (0.71 mm).

- For best results, the maximum total paper thickness you should attempt to slit is 0.024 in. (0.61 mm) for enamel stock. For example, six panels of 80-lb. enamel with a thickness of 0.004 in. (0.10 mm) will slit acceptably (0.004 in. × 6 = 0.024 in.). Adding a seventh panel will likely result in a rough edge—even if your slitter wheels are brand new. **Note:** Most folders technically can slit 0.050 in. (1.3 mm) or more, but your piece will look like a beaver chewed it.
- For slitting offset stock, 0.028 in. (0.71 mm) is considered the prudent maximum total bulking thickness. (Offset stock tends to be softer and easier to cut than enamel.)
- Since the normal diameter of a fold roller is about 2 in. (51 mm), attempting to slit a final-size piece smaller than 2 in. almost always results in erratic slitting. This is because the piece has left the grip of the fold roller before it is firmly in the grip of the slitter shaft rollers.
- Keep your slitter wheels razor-sharp.

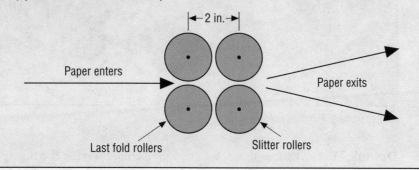

Tips for effective slitting on folders.

Both wide- and small-gap gatefolds are possible. If you need a gap smaller than ³⁄₁₆ in. (4.8 mm) or larger than a few inches, ask.

Green projects can cause production problems. Soy ink tends to scuff more than regular petroleum-based ink. Recycled paper has a tendency to have less strength than pre-consumer paper because of shorter paper fibers. This affects bindery performance. Likewise, recycled paper tends to be less pliable and is subject to more jams, increased tearing, a poorer quality fold, and more wrinkles.

Check for brittleness. For presses with dryers, consistent drying time is important because either oven temperature or web speed variation will lead to paper pliability and brittleness fluctuation.

Memory. Folding plastic is possible, but remember plastic has a "memory" and may rebound.

Properly band your skids to avoid shipping problems. If the stretch wrap is too tight, product corners can be damaged. For coated stock, band at right angles.

Diecut project management. If your project is diecut, be sure to procure a sample, or at a bare minimum a thumbnail sketch, so you can plan around any hidden traps before the project is printed. When folding diecut pieces, sometimes it is possible to get away with uneven or non-right-angle side guides.

An assortment of folded products.

Dry ink. We can't stress this point enough. No matter what the time pressure, resist converting jobs with wet ink. Inks tend to be brittle and may crack when bent, exposing paper fibers underneath.

*   *   *

The Final Word...

Folding is a great way to differentiate your printed products. The first step to smooth folding production is a great layout. Before the piece is printed, be sure your project is taking advantage of the best production-enhancing folding options available. Be sold on the fold. Your printing customers already are.

Contributors:

- *Russ Haines, Rapid Bind, Inc., Portland, Oregon*
  www.rapidbind.com
- *Jack Rickard, Rickard Bindery, Chicago, Illinois*
  www.rickardbindery.com

12 Specialty Folding

To many graphic arts professionals, specialty folding begins and ends with a bemused, "How'd they do that?" Such speculation does a disservice to skilled bindery professionals who accomplish extraordinary feats every day. Rest assured, there's a lot of behind-the-scenes "specialty" work occurring on folding jobs that look downright ordinary.

What You Will Learn

- What is specialty folding?
- Adequate production speed
- Opportunities in small and large formats

Some print sales representatives run and hide when asked to bid on work involving tricky folds. Sales reps who figure out how to produce unusual projects are more valuable than those who say "no" prematurely. Rather than passing on projects with lots of panels, folds at unusual angles, diagonal folds, unusual diecut shapes, or those with no obvious side guides (and thus opening the door for your competitors), you owe it to yourself to seek expert advice.

Trade binderies should be thought of as extensions of printing facilities. Knowing where to get something done effectively and efficiently is much more important than anyone's ability to do it infrequently. If a buyer sends a quote to his usual printers and only one knows where to go for specialty folding, guess who gets the job? Iron cross folds, swinger folds, pop-up folds, miniature gatefolds, 17-accordions, tight normal gatefolds, right-angle gatefolds, and folding without side guides are all possible and practical.

The point here is: Don't give up on jobs with specialty folds. Shops that are willing to tackle jobs with specialty folding requirements are very valuable in the marketplace. There are skilled binding specialists out there who can help you make money on them.

What Is Specialty Folding?

Specialty folding means more than automatically producing "tricky" folds. Should a company's ability to reduce or eliminate wrinkling qualify as specialty folding? What about holding brittle paper together as it travels though fold rollers and designing fold sequences that travel through machinery with minimal stress? Yes: Each of these capabilities solves difficult problems and is an example of specialty folding.

Sometimes specialty folding simply means the ability to work with thick, thin, or unusual paper stocks. Specialty folding experts need to know what pieces of equipment are suitable for which jobs. Knowing which resources to use prevents a lot of potential snags from morphing into full-blown production problems. Some types of unusual miniature and large-format work qualify as specialty folding, as does the in-line application of easy-release, permanent, or removable glue.

Should a company's ability to accept exceptionally large jobs qualify as specialty folding? As long as it isn't commodity-type work, the answer is "yes." Companies that claim to be specialty producers should be able to turn around large jobs fast—and have the redundant machines that enable them to do it.

There are few universal rules about what is or isn't possible in this area. Here is a short list of some "how'd they do that?" folds that are both realistic and image-enhancing:

- Iron cross folding
- Pop-up folding
- Multi-directional diecut folding
- Paper-doll style folding
- "Swinger" folding
- Narrow gap, no gap, and wide gap gatefolding
- No apparent side guide folding (ovals, circles, etc)
- Miniature folding with panels as short as $7/16$ in.
- Lay-flat miniature folding (with or without using glue)
- Folding sheets as large as 80 in. long

Managing Production Speed

Specialty folding also means knowing when to employ which manufacturing process. Doing something in the fastest way possible rarely produces the best quality. If a client has endured the expense of putting a beautiful six-color job on a 100-lb., No. 1 enamel sheet, it is a good bet that ragged or crooked edges won't be tolerated. On the other hand, if a job is printed on groundwood stock, time- and cost-saving suggestions are valued, if not expected. If product quality is essential on a right-angle folding project, the job plan should allow for one-up bindery production. While split-side guides certainly permit faster production, they also cause out-of-balance roller tension and result in poor quality.

Although one-up work is not affected by running gatefold projects with loose fold rollers, multiple-up work certainly is. In fact, running gatefolds multiple-up is fraught with danger. To avoid gatefold "pullout" (an unintended fold located approximately ⅛-in. away from the intended fold), fold rollers should be set loosely. Since operators can't get a solid grip on gatefolds as they travel though the slitter shaft, slits are usually crooked, ragged, or both. Since two-up formats don't yield much more

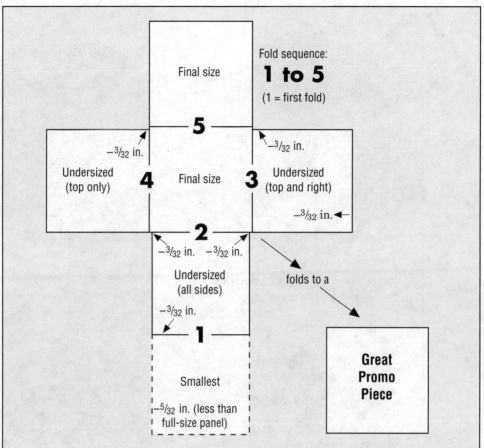

Iron cross folds.

Fold sequence:
1 to 5
(1 = first fold)

5

Final size

4 Final size **3**

Undersized
(top only)

Undersized
(top and right)

−³/₃₂ in.

−³/₃₂ in.

−³/₃₂ in.

2

−³/₃₂ in. −³/₃₂ in.

Undersized
(all sides)

−³/₃₂ in.

1

Smallest

−⁵/₃₂ in. (less than
full-size panel)

folds to a

**Great
Promo
Piece**

- Panels may open in any sequence, but panel sizes must be adjusted based on which panels open first.
- Plan opening sequence carefully for maximum marketing effect.
- Additional hanging panels may be attached to the first leg in the fold sequence (as in example).
- Minimum paper weight is 70-lb. enamel text or 60-lb. offset text. Don't use any sheet heavier than 100-lb. coated cover.
- Channel-score when diecutting.
- 6×6-in. (152×152-mm) and 8×8-in. (203×203-mm) products are very popular sizes.
- Panels may be rectangular-shaped instead of square. Also panels can be eliminated or added to create "T" and "L" shapes.
- Large quantities are fine. Rickard Bindery, for example, has modified over a dozen folders to fold iron crosses.
- Many projects are wafer-sealed and can be manufactured in-line for use as self-mailers.

product than one-up production, designing multiple-up gatefolds projects rarely makes sense.

Gatefolds may have short gaps (less than ¼-in. total gap), no gaps, or wide gaps (more than 2 in.). Since most commercial gatefolding plates don't handle these types of projects very well, make sure you have the necessary specialty machinery for your job, or at least know where to go to get it done.

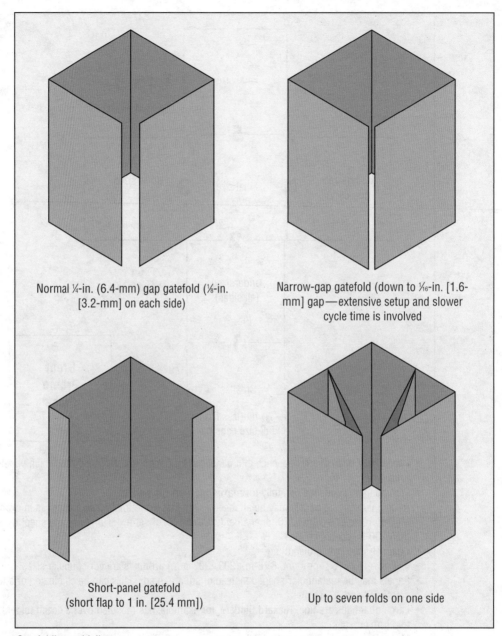

Gatefolding guidelines.

Swimming Downstream

One of the trickiest things about folding diecut products is getting them to feed cleanly. When a diecut sheet emerges from a feeding unit, its edges and corners may catch on the sheet below it. Feeding considerations should be thought out carefully during the planning stage to avoid these very common errors.

Getting product successfully delivered out of a machine and properly packed is also important, especially when automated downstream operations are required.

Miniature & Small-Format Folding

As the size of consumer packaging continues to shrink and new products hit the market, shelf space is at more of a premium than ever before. To cope, marketers are learning to take advantage of small-format printed pieces to draw attention to their products.

Miniature and micro-mini folding typically refers to any folded piece with at least one final-size dimension of 2-in. or less. Pieces can be automatically folded down to panels as small as $\frac{7}{16}$-in. Products this small must be produced on specialized equipment by experienced operators.

Micro and miniature folding is used to create products such as bottle hang tags (left) and product inserts (right).

Common Applications

As mentioned above, attachments to consumer goods are an increasingly popular application, including hang tags for bottles and clothing and product inserts and outserts. Micro and miniature folding are also used to create standalone products such as coupons, game pieces, instruction sheets, and schedules.

Before embarking on miniature folded projects, check downstream production requirements. Some automatic inserting machinery requires that pieces lie flat. If glue is objectionable, ask your miniature-folding company whether they can get the product to lie flat without it. There are ways to overcome this problem. Also, be sure to discuss paper options with your bindery because miniature-folding machines handle less stock variation than regular-sized folders.

For example, pharmaceutical manufacturers often require miniature folded-paper products to be automatically inserted into boxes, bottles, and other containers. This, in turn, usually requires folded work to lie flat and be neatly packed. Even if a bindery's miniature folding is produced on budget and looks beautiful, it is still a failure if it jams up downstream pharmaceutical inserting machinery.

There are several available packing options to facilitate subsequent handling. Rubber banding is convenient but tends to leave a crease or kink in the product. Placing folded products in trays is a better solution, as they allow products to be removed easily. Again, it's important to coordinate packing options with those handling the products downstream.

Oversized Folding

Projects that require large-format or oversized folding capabilities are becoming increasingly attractive to printers with larger presses. Posters, display graphics, calendars, maps, promotional materials, diagrams, and even direct mail are a few of the types of projects that can benefit from the efficiency of large-format and oversized folding.

Since most large-format folding projects require several folds to get down to their final size, the type and sequence of the folds is a significant factor. For example, map projects often use accordion folds followed by a series of parallel folds. This allows air to escape during folding, which helps prevent paper wrinkling and other production issues.

Depending on the sheet size, final size, and folding style of your project, one folding sequence may be much more economical than another. If your oversized folding application will be placed inside a publication, keep in mind that the final size of the product must be slightly smaller than the trim size of the publication.

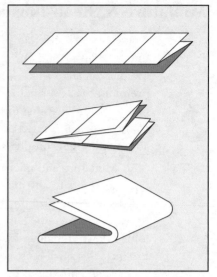

Oversized folding projects such as maps benefit from a series of accordion folds (top) followed by parallel folds (middle) to achieve their final size.

Another common problem in oversized folding occurs on products with more than forty panels, such as very thick maps. If final product bulk is not accounted for when designing the cover and back panel, the piece may look terrible if there are color break problems.

Specialty binderies should look beyond their own processes and consider how their work affects the operations that follow or precede them in the manufacturing chain. In order to provide troubleshooting and design advice to their clients, many specialty-folding companies employ staff machinists and engineers to customize bindery equipment. If you have a creative eye and a lot of real-world experience, "how'd they do that?"-type folding projects can be both doable and profitable.

*   *   *

The Final Word...

As we've discussed, specialty folding is much more than tricky folds. It is participating in the design stage, choosing the right processes and equipment for each job, having large-volume capacity, and being able to offer creative solutions to formidable challenges. The bottom line? Put your knowledge of specialty folding in your briefcase and use it to win more printing business.

Contributor:

• *Jack Rickard, Rickard Bindery, Chicago, Illinois*
  www.rickardbindery.com

13 Adhesive-Binding Glue Options

The glues used in adhesive binding need to be strong enough to hold together hundreds of book pages and a cover, yet flexible enough to allow the book to be opened easily. Adhesive-binding glues fall into three main categories:

- *EVA hot-melt (ethylene vinyl acetate)*
- *PVA (polyvinyl acetate)*
- *PUR (polyurethane reactive)*

Here is a brief overview of each, giving their comparative strengths and weaknesses.

What You Will Learn

- When to choose EVA, PVA, and PUR glue
- EVA limitations
- PUR is the king of adhesive binding glues

EVA

As the "standard" adhesive used in traditional perfect binding, EVA hot-melt is available in literally hundreds of formulations, although some characteristics are common to all of them. Hot-melt EVAs are made from a combination of solid thermoplastic polymers, tackifying resins, and waxes that function with the right viscosity when properly heated in a glue pot. As the name implies, EVA hot-melt adhesives are heated just prior to application, making them malleable.

EVAs are versatile enough to be used on coated and uncoated stock. They demonstrate strong adhesive properties under most conditions, "set" quickly, are relatively inexpensive, and are available in a variety of formulas for applications beyond perfect binding. (A "roundable" hot-melt adhesive can be used to create a rounded spine on Smyth-sewn books, for example.) After application, most EVA glues rigidly bind pages together. Pressure-sensitive hot-melt formulas can be used as side glues for padding and cover hinges.

Modern EVA formulations are subject to less chemical breakdown as they age, but tend to stiffen when cooled. As a result, EVAs are subject to cold crack when stored in very cold warehouses, although newer formulations display good flexibility.

It can be difficult to use hot-melts on heavily coated stocks or stocks heavier than seventy pounds. Hot-melt glue also can be hard to apply without contaminating the applicator heads. Contamination occurs more frequently in jobs requiring small applicator orifices because overheating of the glue pot creates clog-causing char. Moreover, since hot-melt units have a working temperature in excess of 300°, fixing problems under operating conditions is difficult. Hot-melt contamination usually requires a time-consuming system flush that wastes expensive glue. One way to reduce hot-melt glue waste is to clean contaminated applicator heads with hot vegetable oil.

Hot-melt padding glues are very flexible, but not very strong. These glues are suitable for projects that do not have thick, heavy pages that will pull away from the bind after repeated use. Desk calendars and pads are bound with this glue, which enables the sheets to be detached easily.

PVA

PVA glue is applied cold. As it dries, the resins penetrate deep into the structure of the paper stock, forming a solid bond. PVA glues cure to a semi-soft state, providing a more flexible backbone than hot-melts. Unlike hot-melt glues, PVAs won't crack in extreme temperatures.

PVA is not generally used in softcover bookbinding because of its long curing time and because most machinery is not very adaptable to the need for cleaning from job to job. Like EVAs, PVAs also can be difficult to apply and yield inconsistent results when applied improperly. Because PVA glues do lie relatively flat, they are used mostly on telephone books and with extremely porous stocks.

PUR

Many bindery experts consider PUR to be the most flexible and durable bookbinding glue on the market. Originally designed for use on furniture and automobiles, PURs consist of solid polymer moisture-curing elements and are appropriate for difficult-to-"impossible" bookbinding projects.

PUR glues can withstand an exceptional amount of punishment, and are resistant to remelting and cold cracking. This makes them ideal for high-abuse applications like high school textbooks and automotive shop manuals, as well as for other frequently used books printed on heavyweight, coated stock, including synthetics and UV. PUR glues cure when exposed to moisture in the air and will bind with ink or coating bleeding into the spine gutter. They work with all stocks and coatings, including synthetics and UV.

*   *   *

The Final Word...

Today's adhesive binding methods have the flexibility to allow for a wide range of design and layout possibilities. Armed with the latest high-tech glue formulations, the knowledgeable bindery representative will never again have an excuse for choosing the wrong adhesive-binding glue.

Contributors:

- *Marty Anson, Bindagraphics, Inc., Baltimore, Maryland*
  www.bindagraphics.com

- *Kris Koch, Allied Bindery, Madison Heights, Michigan*
  www.alliedbindery.com

- *Peter Pape, The Riverside Group, Rochester, New York*
  www.riversidegroup.com

14 Adhesive-Binding Testing Methods

There are many ways to test the strength of perfect-bound books. In general, binderies err on the side of strength, not flexibility, when making glue decisions. Since strength is so important, good binderies test all jobs as they are being run. The industry standard for page-pull strength is 2½ pounds per linear inch, which means that a page in a book with an 11-in. binding edge must withstand at least 27½ pounds of applied pressure before pulling loose from the spine. The best binderies maintain more stringent page-pull standards and routinely reject books if testing results fall below 3 pounds per linear inch.

What You Will Learn

- Page-pull test
- Flex test
- Temperature test

According to Chuck Cline, technical manager of National Starch and Chemical Company's bookbinding division, "If everything is the same—paper, spine preparation, application, everything—then EVA (ethylene vinyl acetate) traditional hot-melts will test at one level, PVA (polyvinyl acetate) cold-emulsion glues will test at 10–20% higher than EVAs, and PURs will test 20–30% higher than PVAs." Of course, Mr. Cline advises careful consideration of all factors. For instance, the glue is only as strong as the paper. If you are using 40-lb. stock, most properly applied adhesives are stronger than the paper, resulting in paper yielding before the glue.

Page-Pull Test

A page-pull testing machine measures how many pounds of pressure a page can withstand before it is either torn or pulled from the binding. During this process, a page is mechanically gripped and pressure gradually applied until the page pulls away from the spine. As expected, PUR glues withstand these tests better than hot-melts. As mentioned above, any bound page should withstand a minimum of 2½ pounds of pressure per linear inch before yielding from the spine. PURs routinely withstand 4 to 7 pounds of pressure per linear inch before becoming dislodged. Hot-melt glues generally withstand from 3 to 4 pounds.

Flex Test

The flex test, another way of testing the strength of perfect-bound books, is performed by using a machine that simulates a person turning a page back and forth, mechanically pulling a book leaf in 120° arcs. This machine measures the number of turns a page will withstand before breaking from the spine. Again, PUR and other cold glues hold up better than hot-melts in this test. Minimum standards are 200 flexes. Conventionally bound pages generally withstand 300–400 flexes. However, many books routinely test well over a thousand flexes.

A page-flex testing machine.

Temperature Test

Temperature tests measure glue strength in varying climates by subjecting books to extreme climate conditions and then pulling their pages. Hot-melt glues are weaker in this test because they will crack in low temperature conditions, causing pages to break away from the binding. In sample tests, PUR temperature resistance ranged from –40°F (–40°C) to 200°F (93°C), typical EVA glues ranged from 10°F (–12°C) to 120°F (49°C), emulsions –40°F (–40°C) to 120°F (49°C), and rubber-based hot-melts performed adequately between –20°F (–7°C) to 130°F (54°C).

As a rule of thumb, when measuring the tensile strength of adhesives, liquid glues average 300 pounds per square inch (psi), PVA and hot-melt glues log in at 500–800 psi, PUR glues test at 1600–2200 psi, and your average paper tensile strength is 50–80 psi.

A product's end use is critical in choosing the right glue and binding method. Consult with your finisher to determine the best glue and binding method before specifying a project.

A Horror Story

A small-format map book using hot-melt glue was outsourced to a trade bindery we know. As with all perfect-binding jobs run at this facility, books were pulled for testing throughout the run, and the results were logged. The company's quality standards were met, and the job was shipped out.

However, they were shocked when informed that some books had literally fallen apart. As it turned out, the product was distributed in the southern United States during the heat of the summer. Had the book's final destination been communicated in advance, a recommendation could have been made that would have saved the job.

Many of these books had been left on car window ledges in 100°F (38°C) heat, and, as we all know, the inside of a closed car heats up far warmer than the outside air. Also, because the books contained maps, users regularly bent the book in half. Clearly the hot-melt glue was not up to the task. Either PUR glue or mechanical binding would have been a better choice.

With many publishers planning for worldwide distribution, and given today's competitive markct, bookbinding glues must perform better than ever. For instance, software publishers should pay particular attention to end-use since their manuals can end up anywhere in the world. They must be able to withstand a wide range of climates and user habits.

Even domestic publishers should be knowledgeable about binding methods and durability. Books must not only catch a buyer's eye when on the shelf, but also should be able to withstand a lot of abuse. In addition, factors such as cost-competitiveness and turnaround times make glue selection significant.

*   *   *

The Final Word...

Choosing the perfect glue for an adhesive-binding job isn't always easy. Your sales force should be armed with information about all glue and binding methods. Once you win a job, communicate as much information as possible about the project's end-use to your bindery. This is critical to making the right glue selection for your project.

Contributors

- *Marty Anson, Bindagraphics, Inc., Baltimore, Maryland*
  www.bindagraphics.com
- *Kris Koch, Allied Bindery, Madison Heights, Michigan*
  www.alliedbindery.com

15 Perfect Binding

Every perfect-bound project should achieve four objectives. First, the book's appearance must be the right shape with all copy properly positioned. Second, the pages need to be bound in the right sequence. Third, the book has to be durable. And fourth, the project should run efficiently to be cost-effective.

What You Will Learn

- Appearance, sequence, durability, and production efficiency
- Project planning
- Tricks and traps

Good planning and communication with your perfect-binding partner will help assure perfect-binding success. Start by selecting the right raw materials. Your decisions regarding cover and text stock, ink, paper coatings, tabs, fly sheets, bind-ins, blow-ins, and postproduction packaging are all important. Next, consider having your bindery make a preproduction sample (dummy) so you know where to place copy. Pay special attention to spine printing, crossovers, borders, and your bindery's grind-off margin preferences. As you're pulling the whole perfect-binding job together, keep the following additional rules in mind so that everything proceeds smoothly.

Product Appearance

Preproduction samples. Your bindery should give you a dummy upon request. Some charge for this service, but many do not. These samples are especially important if the final product will be mailed and the total weight is near 1 lb. (454 g). Because mailing charges increase significantly when a package crosses the 1-lb. barrier, all weight factors such as glue, companion pieces, and packaging materials need to be considered.

Grind-off margin. Before laying out any image, check with your bindery to determine their desired grind-off margin. For example, most companies prefer a grind-off margin of ⅛ in. (3.2 mm), but some may want more, such as ³⁄₁₆ in. (4.8 mm). If your relationship with your bindery is new, it's important not to assume anything. Crossovers (i.e., images that straddle two pages), perforations close to the spine, and gatefolds all require grind-off planning to avoid disasters, such as lost business-reply card (BRC) perforations or foldout pages that are glued shut or trimmed off.

- Keep grain direction parallel to the spine, if possible.
- For top quality, score your hinge scores on a diecutter. On thin books, avoid using thick covers (>10 pt.).
- Ink, varnish, and UV coating on the inside front cover shouldn't enter the hinge score and/or spine area by more than ⅟₁₆ in. (1.6 mm).
- Keep signature ink and coatings away from spine edge.
- Send cover press sheets with press gripper and side guides marked.

⅟₈-in. head trim over and above signature trim.

¼-in. hinge score (from spine edge)

Ideally, face and signature trims should be the same size.

⅟₈-in. foot trim over and above signature trim.

Perfect-binding cover layout guidelines.

Spine color breaks. If your book has color breaks on the spine edge, it would be wise to request a dummy from your bindery to assist with proper cover copy layout. Spine printing problems on books are frequent but easily avoidable. Paper bulk varies from manufacturer to manufacturer, and these variances, combined with changing atmospheric and moisture conditions, can measurably alter your book's thickness.

Consistent signature jogging. Don't lay out your signatures with different head and foot trim margins. A book block (i.e., a book that has been folded, gathered, and stitched but not cased-in) traveling down a perfect-binding line will jog either to the foot or the head. It usually doesn't matter which you choose, but be consistent.

Crossover image alignment. Planning for perfect-binding crossovers is part art and part science. In addition to grinding ⅛ in. (3.2 mm) off the signature spine, accurate crossovers depend on your layout and how the books are opened. For maximum operator flexibility, place your crossover images ³⁄₁₆ in. (4.8 mm) from the spine edge. Your crossovers should appear to meet right at the spine. To achieve this effect, strip your copy ⅟₁₆ in. (1.6 mm) short of the grind-off area. If your book is thick or is printed on heavy paper, nudge the image outward, perhaps another ⅟₃₂ in. (0.8 mm).

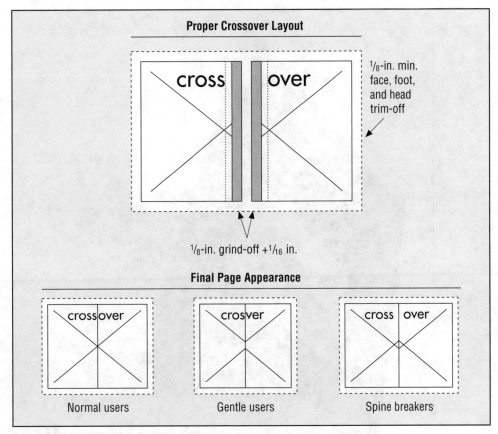

Crossovers for perfect binding.

If your book is thin, nudge the image closer to the grind-off area. In general, diagonal lines are among the toughest to line up visually.

When you have crossovers between signatures, folding accuracy is a huge factor. In these cases, if you're using a trade bindery, do yourself a favor and let them do all the signature folding.

Hinge scores. Top-quality hinge scores can be done on most perfect-binding machines. For thin books, always use hinge scores that are placed ¼ in. (6.4 mm) away from the spine edge. For a dressed-up professional image, consider using hinge scores on all your perfect-bound books.

Ultra-thin books. You can successfully perfect bind books as thin as ³⁄₃₂ in. (2.4 mm). When doing so, however, your cover should be grain-long to prevent a wavy spine. Also, your cover stock shouldn't be thicker than 10 pt. When your book block is thinner than ⅛ in. (3.2 mm), avoid spine printing if at all possible.

Cover protection. Any time your cover has heavy coverage in a dark or metallic ink, it is best to laminate, UV-coat, or dry-trap-varnish it. For lamination, specify stay-flat laminating film and avoid polypropylene because it scratches too easily.

Thin perfect bound book with staggered pages.

Product Durability

Inside cover copy. For maximum adhesion between cover and text, your ink and paper coatings shouldn't enter the inside cover's hinge score and spine areas. If a full-bleed image is used on the inside front cover, a ¹⁄₁₆-in. (1.6-mm) overlap into either area should be acceptable.

Paper coatings. Beware of flood coatings. Aqueous, UV, beauty coat, varnish, web-applied silicon, as well as regular ink all reduce glue adhesion. Glue must directly contact exposed raw paper fibers to create a strong bond. Spot-coating your image is fine as long as your coatings don't enter the gutter margin. Give your bindery production flexibility. Keep ink and paper coatings ⅛ in. (3.2 mm) away from the gutter.

Small-format perfect bound book

Although ¹⁄₁₆ in. (1.6 mm) may be acceptable, a full ⅛ in. allows your bindery to adjust the grind-off margin for best copy appearance.

Paper. As stated earlier, the more surface contact that glue has with raw paper fiber, the stronger the book will be. This does not mean, however, that you should always avoid coated stock. When bidding on a perfect-bound project with coated text, ask your bindery to make a few dummies so that you and your customer can make an educated decision on the feasibility of using coated stock. Working with people experienced in binding difficult stocks will increase your chances for success. Proper testing and quality control systems will help you get a durable book, even if it has coated paper inside.

Grain direction. Run your text and cover grain-long (parallel to the spine). Grain-short text reduces the book's page-pull strength and shelf life. Grain-short covers crack more easily on the edges of the spine.

Two-page forms. Avoid two-page forms if possible. When you can't, bury them somewhere in the middle of your book. Because they look so good, fly sheets are common. When bidding on books with fly sheets, such as annual reports, advise your customers that the perfect-binding machine may run between 25% to 50% slower than normal. However, because fly sheets hardly impact makeready times, small job quantities rarely are a problem. As quantities increase, though, poor production speed becomes an issue. When selecting your fly sheet, remember that the slicker the paper surface, the farther your glue will spread.

Notch perfect binding. When you need stronger glue adhesion, consider notch perfect binding, which creates small serrations that are cut into the spine of a perfect bound book. The downside is that notched book spines sometimes acquire a nail head appearance, where the glued edge is thicker than the book. Experienced perfect binding companies, however, armed with the latest in glue technology can usually achieve excellent adhesion results on most projects with normal perfect binding.

Production Efficiency

Cover glue traps. Allow enough head and foot cover overhang to function as glue traps. If your signature spine length is 11½ in. (292.1 mm), then your cover length needs to be at least 11¾ in. (298.4 mm) and center-positioned with ⅛-in. (3.2-mm) overhang on both the head and foot. When the cover is the same size as the signatures, perfect-binding operators must "cam-stop" both the spine and side glues. (A cam stop allows an operator to stop the flow of glue on an application wheel by using mechanically timed scraper blades.) This may result in poor production rates and lesser product quality.

Signature preparation. Perforate the spine and head of your signatures to allow trapped air to escape. This will reduce paper wrinkling and improve clamp grip. Then, bundle-tie them with end boards to compress your forms as tightly as possible.

The way signatures are stacked is also important. Don't crisscross signatures in a lift; instead, stack them so they're all going the same direction. Forms with reverse curling patterns (e.g., concave vs. convex) will work against each other in a book block. Good perfect binding requires tightly clamped books to go through the grind and glue wheels prior to adhesion with the cover. Poorly clamped book blocks may lead to unattractive spiked glue creeping up between signatures. Once your signatures have developed opposing memories, your job simply won't run or look as nice.

NOTE: Plan your perforations to pass the low-tech "finger-flick" test. They should be numerous enough to easily let out trapped air but not so deep that the sheets separate upon a light flick of the finger.

An assortment of perfect-bound products.

Preflight. Preflight your perfect-binding jobs. This process consists of gathering signatures, cutting off the spine, trimming the cover, collating the piece, and assembling it. Careful examination of each page will reveal incorrect dimensions and poorly positioned copy. Good trade binderies and finishers routinely preflight.

Spine markers. To help ensure that your signatures are loaded in the right order and direction, stepped markers should be printed on the spine of each form. This allows for either an operator or an electronic eye to determine instantly if your pages are properly positioned in the clamp. For complete removal during the grinding process, your signature spine markers should be no wider than ⅛ in. (3.2 mm) and straddle the signature fold (1/16 in. [1.6 mm] on each side).

Foldouts. For gatefolds, half-cover folds, roll folds, map folds, and so forth, allow for the proper grind-off margin plus an extra ⅛ in. (3.2 mm) so your foldout doesn't get glued. Also, give ⅛-in. face-fold margin so your fold isn't trimmed off during the face trim. Providing less of a margin reduces the perfect-binding operator's ability to make adjustments for such elements as crossover image positioning. Similarly, glued pockets on the inside back cover also need ⅛-in. foot and face clearance. Check to ensure your foldouts will feed properly in the loading pockets.

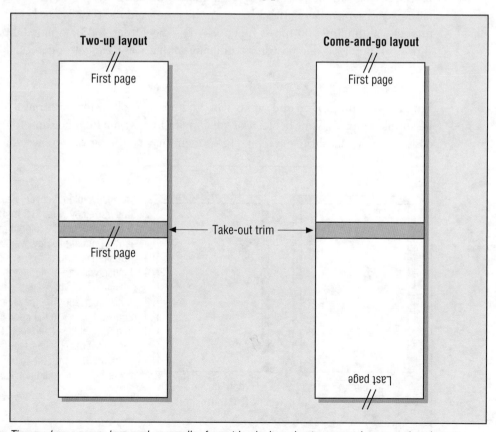

Time and money can be saved on smaller-format books by using two-up and come-and-go layouts.

Two-up layouts. To double your production speed and greatly reduce your price on long runs of smaller-format books, consider two-up perfect-binding layouts. The "come-and-go" layout (see illustration on preceding page) is a popular choice. Since many perfect-binding machines can't do two-up perfect binding, you may need to search for a binding source. For unusual layouts, ask for assistance.

Consistent stock. Changing stock during a signature run can create a bindery mess because book block thickness must be consistent to ensure the proper functioning of clamps and electronic sensors.

No saddle-stitching layouts. Some mistakes can be very costly. It's a real shame whenever perfect-bound books are stripped with saddle-stitching layouts. In order to save these poorly conceived books, they must be gathered on a saddle stitcher, cut in half along the spine, and re-collated. Needless to say, this is very inefficient, the quality is poor, and the price is astronomical.

Peripherals. Foldout Mylar® (trademark of DuPont) tabs falling between signatures increase the value of perfect-bound reference books, buyer's guides, and similar products. Staggered tabs can provide an interesting look. Keep blow-ins between signatures and avoid placing them between the cover and the text. Try to keep your project with multiple postpress functions (e.g., diecutting, foil stamping, tabbing, and shrink-wrapping) at one postpress company so that you have better coordination and accountability.

Shrink-wrapping. Don't be penny wise and pound foolish. Prevent transit scuffing by shrink-wrapping your books. For small quantities with a high per-unit total project cost, your minimal shrink-wrapping investment may be the best insurance you can buy.

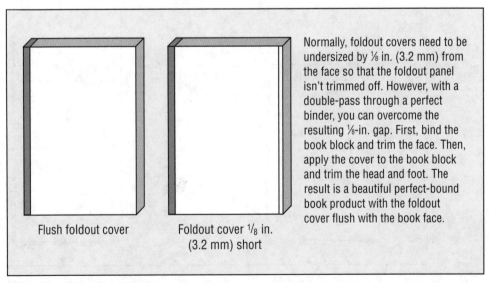

Flush foldout cover

Foldout cover ¹/₈ in. (3.2 mm) short

Normally, foldout covers need to be undersized by ⅛ in. (3.2 mm) from the face so that the foldout panel isn't trimmed off. However, with a double-pass through a perfect binder, you can overcome the resulting ⅛-in. gap. First, bind the book block and trim the face. Then, apply the cover to the book block and trim the head and foot. The result is a beautiful perfect-bound book product with the foldout cover flush with the book face.

Production tricks with foldout covers.

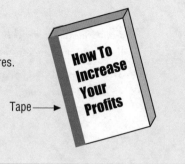

- Eye-catching new look.
- Mix and match paper stock.
- Use any form thickness—e.g., 2-, 4-, or 16-page signatures.
- Flysheet covers look great.
- Use foldouts, foldups, diecuts, and more.
- Variety of tape colors and textures.
- Functions as "capping" for case-bound books.

Tape →

Using adhesive tape binding to get a different look.

Packing. Select the right boxes for your project. Predetermining box counts reduces the bindery line packer's ability to tightly pack books and may necessitate adding foreign filler material. When books are packed loosely, your chances of cover rubbing, scuffing, and scratching greatly increase. Encourage your customers to give you packing guidelines, not specifics.

* * *

The Final Word...

To ensure that your job goes well, make sure your customer communicates the product's end use to you. A book intended to last ten years may require different treatment than a throwaway advertising piece with a shelf life of a day.

Contributors:

- *Mark Beard, Finishbinders, Inc., Des Moines, Iowa*
  www.finishbinders.com

- *Fred Daubert, The Riverside Group, Rochester, New York*
  www.riversidegroup.com

- *Chris Eckhart, Eckhart & Company, Indianapolis, Indiana*
  www.eckhartandco.com

- *John Helline, Spiral of Ohio, Inc., Cleveland, Ohio*
  www.spiralohio.com

- *Dave Gischel, Victor Graphics, Baltimore, Maryland*
  www.victorgraphics.com

- *Kris Koch, Allied Bindery, Madison Heights, Michigan*
  www.alliedbindery.com

- *Chuck Manthey, Sentinel Printing Company, St. Cloud, Minnesota*
  www.sentinelprinting.com

- *Bill Seidl, Seidl's Bindery, Houston, Texas*
  www.seidlsbindery.com

- *Frank Shear, Seaboard Bindery, Woburn, Massachusetts*
  www.seaboardbindery.com

- *Mike Welsch, Muscle Bound Bindery, Minneapolis, Minnesota*
  www.mbbindery.com

16 PUR Glue Binding

With the exception of machine setup times and running speeds, major technological advancements in the postpress world are relatively few. However, one technology that has markedly improved the adhesive-binding process is polyurethane reactive (PUR) adhesive. PUR glue offers several clear advantages over traditional perfect-binding adhesives—so much so, in fact, that some experts believe that PUR adhesive binding eventually may spell the end of perfect binding.

What You Will Learn

- The strength advantages of PUR glue
- Applying the glue
- Extended curing time

Do adhesive-bound books need to stay together? Of course they do. For the ultimate in raw strength and flexibility, don't trust anything less than PUR glue. PUR lasts far longer than ordinary hot-melt and cold-emulsion adhesives, stands up to extreme temperatures better, looks great, and holds difficult coated stock with an iron-clad grip.

More Strength, Better Flexibility

PUR glues are considered by bindery experts to be the most flexible and durable bookbinding adhesives on the market. Those properties have also made them popular for use in automobiles and aircraft—a good indication of how well it holds books together. PUR glues yield products that lie flatter and require less backbone preparation than other types of glue. PUR dries clear, less of it is needed to create a solid bond, and it yields stunningly beautiful products. And, since PUR cures to a semi-soft state, books bound with PUR glue "lay flatter" than those bound with traditional EVA hot-melts.

The page-pull strength of a PUR-bound book is more than 2.5 times that of a standard EVA perfect-bound book. Books bound with PUR adhesive simply will not fall apart, even under heavy usage in the most demanding conditions.

Over time, hot-melt perfect-bound books lose both their strength and pages. This isn't a problem for books with a short life expectancy, but for many types of products, failing glue can be a serious flaw. Until PUR glue hit the bookbinding scene in the late 1980s, there was no cost-effective solution to the problems caused by aging glue.

Why PUR?

PUR glues transcend the normal limitations of hot-melt glues, even when exposed to the most difficult environmental conditions. Try holding a PUR-bound book under water. The pages will get soggy and lose their structural integrity, but the glue will hold fine. Not only do page-pull tests conclusively demonstrate that PUR is at least 20 percent stronger than traditional hot-melts, but simulated aging tests prove that PUR lasts far longer than paper.

PUR's bond is so strong, in fact, that it routinely replaces previously Smyth-sewn and notch-perfect-bound books for some applications. Today, many museum-quality art books, coffee table books, and frequently used library reference materials are bound with less costly PUR.

As we have seen, the choice of glue and binding method depend on the printed product's proposed end use. Products likely to benefit from the use of PUR glue include:

- Perfect-bound books with 80-lb. coated text or heavier.

- Signatures with ink, varnish, UV, or aqueous coating bleeding into the gutter.

- Books that are frequently opened and closed.

- Books used in extreme environmental conditions.

- Otabind and RepKover "lay-flat" adhesive binding.

PUR also can be used to rescue-bind books that already have "failed" during conventional perfect binding. For example, a bindery once was asked to bind a cata-log with 80-lb. coated text. The previous version of the project had failed because it was subjected to exceptionally heavy use: End-users cracked spines and lost pages as they repeatedly opened the books for photocopying. After the next version was bound with PUR, customer complaints disappeared.

Technical Considerations

Unlike hot-melt adhesives that cure within seconds of application, PUR glue needs at least six hours to cure. During this time, PUR books must remain exposed to natural air because the bonding chemicals in PUR cure by drawing moisture out of the air. (Contrary to the behavior of regular hot-melt glues, PUR glues actually cure faster on humid days.) If uncured PUR-bound books are shrink- or stretch-wrapped, stringy strands of glue may wind up clinging to poorly bound pages.

NOTE: Although a six-hour cure time may sound long, this is a big im-provement. It was only a few years ago that a twenty-four-hour curing period was mandatory!

When sending a job out for PUR binding, let your bindery know what type of printing press was used. Heatset web-run jobs should have time to acclimate to the surrounding atmosphere and absorb moisture before the PUR-binding process is begun. As soon as these heatset web jobs arrive at the bindery's loading dock, all stretch-wrap should be removed so that the process can begin.

In addition, PUR produces smoother, less-wavy spines than traditional perfect binding because it runs at cooler temperatures and draws less moisture out of the paper itself. In general, very thin books (approaching ¹⁄₁₆ in.) as well as those with cross-grain signatures should be bound with PUR glue.

Testing Strength

Most PUR formulations cure too slowly to be tested during production. Although PUR glue is clear, some formulations now have a built-in ultraviolet indicator that enables operators to view these glues under a black light and determine the quality of application. Regular hot-melt-bound pages should withstand a minimum pressure of $2\frac{1}{2}$ pounds per linear inch before yielding from the spine. PUR glues routinely withstand from 4 to 7 pounds of pressure before being dislodged.

Another PUR test is called the "subway" test. Here, the PUR operator folds back the product cover to cover and looks for adequate connecting filaments of glue crossing the spine, a phenomenon commonly called "stringing." If you see consistent stringing from head to foot, and if the entire spine is tacky to the touch, you can rest assured you have good coverage and that your product will be strong.

In short, PUR is so good that some binderies are now using PUR glue for all of their adhesive-binding applications. Because there are no adhesive setup processes to perform, scheduling and turnaround times are greatly reduced.

*   *   *

The Final Word...

The strength, flexibility, and durability of PUR adhesive overcome many of the inherent concerns of perfect binding. Designers are free to use inks and coatings liberally, as PUR will form a super-strong bond in their presence. Books can also be planned to last many years, as pages will not fall out of a PUR-bound book. They key to the success of a PUR binding project is to find a postpress services provider that's not only experienced in the use of PUR adhesive but can also perform ancillary services such as diecutting, folding, cutting, and shrink-wrapping. Should PUR glue be used on a standard short-life 96-page book containing 60-lb. offset text with no ink or coatings bleeding into the gutter? No. The additional expense isn't worth it. However, for many other products requiring more durability and flexibility, choose PUR, the strongest bookbinding glue available.

Contributors:

- *Marty Anson, Bindagraphics, Inc., Baltimore, Maryland*
  www.bindagraphics.com

- *Fred Daubert, The Riverside Group, Rochester, New York*
  www.riversidegroup.com

- *Kris Koch, Allied Bindery, Madison Heights, Michigan*
  www.alliedbindery.com
- *Bill Seidl, Seidl's Bindery, Houston, Texas*
  www.seidlsbindery.com
- *Frank Shear, Seaboard Bindery, Woburn, Massachusetts*
  www.seaboardbindery.com

17 Lay-Flat Adhesive Binding

Columbus may have proved that the world is round, but some things should lie flat. Some volumes, like cookbooks, are more useful when people can use them hands-free. Likewise, software and computer manuals, instruction books, and similar types of products all should lie flat. Until recently, mechanical binding (Wire-O, plastic spiral, spiral wire, and GBC) was the only so-called "lay-flat" binding solution available. When perfect binding isn't a good solution because the user is apt to break the spine, and when price is a major consideration, ruling out too-expensive mechanical binding, your best solution may be "lay-flat" adhesive binding.

What You Will Learn

- The Otabind process
- The RepKover process
- Layout tips

There are several options for lay-flat adhesive binding. As with any binding style, understanding and managing the production process will ensure your project will be completed without any hitches.

Otabind Lay-Flat Adhesive Binding

The premier lay-flat adhesive binding process is Otabind. Developed in the 1980s by the Finland-based Otava Publishing Company, Otabind has gained widespread favor in the United States, becoming the preferred method for many companies that produce software manuals, cookbooks, textbooks, reference books, and instructional materials.

The Otabind process requires two applications of cold-applied polyvinyl acetate (PVA) glue down the spine of the book block to adhere pages to a crash paper liner. The cover is then attached with glue on the side of the book block, rather than across the entire width of the spine as in traditional perfect binding. The use of PVA adds to the book's flexibility because cold glues cure to a semisoft state and don't crack like hot-melts.

The Otabind method not only yields a higher-quality binding but also is significantly cheaper than its nearest substitute product—mechanical binding. For example,

A publication bound using the Otabind method.

one postpress company has bound more than one million copies of a 496-page cook-book. Early editions of the book had been plastic comb-bound at a bindery price of $2.06 each. Using Otabind, the cost dropped to $0.31 each. Otabind is now widely accepted in the United States, and major companies routinely specify it when placing book orders.

There are certain guidelines to keep in mind when considering Otabind lay-flat adhesive binding. Typically, it is used on books up to 1½ in. (38.1 mm) thick. For maximum binding strength, paper grain should run parallel to the spine, as with all adhesive binding. Although some binderies initially shied away from Otabind because of difficulties with coated stock, generally it can be successfully used if the coating is light and the grain runs parallel to the spine. On occasion, some companies have been able to use Otabind on 70- to 80-lb. stock, with grain running in the wrong direction. In other instances, Otabind has been used for directories with tabbed pages on cover stock.

When laying out Otabind projects, keep artwork at least ½ in. (12.7 mm) away from the spine for the inside front and back covers, as well as for the first and last text pages of the book block. Because side glue is used to bind the cover to the book block, this ½-in. clearance is needed for artwork to clear the extra hinge scores required by Otabinding.

RepKover Lay-Flat Adhesive Binding

One lay-flat adhesive binding option well-suited for short-run projects is RepKover. Developed by RIT Professor Emeritus Werner Rebsamen, RepKover is frequently used as an alternative to Otabind. Covers for the RepKover binding method are pro-duced separately from the book block. A wide cloth strip is glued along the spine of the inside front and back covers with cold PVA glue. Next, glue is applied to the book

A publication bound using the RepKover method, which uses a cloth strip mounted on the inside of the spine to reinforce the soft cover of a book

block and the preassembled cover is properly positioned and affixed into place. Since RepKover entails a quick makeready, it is a cost-efficient alternative to Wire-O, spiral wire, or any other form of mechanical binding.

Because RepKover involves extra production steps and specific types of equipment, it is best to discuss both methods with your bindery before making your choice. When laying out a RepKover project, ask your bindery how far the cloth strip will creep up the inside front and back cover. Then, keep your inside cover artwork away from the spine by at least this margin. Copy can run right next to the spine (after allowances for grind-off) for first and last text pages of the book block.

PUR Glue As a Lay-Flat Adhesive-Binding Method

Some binderies use PUR hot-melt glue as lay-flat adhesive binding. This adhesive is more flexible than older types of glues, works well with any type of stock, and is acceptable for some applications. PUR-only lay-flat adhesive binding doesn't have a flexible crash sheet and usually won't lie as flat as either Otabind or RepKover.

If you are outsourcing lay-flat adhesive binding, ask your bindery representative what type of lay-flat binding they use. The marketplace is full of Otabind knockoffs, and while some of them may function as promised, others may cause disappointment. When in doubt, ask.

* * *

The Final Word...

By consulting with a postpress house on unusual or unfamiliar binding and finishing requirements, you'll not only avert high costs, but you may also discover unexpected solutions that uniquely and effectively meet your customers' needs.

Contributors:

- *Marty Anson, Bindagraphics, Inc., Baltimore, Maryland*
  www.bindagraphics.com
- *Fred Daubert, The Riverside Group, Rochester, New York*
  www.riversidegroup.com
- *Kris Koch, Allied Bindery, Madison Heights, Michigan*
  www.alliedbindery.com
- *Bill Seidl, Seidl's Bindery, Houston, Texas*
  www.seidlsbindery.com
- *Frank Shear, Seaboard Bindery, Woburn, Massachusetts*
  www.seaboardbindery.com
- *Mike Welsch, Muscle Bound Bindery, Minneapolis, Minnesota*
  www.mbbindery.com

18 Saddle Stitching

Saddle stitching describes the art of inserting forms on top of other forms over a saddle and driving stitches through the "backbone" of the gathered piece. Companion operations such as in-line trimming, drilling, punching, inkjet printing, refolding, wafer sealing, shrink-wrapping, and packaging all increase the value of stitched products.

What You Will Learn

- Layout basics
- Maximums/minimums
- Using glue in stitching

The world of saddle stitching is much broader than simply stitching forms and trimming them to 8½×11 in. (215.9×279.4 mm). Product sizes can be smaller than 1×1½ in. (25.4×38.1 mm) or as large as 19×22 in. (482.6×558.8 mm). Foldouts, fold-ups, self-mailers, business-reply cards (BRCs), business-reply envelopes (BREs), diecut forms, tabs, and undersized and overhanging forms all add pizzazz and real customer value. Glue opens even more options because it can be applied in trim-off areas allowing stitched products to have gatefolds and multiple foldouts. Twelve-pocket saddle stitchers offer a variety of mixing and matching of forms and incredible design flexibility.

Job Planning

When executing projects with unfamiliar layouts, involve your saddle-stitching expert early on because simple layout changes can make huge differences in time and cost. Many times your least expensive printing and prepress layout will end up costing you more because of downstream bindery inefficiency.

While there are very few saddle-stitching absolutes, most stitching machines can run one-up pieces from 5×6 in. (127×152.4 mm) to 12×17 in. (304.8×431.8 mm). Specialty stitchers can run products as small as 3×3⅞ in. (76.2×98.4 mm) one-up. Although there are some exceptions, the smallest product that can be stitched two-up and trimmed in-line is 3×3 in. (76.2×76.2 mm). While still practical, smaller products usually need to be trimmed offline.

Big and Small

When your bound product is huge, there's no solution like oversized saddle stitching. Although they're rare, some stitchers can accommodate a 19×22-in. (482.6×558.8-mm) final-size product. If you have an oversized stitching resource, selling large-format

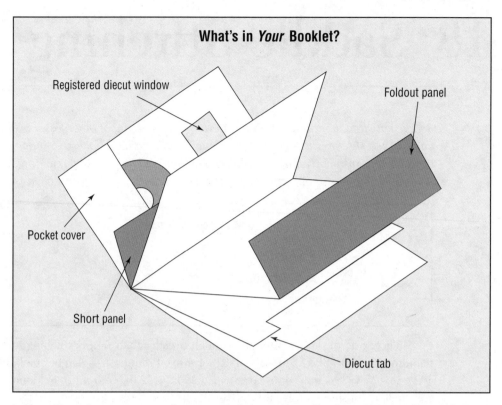

high-end products is practical. However, be sure your bindery resource has wide enough folding capabilities to accommodate the long drop of the oversized product. (Note: a 39-in.-wide [990.6-mm-wide] folder is needed to fold an 8-, 12-, or 16-page signature with a 19-in. [482.6-mm] drop.)

For products that are smaller than standard machine minimums, run them multiple-up or bind them into larger-size booklets. Either way, offline trimming is necessary to get them to their final size. Remember that the minimum distance between stitching heads is usually 2⅛ in. (54 mm). To get closer than this on products with two forms or less, find a saddle stitcher that can do double stroking—two timed sequential stitches on one product. Although production waste may be higher than normal, double stroking allows stitches to be placed ⅛ in. (3.2 mm) apart.

Compensate for Pushout with Shingling

One commonly overlooked element during saddle stitching planning is pushout, which occurs when multiple signatures are folded. To compensate for the effects of pushout on saddle-stitched books, all sheets should be shingled so that the printed area doesn't appear too close to the spine or face once the books are bound and trimmed.

Books with printed index tabs are prime candidates for shingling, as pushout would otherwise cause tabs to appear unevenly along the book's face. A diecut page that registers to print may also require shingling to ensure that tight registration is maintained once the book is bound.

Gluing in Trim-Off Areas

Six- and eight-page gatefolds with glue spots require constant monitoring and frequent sample pulls to ensure accurate glue placement. For example, if glue spreads too far into a piece, it will not be removed in the final trimming process. Easy-release glue should be used in trim-off areas to keep the product functional, even if the glue oozes into the non-trimmed area. When applying glue in trim-off areas, make sure the trim section of your bindery's stitcher can accommodate your trim-off margin choice. Generally speaking, glue only one side of a foldout—either the top or bottom. While ½-in. (12.7-mm) trim-off margin is preferable, ⅜ in. (9.5 mm) is usually fine. Place the large trim-off area opposite the jogging end so the rest of your signatures need only minimal trims.

When planning jobs with bind-ins, check with your bindery for overhang limits. Although the feeding sections and carrier chains of most saddle stitchers can bind panels as short as 2 in. (50.8 mm), not all can work on a project of this size.

Stitching pre-personalized work requires your stitching partner to maintain jobs in sequence. Doing this, however, requires many unusual manufacturing procedural steps. Because component staging, pocket loading, product packing, and quality assurance are all essential in handling pre-personalized material, it is key to find a bindery with years of experience in doing this type of work.

If your job marks or scuffs during production, it is usually because the top of one signature rubs against the bottom of another during pocket feeding. Frequently, the culprit signatures are those with heavy dark ink coverage on one outside panel and light coverage on the other. If you suspect you're going to have a scuffing problem, prudent planning would indicate varnishing the areas of concern. Signatures printed with reflex blue, silver, gold, or other metallic inks are of particular concern. If you're having a scuffing problem during production, try lighter pocket loads.

Oversized and small-format saddle-stitched jobs.

A difficult "Z" double-stitched brochure.

More Tips

The following tips can help your company run its saddle-stitching jobs more efficiently:

- Avoid having a single sheet or a thin signature sticking out of either the head or foot because it will be crushed when joggers position the product for final head and foot trims.

- For jobs with really light or porous stock, such as onionskin, expect slow production rates because reduced machine cycle speeds are needed to avoid pulling doubles.

- All in-feed tables of saddle-stitching trimming sections are not created equal. Those with pull pawls offer better book delivery into the trimming section. This means that registration into the stops is more accurate—giving you more consistent trims. In addition, good in-feeder sections won't collapse or crush the laps (lips) of thin stock.

- Reverse laps on a job will cause slow production rates. Try to keep all of your folios the same size and heading in the same direction. Your jogging-end trim margins should be consistently sized and your "off-end" trim margins should be sized within ⅛ in. (3.2 mm) of each other to ensure adequate production rates.

- When using suction opening, either the head or foot must be closed so suction applied to the outside page of a signature will open to the center every time.

- On thick books, a little tear in the rounded section of the backbone is normal. Because the spine edge isn't fully supported during trimming, knives cut through the supported top pages, but not completely through the bottom pages, causing a small rip at the backbone. With the laws of physics at work here, there is no practical way to eliminate this minor problem.

- When working with a diecut form, carefully plan your job so that nothing catches on the machinery.

- Static can cause problems. Be careful in winter and dry atmospheric conditions.

- Unbalanced signatures may require special handling to keep them from falling off the saddle or the chain. Experienced saddle stitching professionals usually can compensate for this problem with special machine rigs.

*   *   *

The Final Word...

The world of saddle stitching is beautiful and varied. Contrary to popular belief, however, saddle stitching isn't always easy to produce, and there are many ways for problems to develop on "easy" saddle-stitching projects. The good news is that there are ways to keep these problems at arm's length, "wow!" your customers, and fatten your bottom line. So hop in the saddle, ride the big horse, and delight your customers by increasing the value you already add. There's more to this timeless binding method than meets the eye.

Contributors:

- *Jim Egan, Rickard Bindery, Chicago, Illinois*
  www.rickardbindery.com

- *Sue Hein, Rapid Bind, Inc., Portland, Oregon*
  www.rapidbind.com

- *Tony Hoholik, The John Roberts Company, Minneapolis, Minnesota*
  www.johnroberts.com

- *Chuck Manthey, Sentinel Printing Company, St. Cloud, Minnesota*
  www.sentinelprinting.com

- *Joe Piazza, Action Bindery, Norcross, Georgia*
  www.actionbindery.com

- *Bruce Sanderson, Springfield Printing Corporation, Springfield, Vermont*
  www.springfieldprinting.com

19 Loop Stitching

Loop stitching is an alternate saddle-stitching style that's ideal for many ring-binder applications. Loop stitching is preferable to drilling for ring-binder applications since it allows stitched inserts to lay flat in an opened binder. And, like saddle stitching, loop stitching is compatible with products that include multiple stocks and have a wide range of final trim sizes.

What You Will Learn

- When to specify loop stitching vs. saddle stitching
- When to specify loop stitching vs. loose-leaf materials
- Loop-stitching design guidelines

Why Use Loop Stitching?

Have you ever tried to turn the pages of a three-hole-drilled saddle-stitched booklet when it's bound into a three-ring binder? If so, you know that these products are user unfriendly. They won't open easily and they certainly won't lie flat while in binders and therefore must be removed before use. Also, drilling requires either putting holes in copy or allowing extra space in the margin. Loop stitching avoids all these problems.

Loop-Stitching Planning Guidelines

Size requirements. Loop stitching can be performed with as little as 2 in. between stitches (shoulder to shoulder) for small-format applications. The positioning of the loop stitches can be altered to accommodate proprietary ring positioning for binder applications.

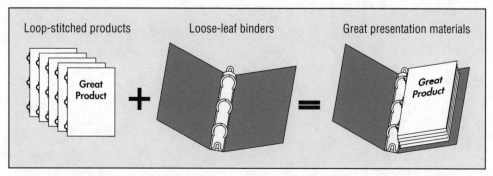

Common application of loop stitching: combining loop-stitched products with a loose-leaf binder to create great presentation materials.

Book thickness. For books printed on a normal text-weight stock, such as 60-lb. off-set, try to limit page counts to 48 pages or fewer. Although thicker books can be loop stitched, more weight places more stress on the stitches. This can lead to damaged stitches if the book is inserted into a ring binder and the binder is shaken or the book is pulled severely when opened.

*   *   *

The Final Word...

Consider loop stitching for price sheets, product catalogs, portfolios, promotional materials, and more.

Contributors:

- *Sue Hein, Rapid Bind, Inc., Portland, Oregon*
  www.rapidbind.com

- *Gary Junge, Rickard Bindery, Chicago, Illinois*
  www.rickardbindery.com

20 On-Demand Book Binding

Every dog has its day. Unfamiliar to most printers just ten years ago, the term "print on-demand" is now a part of our normal frame of reference. Practically speaking, however, "bind on-demand" still leaves many graphic arts professionals lukewarm, if not cold. This is unfortunate, given the profit potential of on-demand stitching (aka booklet binding). However, success depends on finding a partner or partners who really understand what "on-demand" means.

What You Will Learn

- On-demand is important
- Machine options
- Compete successfully

Many trade binderies aren't set up to service the needs of small and instant commercial printers. To be and stay profitable, binderies must feed their large saddle-stitching machines with lots of long runs. From a finishing point of view, however, on-demand projects offer a set of challenges distinct from those associated with longer-run, higher-quantity projects. Because quick setup and turnaround times are the name of the game in this arena, lack of planning will have a severe negative impact on production schedules. Often, for example, long-run jobs are scheduled well in advance, forcing small binding jobs into the queue whenever and wherever they fit. This lack of flexibility isn't your trade bindery's fault; it's just that on-demand stitching isn't yet a normal part of most companies' service offerings.

Trade binderies throughout the country have caught a whiff of the on-demand trend and are trying to decide what to do. Some have already tailored a portion of their services to meet the needs of this emerging market. A few offer twenty-four-hour turnaround and pick-up and delivery at standard prices—something virtually unheard of as recently as five years ago. The trick is getting on-demand printers to understand that outsourcing isn't just for large printers. Large graphic arts companies have been outsourcing bindery services for years, but small-format and on-demand printers have had few, if any, quality bindery solutions available to them.

As the demand for short-run, high-quality bindery solutions continues to grow, on-demand binderies will proliferate. These companies will have the appropriate machinery and internal systems in place to service the outsourcing needs of instant

On-demand saddle-stitched booklet.

and small commercial printers in much the same way on-demand printers service corporate America right now. While partnering with an on-demand bindery is best (if you can find one), working with a commercial trade bindery that understands the on-demand market may be more realistic. At some point, however, you will need to find a company that is oriented primarily toward providing binding and finishing solutions to instant and small commercial printers.

Until then, and as on-demand printing services continue to broaden, postpress services providers that can handle this type of work are becoming increasingly valuable.

Booklet Binding

On-demand stitching machines belong to two distinct categories. One group is comprised of "horizontal" units that collate flat sheets before stitching, folding, and face-trimming the product to final size. For example, a 17-pocket Omnibinder or Multibinder can stitch a 68-page book in a single pass. Once the sheets are stack-collated and stitched, the product travels to a buckle-type folder, gets folded on the stitch, and proceeds toward the trimming blade. Unlike traditional saddle stitchers with three-knife trimmers, most on-demand machines can't make head or foot trims. (This is rarely a problem because on-demand booklets are usually 8½×11-in. or 5½×8½-in.) Depending on the job, horizontal units with fast makereadies can yield up to 4,000 books per hour or more.

Another type of on-demand stitcher is the "tower" unit. These machines may have as many as six connected collating towers, each with at least eight feeding stations, providing up to sixty "pockets" from which to load sheets. With the aid of this type of machine, a shop theoretically can collate 240-page books with sixty different types of stock. This kind of design flexibility far outstrips that offered by the most elaborate trade saddle stitcher. Since most tower systems have knife-folding mechanisms instead of buckle folders, booklets with tough folds on color breaks turn out looking great. In addition, some tower units equipped with automatic servomotor-driven stitching heads and stops offer five-minute makereadies. Many modern tower machines will yield more than 3,000 books per hour.

The marking problems of yesteryear's "friction-fed" on-demand stitching machines have largely disappeared. Today's vacuum suckers don't mark. This means your stock can be as varied as carbon paper, carbonless forms, enamel, onionskin, and 10-point cover. Heavy ink coverage doesn't cause a marking problem either. Because these machines are equipped with accurate measuring calipers, you also can forget about "doubles" and "misses" caused by mismatching stocks.

Begin at the End

In the world of on-demand printing, getting projects on and off press quickly is of paramount importance. However, equal consideration must be paid to how quickly projects can be turned around during postpress production. Layout specifics, ink chemistry, stock selection, and other details all can impact the speed and quality of production both during and after printing. It is important for quick printers to review these details with their finisher to make sure there are no unpleasant "surprises" in store downstream.

Unfortunately, the term "on-demand bindery" raises the expectation of grabbing a project straight off the press and immediately performing finishing work on it. That may be the speed at which production seemingly occurs, but even the shortest production runs require careful planning to turn out properly. As with any other print project, on-demand applications should be planned well in advance of the actual printing by accounting for the product's end use first.

The Opportunity

If you are a small-format printer and can find a bindery that is able to service the on-demand market, you will find yourself competitive on many booklet projects that were formerly out of your reach. For example, if you operate 17-in. presses, you should be competitive with printers that operate 28-in. presses on normal-sized booklet work up to twenty thousand pieces. Personalized covers should further tilt the odds in your favor.

When it comes to 8½×11-in. six-page newsletters, a 17-in. press ordinarily wouldn't stand a competitive chance against a 28-in. press with slit-to-nest folding machine. Add on-demand stitching capability, however, and the 17-in. printer can print two forms, collate the two-pager with the four-pager, turn the stitching head off, and finish by knife-folding the stacked product. And that's that: He winds up back in the horse race with a cost-effective six-page newsletter. If the insert needs to be on a different-colored stock, of course, the job is his.

More On-Demand Booklet Stitching Benefits:

Crossover registration. When a book is stripped for saddle stitching and contains crossovers between the signatures, changing to an on-demand layout should help. Unlike saddle machines, on-demand stitchers fold books at the unit's cutter, giving the operator considerable control over the fold position. As a result, your crossovers should be dead-on.

Single operator. Unlike the traditional fold/saddle stitch/trim process, which requires many operators with different skills, on-demand binding is usually a one-person operation. This efficiency translates into cost savings on short runs.

Design flexibility. Options include diecuts, foldouts, collation-only, mixed-paper stock, bind-ins, corner stitching, side stitching, and small-format books, among others.

Delivery flexibility. In-line possibilities include stagger-stacking, letter- (or tri-) folding, quarter-folding, and more.

Short-Run Adhesive Binding

Perfect-bound books need to have good page-pull strength, square backs, and smooth spines. Getting all these factors right used to mean using large, high-speed production machines, rated at 6,000 books per hour and up. Unfortunately, the longer setup time and high machine hourly rates make short-run production on this class of machine prohibitively expensive. Luckily, there are now short-run perfect-binding machines that turn out perfect-bound books that are virtually indistinguishable from those produced on full-size machines.

At one time, boutique-binding methods, like Otabind lay-flat adhesive binding, were only appropriate for long runs. However, newer processes, like RepKover binding, were developed for the short-run, high-quality segment of the lay-flat adhesive binding market. Many people are surprised that RepKover makes economic sense for quantities as few as 25 books.

Times Have Changed

Once upon a time, short-run printing was a marvel in and of itself. High-quality short-run printing was so rare that binding style and quality hardly mattered. Tape binding, plastic strip binding, and peculiar-sized double-loop wire binding methods were in their heyday because there wasn't any real competition. Machine manufacturers have kept their ears to the ground and developed high-quality binding solutions tailored to the short-run arena. Consequently, print buyers and end users now expect binding and finishing excellence, regardless of run length.

Some digital printing systems offer in-line perfect binding and saddle stitching. Before using these low-cost, in-line binding methods, however, make sure you're satisfied with the quality level. A DocuTech or similar machine may be the right answer for the printing portion of the job, but you may prefer traditional (but still on-demand!) offline bookbinding for better quality.

*   *   *

The Final Word...

Although many postpress functions are applicable to on-demand projects, not all providers are well-suited for short-run work. The key is to find a provider with the equipment, production capacity, and experience to meet your needs and the needs of your customers. Just as customers look for you to provide high quality with fast turn-arounds, you should look for a postpress services provider that will do the same. If you're a small-format commercial or on-demand printer, learn what bindery resources are available to you. When top quality is a must, be sure to look for binderies that understand the nuances of the short-run, high-quality market. Quality is never a given.

Contributors:

- *Mark Beard, Finishbinders, Inc., Des Moines, Iowa*
  www.finishbinders.com

- *Sue Hein, Rapid Bind, Inc., Portland, Oregon*
  www.rapidbind.com

- *Chuck Manthey, Sentinel Printing Company, St. Cloud, Minnesota*
  www.sentinelprinting.com

- *Peter Pape, The Riverside Group, Rochester, New York*
  www.riversidegroup.com

- *Frank Shear, Seaboard Bindery, Woburn, Massachusetts*
  www.seaboardbindery.com

21 Choose the Right Mechanical-Binding Method

The number of products that can benefit from mechanical binding is enormous. Mechanically bound products lay perfectly flat and the format is appropriate for a diverse array of products including desk and wall calendars, cookbooks, instruction manuals, handbooks, and more. This versatility is particularly important for projects with design elements such as diecuts, foldout covers, different-sized sheets, and index tabs.

What You Will Learn

- Mechanical-binding choices
- Common applications
- Manufacturing guidelines

Adhesive binding isn't the best solution for applications that need to lie flat as a board. Anyone who has tried to read a perfect-bound computer manual while clicking away at the keyboard already has an inkling of this. To get the pages to remain open, a perfect-bound spine needs to be heavily creased, a practice that can easily produce a cracked or broken spine.

Now imagine how unappealing a perfect-bound calendar would look, dangling from a wall. Saddle stitching is a low-cost alternative, but it isn't appropriate for thick amounts of paper. As we've already discovered, lay-flat adhesive binding can be a terrific option, but even its pages don't lie perfectly flat. Mechanical binding is a time-tested marriage of form and function that completely solves this lie-flat problem.

Mechanical Binding Choices

Wire-O binding. Also known as double-loop wire binding, Wire-O is an elegant, durable binding style, which, though popular for decades, never looks dated. Wire-O is an appropriate choice for books containing crossover images because its securely bound pages open 360° without a "step-up." Do you want to include foldouts and tabs? With Wire-O, these production options are a cinch. Its contemporary good looks and

Mechanical Binding Type	Opens 360°	Temp. Effects	Shift Up or Down	Print on Spine	Max. Book Thickness*
Wire-O	Yes	No	No	No**	1⅛ in. (28.6 mm)
Plastic coil	Yes	Yes	Yes	No**	1¼ in. (31.8 mm)
Spiral wire	Yes	No	Yes	No**	1¼ in. (31.8 mm)
GBC	No	Yes	No	Yes	1¾ in. (44.4 mm)

——
*Thickness maximums are industry norms only. Larger custom dies can be made. Also, these maximums are for book block bulk, not binding element measurement size.

**Wraparound concealed covers can have printed spines.

Mechanical binding features.

functionality have earned Wire-O a reputation as the "Cadillac" of the mechanical binding world and the reigning king of lay-flat bookbinding.

Plastic spiral. Plastic spiral is popular for use in products such as children's books, high-tech instruction manuals, and cookbooks. Plastic spiral elements are very durable and spring back to their original shape, even after being crushed. For products to be used by children or placed on fine furniture, plastic spiral doesn't scratch and is generally considered to be safer than Wire-O. Like Wire-O, plastic spiral elements are available in a wide variety of colors and sizes. Although plastic spiral can be highly automated, capable machines aren't common, thus long runs usually aren't economical. Like Wire-O books, plastic coil products can be opened 360° for usability. Unlike Wire-O, however, plastic spiral-bound pages do "step-up" when opened; therefore, crossover images should be avoided whenever possible.

Mechanical Binding Type	Pitch	Recommended Copy Distance from Spine	Max. Book Thickness
Wire-O	3:1	⅜ in. (9.5 mm)	½ in. (12.7 mm)
	2:1	½ in. (12.7 mm)	1⅛ in. (28.6 mm)
Plastic coil	5:1	⅜ in. (9.5 mm)	½ in. (12.7 mm)
	4:1	½ in. (12.7 mm)	1¼ in. (31.8 mm)
	2½:1	⁹⁄₁₆ in. (14.3 mm)	1¼ in. (31.8 mm)
Spiral wire	5:1	⅜ in. (9.5 mm)	⅜ in. (9.5 mm)
	4:1	⅜ in. (9.5 mm)	1 in. (25.4 mm)
	2½:1	½ in. (12.7 mm)	1¼ in. (31.8 mm)
GBC	⁹⁄₁₆ C2C	½ in. (12.7 mm)	1¾ in. (44.4 mm)

Normal specifications for common products. Thickness maximums are norms only. Larger custom dies can be made for many pitch sizes.

Spiral wire. Although they are inexpensive, spiral wire-bound products have neither the sturdy elegance of Wire-O, nor the contemporary appeal of plastic spiral. In addition, the popularity of spiral wire appears to be declining. Unless a really thick-gauge wire is used, spiral wire binding isn't as strong as Wire-O because a single spiral wire coil contains less wire than Wire-O's "double-loop" design. Inconveniently, spiral wire-bound pages also "step-up."

Plastic comb. Plastic comb binding (*aka* GBC® Binding, GBC is a trademark of General Binding Corporation) is not an attractive choice for books that need to be held in one hand. Unlike wire- or plastic spiral-bound products, plastic comb binding doesn't open 360°. Although plastic comb binding elements can be imprinted, this advantage is quickly lost since other mechanical binding styles can support printed reversible or fully concealed wraparound covers. Moreover, while plastic comb binding is useful for very thick books, many designers also think that plastic comb elements look dated. As a result, a plastic comb binding has experienced a decline in popularity.

A variety of mechanically bound publications.

Knowing a product's end use is important when selecting the right mechanical binding style. For example, if a book has critical crossovers, such as maps, artwork, or diagrams, it would be best to choose Wire-O or GBC because these styles open without stepping up or down. Likewise, if a book is to be held in one hand, such as equipment manuals or some maps, it would be wise to choose a binding style that opens 360°. If the books will be exposed to extreme temperatures, don't choose plastic binding, such as GBC and plastic coil, because they can melt or crack. If a book is to be sold in retail stores, spine printing might be important.

Calendars

Among the most familiar of promotional products, calendars routinely feature unusual foldouts, PMS-matched binding elements, different-sized pages, gorgeous printing, creative diecutting, foil stamping, and other finishing techniques. Calendars can be long and thin, short and fat, huge, tiny, even round. Mechanical binding adds elegance, as do calendar hangers and matching thumb cuts. For a contemporary look, consider plastic coil. If you want to get back to basics, spiral wire binding is a solid alternative. Just make sure that the form of the calendar matches its intended function.

Calendar Benefits: The Short List

• Most people have the need for another calendar and will hang them somewhere.

• Calendars are displayed for 365 days or more.

• They're cost-effective with round-the-clock exposure at pennies per day.

• You control the distribution—this is target marketing at its best.

• Choose from unlimited design options.

• Calendars are an advertising medium that people actually ask for.

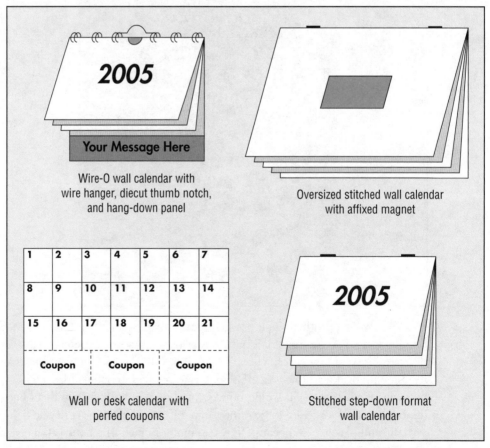

Wire-O wall calendar with wire hanger, diecut thumb notch, and hang-down panel

Oversized stitched wall calendar with affixed magnet

Wall or desk calendar with perfed coupons

Stitched step-down format wall calendar

A few popular calendar design options.

Consider plastic coil binding instead of Wire-O if calendars are to be mailed. Even if someone steps on a plastic coil-bound book, the resident "memory" of the plastic will cause the binding element to spring right back into shape.

*   *   *

The Final Word…

Projects that require a versatile and attractive binding style are ideal candidates for mechanical binding. Mechanical binding's lay-flat capabilities enable easy handling, while the wide choice of binding element colors encourages creativity. Mechanical binding integrates easily and economically with products that include foldouts, tabs, and other finishing options, providing maximum design flexibility and adding value. As always, careful preplanning is a prerequisite for success.

Contributors:

- *Chris Eckhart, Eckhart & Company, Indianapolis, Indiana*
  www.eckhartandco.com

- *Russ Haines, Rapid Bind, Inc., Portland, Oregon*
  www.rapidbind.com

- *Gary Markovits, E&M Bindery, Clifton, New Jersey*
  www.embindery.com

- *Peter Pape, The Riverside Group, Rochester, New York*
  www.riversidegroup.com

- *Bill Seidl, Seidl's Bindery, Houston, Texas*
  www.seidlsbindery.com

- *Frank Shear, Seaboard Bindery, Woburn, Massachusetts*
  www.seaboardbindery.com

22 Wire-O Binding

Other mechanical binding styles—plastic coil, plastic comb, spiral wire—have short-comings that Wire-O doesn't share. Plastic coil, for example, has a contemporary look, but it "steps up" when opened and is subject to fluctuations in temperature. In the winter, plastic coil may crack; in the summer, it may lose its shape when left out in the hot sun. Likewise, plastic comb binding also is subject to extremes of temperature; worse, it also looks dated and can't be opened 360°. Spiral wire also steps up when opened, complicating crossover image registration. Moreover, because less wire is used per linear inch, it is not as strong as Wire-O.

What You Will Learn

- Job planning and production issues
- Wire-O cover options
- Get the book block bulk right

Job Planning and Production Issues

Since most Wire-O jobs contain a lot of separate components, you must work with complete job information from the beginning. End users want books that are modern and attractive yet durable and easy to use. Designers continue to pack more information into less space, making options such as foldouts and tabs increasingly necessary. As if these demands weren't enough, tighter budgets mean that maximum productivity must be squeezed out of every dollar.

Wire-O bound book.

Start with a sample. The shortest and simplest way to get the results you desire is to provide your finisher with a sample of the project. This allows your finisher to measure all margins, copy placement, final trim size, tab placement, and more. It's important that the sample be produced on the exact stock to be used for the production run. This allows the book bulk to be measured to determine the proper binding pitch. For books bulking ½ in. or less, 3:1 (three holes per inch) wire will be used. Books thicker than ½ in. will require 2:1 binding.

Height and width. If you're working on a semi-concealed book, make a bulking dummy and choose the right Wire-O size and these dimensions before laying out your cover.

Signatures. If split-back Wire-O pages are printed in signature form, the signatures first must be folded. All forms then must be gathered, glued, then three-knife trimmed on a perfect binder. The manufacturing process diverges from traditional perfect binding when the fourth side of the book blocks is trimmed off. Finally, the collated stack of loose sheets is punched and the individual books are Wire-O bound.

Cutting and collating. If your project has a low page count, small quantity, or uses variable-size leaves, different stocks, foldouts, diecuts, tabs, or bind-ins, consider cutting sheets to final size and collating them on a single sheet-style collating machine prior to punching and binding.

Scoring. Semi-concealed covers should be scored in opposing directions. Unglued, fully concealed six-page covers must have all scores going in the same direction. If the back two panels are glued together—turning your cover into a four-pager—it will be necessary to add a fourth opposing score.

Punching into copy. All images and text should be kept clear of the spine area to avoid the punched binding holes. This is a common mistake on Wire-O projects. It's also easy to avoid. Appropriate margins are dictated by the size of the Wire-O binding elements. Books that bulk thicker than ½ in. require 2:1 (two holes per inch) Wire-O elements, while thinner books use 3:1 binding. For 2:1 Wire-O projects, a margin of $\frac{7}{16}$ in. from spine edge to the outer edge of the binding hole is appropriate. On 3:1 books, the margin should be at least $\frac{5}{16}$ in. For 2:1 Wire-O books bulking over ½ in. thick, allow at least $\frac{9}{16}$ in. margin.

Projects with overhanging covers. Overhanging covers are ideal for books with tabs, where the cover will be flush with the tab to prevent bending and tearing. Make sure your bindery is capable of fully automatic production on projects with several spine-to-face trim sizes.

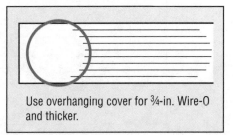

Use overhanging cover for ¾-in. Wire-O and thicker.

Let your bindery do the cutting and collating. Most Wire-O projects involve functions such as cutting, folding, and collating. Cutting and collating go hand in hand with Wire-O binding; when your bindery can work with uncut, uncollated sheets, the result is often better-looking and more efficiently produced. A finisher that can perform these operations in-house can save you time, money, and aggravation.

Plan tabs properly. For projects that include tabs, look for a company that can diecut the tabs and collate them along with the rest of the book just before binding. In order to bind in tabs automatically with the text sheets, leave at least a ¼-in. "shoulder" from the edge of the tab to the head or foot of the sheet. To realize greater production efficiencies, have your finisher collate the tab pages. This not only will ensure that page-specific tabs are located properly, it also makes binding different-sized pages easier.

Skip-binding. This binding style has two or more separate Wire-O binding elements on the same binding edge. Though skip binding is appropriate for almost any Wire-O book application, calendars benefit even more when a wire calendar hanger is inserted between the two wire banks, providing a sturdy and attractive hanging option. No wall-hanging printed product looks better than a thumb-notched calendar with "hangers" inserted between the separate Wire-O elements. Don't settle for drill holes when hangers are available.

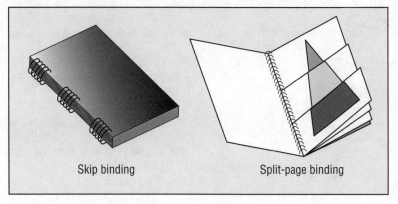

Creative Wire-O binding styles.

Skip binding   Split-page binding

T-slotting. This attractive and functional option enables end users to insert or remove pages quickly. Instead of standard square holes, the book block is punched with a T-shaped die, which allows pages to be easily inserted and removed from a Wire-O book. This is particularly useful for projects such as instruction manuals, where the contents may change frequently.

Layout Concerns

Different machines that are producing the same job sometimes require different layouts for production efficiency. For example, some binderies may want to fold and cut a job, whereas others might prefer to cut and collate the same job. When in doubt, don't guess because your turnaround time and price is dependent on your layout decisions. Poor communication from the bid stage through production can be costly.

Consider another example. An oblong 4×6-in. (101.6×152.4-mm) product (bound on the 4-in. side) should be laid out two-up for automatic punching. If not, your bindery will have to hand-feed lifts into a manual punching machine. What if a similar product is bound on the 6-in. side? If the stock is 12 pt. or thicker, grain direction becomes very important. In this case, the grain should be long because if it isn't, the book may not automatically punch or collate.

Product Thickness

Book thickness greatly affects page layout. Thick books require stronger and larger binding elements, which in turn demand larger punched holes. Bigger holes need to be punched deeper into the page, affecting the positioning of the artwork.

For example, the two most common Wire-O® pitch sizes are 3:1 (i.e., three holes per linear inch) and 2:1. Any book ½ in. (12.7 mm) thick or less will require 3:1 pitch wire, which means copy should be kept ⅜ in. (9.5 mm) away from the spine edge to avoid punching into type. Books that are more than ½ in. thick will use 2:1 pitch wire and, because larger holes will be needed, add more punching margin by keeping copy ½ in. away from the spine. Punching into type is a common problem, but one that is easy to rectify.

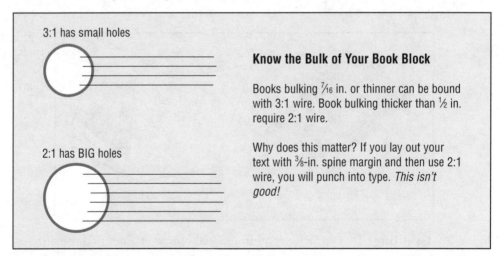

3:1 has small holes

2:1 has BIG holes

Know the Bulk of Your Book Block

Books bulking ⁷⁄₁₆ in. or thinner can be bound with 3:1 wire. Book bulking thicker than ½ in. require 2:1 wire.

Why does this matter? If you lay out your text with ⅜-in. spine margin and then use 2:1 wire, you will punch into type. *This isn't good!*

Choose the Right Cover Style

If your book will be stacked on a shelf and/or when spine printing is necessary, reversible and one-piece spine styles are good choices. These semi-concealed and cased-in multi-panel covers give mechanically bound volumes the look of perfect-bound books, in addition to providing extra real estate for advertisements. All of these options can incorporate diecuts and capacity pockets. And, because mechanically bound books are trimmed prior to binding, foldouts are easily accomplished.

Well-conceived cover designs can improve the appearance and functionality of Wire-O projects. There are many cover styles to choose from, but among the most common designs are:

- Split-back
- Semi-concealed
- Fully concealed wraparound

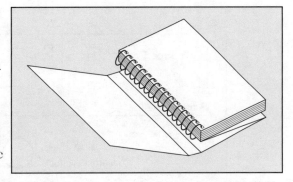

Fully and semi-concealed "wraparound" covers are useful for spine imprinting, protection of inside content, and products with a lot of cover copy. Both styles offer tremendous design flexibility, as well as a printable spine that hides the binding elements without sacrificing functionality. It's up to graphic arts service providers to help their customers design covers that are pleasant to look at, yet retain all the advantages of Wire-O. For projects that feature significant cover copy or multi-panel images, semi- and fully concealed Wire-O are ideal solutions.

Fully concealed covers are more expensive to produce than semi-concealed because they require more paper and tend to slow turnaround times. Longer six-page forms are even more difficult to handle and frequently must be hand-punched because of their length.

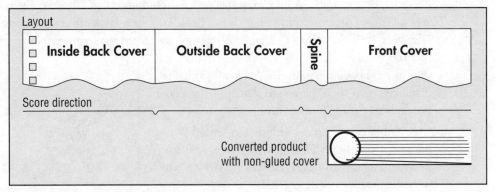

Six-page fully concealed Wire-O cover design.

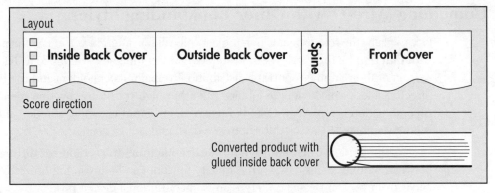

Four-page fully concealed (two panels glued) Wire-O cover design.

In contrast, four-page semi-concealed covers usually can be punched automatically, provided the cover is thin enough. One advantage of leaving fully concealed covers unglued is that the extra cover space will be available for easy reference or high-priced advertising.

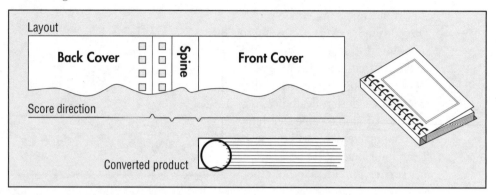

Semi-concealed Wire-O cover design.

For books that will incorporate paid advertising, fully concealed Wire-O can be produced with a six-panel cover that offers plenty of prime real estate for ads or coupons. The last panel also can be glued to form a traditional four-panel cover.

Split-back style is the "standard" Wire-O cover choice. Attractive, two-piece split-back covers are a solid choice when you are battling limited budgets and striving for quick turnaround. As long as your book has common page dimensions, no tabs, and a Wire-O diameter of ⅝ in. or less, "flush-cut" split-back covers are hard to beat.

However, if thicker Wire-O is needed, design your two-piece cover with ⅛-in. "overhang" to compensate for text page pushout. If your books must be displayed on a shelf, be aware that split-back covers do not permit spine printing.

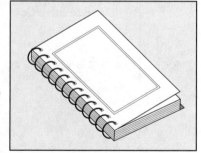

Other cover choices include top-bound Wire-O books with pop-out "easels," which are great for self-standing displays, and "cased-in" Wire-O, which we will consider in Chapter 26.

Combining Wire-O with Other Bookbinding Styles

Occasionally, the requirements of a project will call for different versions to be produced with different binding styles. For example, many companies would like a "high-end" version of their annual report for distribution to major stockholders and the board of directors and for placement in lobbies and other high-traffic areas within the company. A combination run of Wire-O and either perfect-bound or saddle-stitched annual reports can handle the need for both standard and "elite" versions.

Combination runs require a little extra planning to account for differences between binding styles, however. A quality finisher can help you minimize the differences from version to version. Here are some additional design tips:

Semi-Concealed Wire-O Cover Planning Process

Determine	3:1 Wire-O Sizes	2:1 Wire-O Sizes
1. Wire size	For book blocks thinner than ½ in., add ⅛ in. to your book block thickness (bulk) and round to the nearest ¹⁄₁₆ in.	For book blocks ½–⅞ in. thick, add ⅛ in. to bulk and round up to nearest ⅛ in.
2. Spine width	Subtract ¹⁄₁₆ in. from wire size.	Same as 3:1.
3. Cover width plus ¹⁄₁₆-in. overhang	Text page width, plus Wire-O size, then subtract ⅛ in.	Same as 3:1, except subtract ³⁄₁₆ in.
4. Cover score placement	Place *punching score* ⁵⁄₁₆ in. from the nearest spine score.	Same, but *punching score* is ½ in. away.

Perfect bound/Wire-O. Although perfect binding isn't suitable for projects with mixed or heavily coated stocks, a combination perfect-bound/Wire-O run enables easy stock changing for each binding style. Run the Wire-O books first with a high-quality No. 1 sheet, then switch to uncoated stock for the perfect-bound copies without changing plates. On-press UV or aqueous coatings also give Wire-O sheets a premium look.

Saddle stitched/Wire-O. Unlike perfect binding, several different stocks can be used for books with both saddle-stitched and Wire-O versions. Signatures that are laid out for saddle stitching can be used for mechanically bound reports without re-jogging the copy. Sixteen-page signatures are ideal for a combination saddle-stitch/Wire-O run, enabling all the signatures to be folded as for saddle stitching, and trimming those that will be mechanically bound.

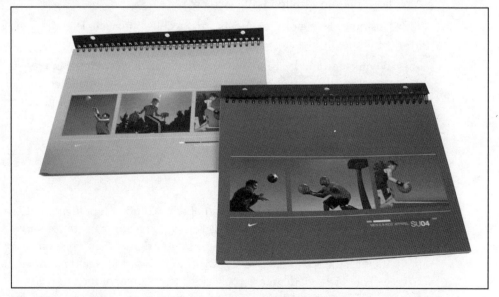

Wire-O bound catalogs with short flap three-hole-punched for insertion into loose-leaf binders.

More Tips

- Embossing or debossing may shorten a cover's width. This needs to be compensated for in design.
- For semi- and fully concealed mechanical projects, a dummy with the right text and cover stock should always be made prior to printing. An unexpectedly high bulking measurement could require a larger binding element size and negatively impact your score placement and copy positioning. Page pushout and hole-to-edge margin adjustments may have similar effects.
- Diecut window registration to ink for mechanical binding is different than in perfect binding or saddle stitching because loose pages move.
- Some binderies are not able to punch double-thick stock.
- Tin (plain) wire may leave undesirable marks on some coated stocks.
- The mechanical binding process can scratch, pick, or feather sheets with full ink coverage. UV coating, aqueous coating, dry-trap varnish, or laminating usually alleviates this problem. In-line machine-applied varnish, however, rarely does.
- Make sure your client isn't expecting a particular style of punched hole. Squares, rectangles, circles, and ovals are common, but most binderies do not have a die for every hole shape and size.
- Consider how a job should be packed. Slip sheeting or individual shrink-wrapping offers additional and sometimes necessary protection from production or transit marking and scuffing.
- One-sided lamination can cause unsightly curling as products age. To alleviate this problem, use double-sided or lay-flat lamination.
- When producing a printed GBC spine job, be aware of normal three-week lead times for printed GBC elements.
- Custom color binding elements are possible, but again, lead times are long and minimum orders large.
- When confronted with inflexible design situations, ask your bindery if the back gauge on their punching machines can be moved. Sometimes this can buy you up to $\frac{1}{16}$ in. (1.6 mm) without significantly sacrificing page-pull strength.

* * *

The Final Word...

Wire-O binding looks great, lays flat, and opens without "stepping up." It's durable, available in a wide array of colors, and is compatible with many different cover styles. It gives design freedom to creative directors and product managers, enabling them to mix and match stocks and page sizes, as well as to insert tabs and indexes. The more you learn about Wire-O, the more you'll agree that it's one of the most versatile binding solutions on the market. What's not to like?

Contributors:

- *Fred Daubert, The Riverside Group, Rochester, New York*
  www.riversidegroup.com
- *Chris Eckhart, Eckhart & Company, Indianapolis, Indiana*
  www.eckhartandco.com
- *Russ Haines, Rapid Bind, Inc., Portland, Oregon*
  www.rapidbind.com
- *John Helline, Spiral of Ohio, Inc., Cleveland, Ohio*
  www.spiralohio.com
- *Gary Markovits, E&M Bindery, Clifton, New Jersey*
  www.embindery.com
- *Joe Piazza, Action Bindery, Norcross, Georgia*
  www.actionbindery.com
- *Bill Seidl, Seidl's Bindery, Houston, Texas*
  www.seidlsbindery.com
- *Frank Shear, Seaboard Bindery, Woburn, Massachusetts*
  www.seaboardbindery.com

23 Plastic Spiral Binding

When planning a job for mechanical binding, it's easy to assume that plastic spiral binding (aka plastic coil) and spiral wire binding are interchangeable. Both involve winding a coil of material through holes punched in the book block. They both offer lay-flat capabilities and can also be folded 360° for single-handed use.

What You Will Learn

- Plastic spiral's advantages
- Available options
- Production tips

Why Plastic Spiral?

Like Wire-O, plastic spiral binding looks great and allows bound pages to lie flat as a board (either 180° or 360°) for the ultimate in user friendliness. However, unlike Wire-O, plastic spiral's crush resistance makes it a popular binding method for heavily used products such as cookbooks, manuals, appointment books, and reference materials. Even when stepped upon, plastic coil binding elements spring back to life with the same great looks and functionality as before.

Plastic spiral is available in a wide variety of colors. In addition to more than twenty standard ones, you have dozens of pastels, neons, and other specialty colors to choose from. If you really want to make an impression, plastic spiral elements can even be manufactured to match any PMS color.

Plastic spiral binding elements are widely available in standard sizes from ¼-in. to 2-in. diameter. Thicker sizes are available, but the coiling process becomes slow. A rule of thumb in choosing the right spiral size is to add ⅛ in. to the book block thickness. As few as two sheets of paper can make the difference between running the job automatically or not.

Technical Tips

Crossover images. Unlike Wire-O, plastic spiral-bound books step up when opened. This means that you should be careful with crossover images that jump the spine.

Crimping. The crimped ends of the spiral binding element shouldn't extend past the diameter of the spiral. Improperly bound protruding elements can catch on clothing or scratch fine furniture.

Page size. For pre-collated plastic spiral binding jobs, it's very important that each page is the same size. If not, you risk incurring hand punching, which is neither time nor cost effective. If your job has different page sizes, let your bindery punch and collate it.

Bulking dummy. Before having your bindery order plastic spiral-binding elements, send them a bulking dummy on the exact paper you will be using. Paper bulk varies between different brands of paper and even between different lots of the same paper. If the binding element is too tight, production will be slow and the pages won't turn easily. If the binding element is too loose, the pages will be dwarfed and the whole book will look ungainly. In addition, some colors require advance lead time for prompt delivery.

Punching considerations. Unlike Wire-O, plastic spiral binding requires holes to be punched to the top of the sheets. The height of the book determines how many holes need to be punched. In order for books to look and function properly, these holes should be centered along the binding edge. Also, avoid punching into copy by leaving at least a ⅜-in. margin between the binding edge and the outer edge of the holes.

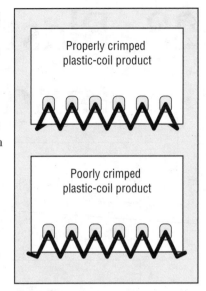

Properly crimped plastic-coil product

Poorly crimped plastic-coil product

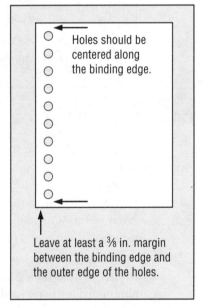

Holes should be centered along the binding edge.

Leave at least a ⅜ in. margin between the binding edge and the outer edge of the holes.

*   *   *

The Final Word...

Automating the plastic spiral manufacturing process has been difficult. Often production is a semiautomatic process that significantly depends on operator skill for consistent production results. There is some automatic in-line machinery available that punches book blocks, forms the spiral elements from a spool of plastic, trims it to the proper length and binds it into each book. This is by far the fastest plastic spiral-binding method available and yields production speeds approaching those of spiral-wire binding.

Contributors:

- *Fred Daubert, The Riverside Group, Rochester, New York*
  www.riversidegroup.com

- *Chris Eckhart, Eckhart & Company, Indianapolis, Indiana*
  www.eckhartandco.com

- *Russ Haines, Rapid Bind, Inc., Portland, Oregon*
  www.rapidbind.com

- *John Helline, Spiral of Ohio, Inc., Cleveland, Ohio*
  www.spiralohio.com

- *Joe Piazza, Action Bindery, Norcross, Georgia*
  www.actionbindery.com

- *Bill Seidl, Seidl's Bindery, Houston, Texas*
  www.seidlsbindery.com

- *Jim Shear, Seaboard Bindery, Woburn, Massachusetts*
  www.seaboardbindery.com

24 Spiral-Wire Binding

Spiral-wire binding lays flat and generally is considered the most economical of all mechanical-binding options. Spiral wire can be coated with colored plastic, is available in a wide selection of colors, and can accommodate nearly any size book.

What You Will Learn

- Why spiral wire?
- Design options
- Technical tips

Spiral-wire binding does have a lot of advantages, including:

- Lay-flat capabilities
- A traditional look
- Compatibility with mixed stocks
- Quick turnaround times for long runs
- Economical production

However, keep in mind that it will be permanently crushed if stepped on, and, like plastic coil, pages step up, making crossover alignment difficult.

Spiral-Wire Design Options

Spiral wire is available in many standard colors. For large production quantities, PMS-matched wire can be ordered to perfectly match corporate logos. Also, spiral-wire binding allows for plenty of cover options. Stocks can range from thin paper to 10-pt. board up to hard covers of 50 pt. or more. Additional softcover options include foldout and pocket covers, as well as diecut covers that can register to print for a dramatic opening.

Spiral-wire binding comes in three main sizes: 5 holes per linear inch (5:1), 4 holes per linear inch (4:1), and 3.2 holes per linear inch (3.2:1).

- 5:1 punching is appropriate for books bulking $\frac{5}{16}$ in. or thinner.
- 4:1 punching is for book blocks $\frac{3}{8}$–$\frac{5}{8}$ in. thick
- 3.2:1 punching is for book blocks $\frac{11}{16}$–$1\frac{1}{8}$ in. thick

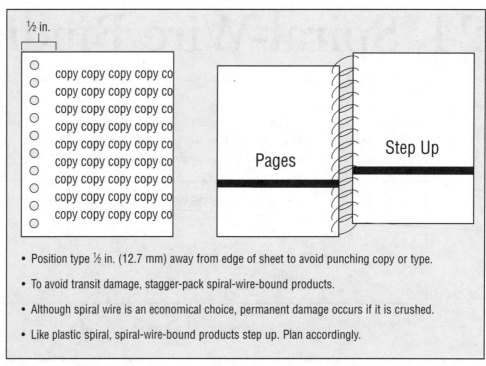

½ in.

copy copy copy copy co
copy copy copy copy co
copy copy copy copy co
copy copy copy copy co
copy copy copy copy co
copy copy copy copy co
copy copy copy copy co
copy copy copy copy co
copy copy copy copy co

Pages

Step Up

- Position type ½ in. (12.7 mm) away from edge of sheet to avoid punching copy or type.

- To avoid transit damage, stagger-pack spiral-wire-bound products.

- Although spiral wire is an economical choice, permanent damage occurs if it is crushed.

- Like plastic spiral, spiral-wire-bound products step up. Plan accordingly.

Spiral wire binding basics.

Technical Tips

- For best product appearance and maximum production efficiency, encourage your customers to let you collate and trim the book block to final size. If furnished trimmed books are off by as little as $\frac{1}{16}$ in., production speed and/or product appearance may be sacrificed. For example, if the distance between the edge of the paper and the first hole is too great, re-trimming may be necessary.
- Spiral-wire binding is available in dozens of gauges that fit a wide range of book bulks.
- Uncoated silver wire has a tendency to mark when it rubs against matte-coated stock.

＊　　＊　　＊

The Final Word...

Spiral-wire binding is an economical choice for a wide range of products, including wall and desk calendars, notebooks, memo pads, shop manuals, and flip charts. Like plastic spiral and Wire-O, index tabs and foldouts are a breeze to include, and even multiple stock weights and finishes can be used.

Contributors:

- *Marty Anson, Bindagraphics, Inc., Baltimore, Maryland*
  www.bindagraphics.com
- *Fred Daubert, The Riverside Group, Rochester, New York*
  www.riversidegroup.com
- *Chris Eckhart, Eckhart & Company, Indianapolis, Indiana*
  www.eckhartandco.com
- *John Helline, Spiral of Ohio, Inc., Cleveland, Ohio*
  www.spiralohio.com
- *Joe Piazza, Action Bindery, Norcross, Georgia*
  www.actionbindery.com
- *Bill Seidl, Seidl's Bindery, Houston, Texas*
  www.seidlsbindery.com

25 Plastic Comb Binding

While plastic spiral, Wire-O, and spiral-wire binding are popular for most mechanical-binding applications, plastic comb binding is another option that gives books a distinctive look.

What You Will Learn

- Plastic comb's advantages
- Available options
- Manufacturing process

Although plastic comb binding does not open 360° like other mechanical-binding styles, it does offer two distinct advantages. First, plastic comb-binding elements can include silk-screened lettering in many colors, allowing books to be identified on store shelves. Second, pages can be added or removed as desired, making plastic comb binding suitable for extended-use applications.

Applications

Plastic comb-binding elements are available in more than a dozen colors—including PMS-matched tones—to give you the creative freedom to blend them in with the design of the book. Binding combs are available in diameters from $\frac{3}{16}$ in. up to 2 in. and beyond, making plastic comb binding suitable for thicker applications such as cookbooks, children's books, and technical and reference manuals. Most comb-binding elements 2 in. and thicker have a locking mechanism to ensure that pages don't fall out.

The Plastic Comb-Binding Process

The first step in the plastic comb-binding process is to gather and punch the text sheets. The comb elements are then opened on a machine, and the text block is placed on them. Since this is a semiautomatic process, plastic comb binding is most suitable for shorter-run projects.

Unlike some other mechanical-binding styles, plastic comb binding can be centered easily along the binding edge of the book. That allows you to design books of any length without worrying about the location of punched binding holes.

*   *   *

The Final Word...

Plastic comb binding can be produced as either a semiautomatic or manual production process. This allows relative production efficiency for short and medium run lengths. However, plastic-comb production rates never will approach Wire-O, which is certainly more automation-friendly.

Contributor:

- *Chris Eckhart, Eckhart & Company, Indianapolis, Indiana*
  www.eckhartandco.com

26 Cased-In Wire-O Binding

For most book projects, the appropriate binding style falls into one of four categories: mechanical binding, adhesive binding, case binding, or saddle stitching. Binding options narrow considerably for complex books that need a solution that combines several of these elements. Consider a project with these divergent requirements: lay-flat capabilities, a printable spine, an elegant appearance, and sturdy construction that will withstand frequent, long-term use. It's a tall order, but cased-in Wire-O binding can fill it.

What You Will Learn

- What is cased-in Wire-O?
- Create market awareness
- Production tips

Cased-in Wire-O is an attractive combination of a thick, wraparound cover with the lay-flat capabilities of Wire-O binding. This gives it the characteristics of both case binding and mechanical binding, without compromising the advantages of either. Cased-in Wire-O is sturdier than most adhesive-bound books because the weight of the book isn't concentrated in the bind itself and because the cover isn't attached directly to the binding elements.

The durability of cased-in Wire-O makes it ideal for books that will receive extended and repeated use. Books that will be featured in retail locations are also prime candidates for cased-in Wire-O, thanks to the high visibility of the wraparound cover, which can accommodate spine printing.

Cased-in Wire-O products can be bound with a wire diameter of up to 1¼ in. (31.75 mm). Cover materials include cloth, offset-printed and film-laminated paper, leather, and more. Decoration options include foil stamping, embossing, and screen printing. In addition to foldouts and diecut pockets, covers can be designed to contain everything from audiocassette and compact disc holders to pens, pencils, and other small giveaways.

Despite these advantages, however, cased-in Wire-O is relatively underutilized because many print buyers and book designers aren't yet aware of this option. As a result, cased-in Wire-O represents a selling opportunity for astute print sales reps who are willing to educate their customers.

Cased-in Wire-O production involves three stages, the first two of which are performed simultaneously.

The first step is to Wire-O bind the book block. Many cased-in Wire-O books are bound using 3:1 wire (3 loops per linear inch), a technique that provides superior strength for extensive use. Binding is performed just as it would be for any other split-back Wire-O book, except that the covers are replaced by thick end sheets that will be mounted to the case. These paper end sheets should be on substantially thicker stock than the text to ensure a proper fit and long life.

The second step is to manufacture the case by wrapping a chosen material around board. This involves mounting a laminated sheet to two pieces of board to form separate front and back covers. Printed, laminated covers are ideal for retail book applications that call for high-quality, high-end graphics and maximum visibility.

The third step is to adhere the Wire-O book block to the case. The two end sheets are glued to the case, enabling the wire elements to move freely under the spine. The most common application calls for a "soft" spine with a rounded appearance, although the spine of the case can have a board in it to create a "hard" or "square" spine.

The last step is where a finisher with automated capabilities can make an important difference. A casing-in machine holds the book on a metal "wing," where glue is applied to the end sheets and the case is attached to the book block in a single pass. Coupled with a high-speed in-line punching and binding system, automation not only drives efficiency and reduced turnaround times, but also yields consistent production quality at competitive prices.

Planning and Production Tips

As you might expect, cased-in Wire-O production requires the efficient exchange of complete information with your finisher. To make sure your project goes smoothly, keep the following tips in mind:

Create a bulking dummy and take exact measurements. As in a regular Wire-O project, properly communicating the thickness and size of a cased-in Wire-O book block is of paramount importance to the quality of the finished product. The case is measured and manufactured based on the bulk of the book block; if that measurement is off by even $\frac{1}{16}$ in., the book may not sit properly in the case. Likewise, if changes are made to the book block after production begins, it could render the cases useless. To avoid surprises, send your finisher a bulking dummy prior to production, or let your finisher know what stock you plan to use and have them create a bulking dummy for you.

Measure trim sizes and text margins carefully. An under- or oversized book block will yield unsatisfactory results, so be sure trim sizes are accurate. As with any other mechanically bound book, text and image margins should be considered. For a book using 3:1 wire, leave at least a $\frac{3}{8}$-in. margin from the spine edge to the punched holes to avoid punching into type.

Avoid "fallout." The weight of the end sheets in the bound book block determines the strength of the cased-in book. If the end sheets are too light, the book will "fall

Cased-in Wire-O.

out" of the case, causing it to sag in the middle when the book is held by the cover. The proper end-sheet weight for your project is based on the weight and number of the text pages. Communicate all details of the book with your finisher to be sure sheets of the proper weight are specified. In general, when casing in Wire-O book blocks, end sheets should be 90-lb. index stock or heavier and extend $\frac{1}{16}$ in. beyond the face of the trimmed book block.

Thick book? Complex project? Consult your finisher early. Books approaching the maximum wire size of $1\frac{1}{4}$ in. require a little more experience and communication to turn out exactly as planned. A single end sheet that wraps around the wire elements for reinforcement may be preferable to separate end sheets in some applications.

*   *   *

The Final Word...

Cased-in Wire-O has been around a long time—with good reason. To add more value to the selling process, sharpen your competitive edge, and win more work, make a point to learn about the benefits of this fine product.

Contributor:

• *Chris Eckhart, Eckhart & Company, Indianapolis, Indiana*
  www.eckhartandco.com

27 Case Binding

For elegance and durability, there is no substitute for case binding. This time-tested, impressive binding style can accommodate not only truly distinctive products but also can be scaled down to fit lean budgets.

What You Will Learn

- Layout/production tips
- Case-binding options
- Speeding up deliveries

Since there are many steps in a typical case-bound job, attention to detail is very important. Carefully preplan your jobs so they will be delivered on time, with consistent quality, at reasonable prices.

Case-Binding Layout Basics

While some binderies may want different trim-off margin allowances, most prefer ⅛-in. (3.2-mm) head trim, ¼-in. (6.4-mm) foot trim, and ¼-in. face trim on the low folio side. When bleeds occur on at least one of the four sides, increase the head trim to ¼ in. However, when combined head and foot trims exceed ¾ in. (19 mm), production rates will start to decline. If they total 1 in. (25.4 mm), the project may even have to be pre-trimmed. Similarly, face trims should not exceed ¾ in.

Sewn book blocks require special planning to ensure maximum sewing efficiency. For this reason, it would be wise to follow these three rules:

1. Never put perforations on the spine side of a signature.
2. When supplying folded signatures, head perforations must be closed. If the perforations are too big, individual leaves within the signature easily peel away and can cause a dramatic loss of sewing efficiency. In the worst cases, expensive hand-fed sewing is required.
3. All signatures must have the same head-to-foot and spine-to-face lengths. Variation will increase delivery time and costs.

Plan your signature lips for consistency. While high-folio lips are preferred, low-folio ones are fine as long as they're consistent. Mixing lip direction is an expensive and easily preventable mistake. For thin signatures (e.g., 16-pages or fewer on 70-lb. text stock or thinner), lips may be as short as ¼ in. (6.4 mm). When folding thicker signatures, pushout from the spine may cause a ¼-in. lip to shrink to the point where it has no benefit. In these cases, ⅜-in. (9.5-mm) lips are preferred.

Many case-bound books have signatures with varying page counts. Pay careful attention to signature order because a product's strength and production efficiency depends on it. First, thin signatures should never be positioned at the front or back of any book block. While 32-pagers are preferred, 16-pagers are usually acceptable for these importantly placed signatures. Likewise, signatures on very thin stock, as well as 2-, 4-, and 6-page forms must be tipped to thicker signatures prior to gathering. In these cases, it's best to tip the thin form to the back page of a high-folio signature.

Plan for end sheets to be tipped onto the front and back of the book block when the book has uncoated text, bulks less than 2 in. (50.8 mm) thick, has a final trim size of 8½×11 in. (215.9×279.4 mm) or smaller, and weighs less than 2 lb. (0.9 kg). Otherwise, the end sheets should be reinforced. When calculating production waste allowances for books with tipped-on end sheets, set aside 100 makeready pieces of each signature plus 2% of the run length. For projects with reinforced end sheets, boost this to 150 pieces plus 2.5% of the run length. Also, add another 2% for the first and last signatures of the book.

Tipped and reinforced end sheets.

When a book has critical crossovers, try to lay out the signatures with crossovers as 8- or 16-pagers to prevent pushout problems. Let your case binder do the folding, especially on jobs with crossovers, because control and accountability will remain with one company.

Grain direction is very important in perfect-bound case binding. If jobs are run against the grain (bisecting the spine), books won't lie flat. Similarly, when applying printed covers to board, the grain must go in the same direction as the binding, or the board may warp. The grain in end sheets should travel in the same direction, too.

Stripping preprinted covers for case-bound books is no more difficult than for perfect binding—as long as you have a dummy to follow. In order to properly position copy on pre-printed covers, you need to know the book block bulk, joint curvature allowances, final board size, and board thickness. Color breaks positioned anywhere near the spine edge or joint make dummies even more important. Since there is a clear trend toward preprinted, laminated covers, this planning is critical on many jobs.

Foil stamping on cloth is different than foil stamping on paper. Foils have many adhesive properties and are not always interchangeable. For example, a foil that works on Roxite C (trademark of Holliston/ICG) probably won't work on Roxite A. Poor foil stamping has ruined many case-bound jobs.

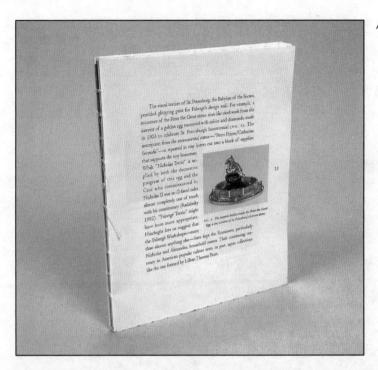

A sewn book block.

Case-Binding Options

There are many ways to alter the appearance or functionality of case-bound books. First, you have your choice of three spine styles: rounded, flat back, and tight back. Rounded is probably the most common. The next grade up, flat back, is common on coffee table and other premium books. For books that weigh more than 3 lb. (1.4 kg), a tight-back spine (text glued to the spine) is recommended for quality and durability reasons.

Another consideration is the type of board you need. For top quality, settle for nothing less than warp-resistant binders' board because metal particles make it stronger and thicker than other boards. If your project is on a tight budget, has a preprinted cover, and is cased-in perfect bound, you may consider lowering the grade of the board to save money. For projects with expected short lives, inexpensive board such as Rock-Tenn (trademark of Rock-Tenn) may be a reasonable substitute even though it tends to warp more than binders' board. Some case-binding companies can even case bind a flexible 21-pt. Lexitone board (trademark of Rexam DSI) as a cover by itself, which saves a lot of money. In general, switching from sewing to perfect-bound case binding usually will save you about 15% to 25% of the binding cost.

Cased-in Wire-O binding offers a truly lay-flat product. When casing-in Wire-O book blocks, end sheets should be 90-lb. index stock or heavier and extend $\frac{1}{16}$ in. (1.6 mm) beyond the face of the trimmed book block.

There are a variety of extras that you can use to dress up your case-bound projects. Reader ribbons, thumb notches, hubs (spine bumps for premium books), gilding (gold edging), multi-pass foil stamping, embossing, debossing, multi-level dies, padded board, round corners, and specialty headbands are all possible and practical. Lastly, nothing looks and feels better than leather binding.

Various spine styles: rounded (top) and flat-back (bottom).

Shortening Turnaround Times

In general, case binding takes longer to produce than other binding styles. Ask your case-binding company whether they have an inventory of board. Companies that don't keep board on hand may face lead times usually measured in weeks, which needlessly delays the starting of jobs. In short, binderies that inventory board will produce jobs faster. Also, search for companies with board slitters in addition to flatbed cutters because slitters prevent draw problems and produce more consistently sized boards.

Normal end sheets are 80-lb. offset. If coated end sheets are required, 100-lb. text stock or thicker should be used to prevent wrinkling. End sheets with special textures or colors can be applied but usually must be specially ordered. If speed is an issue, give a purchase order (PO) to your case-binding company early so they can order all job components well in advance.

If a job is going to be delivered to a bindery in partial shipments, prioritize the printing of the first and last signatures and deliver them ahead of time. If these signatures are already tipped or reinforced with end sheets when the rest of the job arrives, days will be shaved off the delivery date.

＊　　＊　　＊

The Final Word...

Since so many factors go into case binding, finding a case-binding partner with a proactive attitude is important. Minor problems left uncaught or ignored have a way of quickly ruining jobs. Keep in mind that foils can mark or pick, layouts can be wrong, and matte laminated covers can show fingerprints. Unless your bindery offers you the white-glove touch and pays careful attention to detail, you may be disappointed with your end results. In the case-binding world, the sobering reality is that tens and even hundreds of thousands of dollars of product can be destroyed in a flash unless your bindery begins the troubleshooting process before the job is printed.

Contributors:

- *Fred Daubert, The Riverside Group, Rochester, New York*
  www.riversidegroup.com

- *Chris Eckhart, Eckhart & Company, Indianapolis, Indiana*
  www.eckhartandco.com

- *Jerry Nocar, Advantage Bookbinding, Inc., Baltimore, Maryland*
  www.advantagebookbinding.com

- *Mike Welsch, Muscle Bound Bindery, Minneapolis, Minnesota*
  www.mbbindery.com

28 Easy-Release and Seam Glue

Successful gluing work needs a scientific approach and an artistic touch. The four horsemen of gluing—paper, ink, coatings, and glue—are about equal contributors to a job's success. Their combinations are nearly infinite, and unexpected results do frequently occur. Sometimes easy-release glue tears paper fiber. Sometimes permanent glues perform like easy-release. Even the wizard Merlin would be puzzled.

What You Will Learn

- Easy-release glue
- Permanent glue
- Paper surfaces and coating

The process of gluing seems simple enough. You have two printed pieces that need to stick together. What can be so complex about that? For one thing, different glue formulas require different curing times. This can be a key factor in deciding which formula to use. Furthermore, not all glues hold paper together the same way. The interaction between the glued pieces and the end use of the finished product will determine exactly what type of glue is necessary and how it will be applied.

There are literally hundreds of glues available for projects that require gluing. The unique needs of a given job place different demands on the glues that are used. Likewise, the distinct properties of various adhesives make them more or less suitable for a given application. Selecting the right one for your application is critical to the finished look and usability of the piece. Whether you're gluing the sides of a CD sleeve or sealing a multi-page self-mailer, there's an adhesive that will make the job a success.

Graphic arts glues are mainly oil-, resin-, or latex-based. Each type performs as expected most of the time, but there are exceptions.

Both easy-release and permanent oil-based glues offer good adhesive properties and are appropriate for physically heavy or varnished pieces. However, their relative great bulk may result in an unattractive product from a marketing viewpoint. Resin-based permanent glues are cold-applied and provide a good bond with a relatively small amount of residue. Latex easy-release glues are thin, generally reliable, inexpensive to apply, energy efficient (applied cold), environmentally friendly, and FDA-approved for many food packaging applications. Latex, however, is a natural rubber tree product and coagulates when contacted by steel or iron. Coagulation can cause machine applicator problems. Also, latex glue doesn't work well in compressed-air noncontact systems.

Easy-Release Glue

Easy-release glue, also known as removable or fugitive glue, performs well nineteen out of twenty times, but one tough job will prove there's no "easy" release from gluing headaches.

Easy-release glue performs best on penetration-resistant, highly calendered, dense paper with heavily inked and coated surfaces. Matte and other lightly calendered enamel stock, offset paper, or sheets with a heavy clay fill are susceptible to delamination and fiber tearing when the intention is an easy-release effect.

Latex easy-release glues require long setup times (3 to 4 min.) and tend to spread when the opposing sheet is tightly squeezed. Their curing period is really twenty-four hours, even though they appear to be dry after ten minutes. Unfortunately, products that perform properly ten minutes after manufacturing can change in twenty-four hours and pull fiber. Oil-based easy-release glues have a shorter curing time, but glue bulk remains an issue.

Managing variable adhesion and chemical reactions is important. Some easy-release glue solvents, such as ammonia, dissolve aqueous and other coatings and result in unintentional permanent adhesion. Occasionally, permanent resin glues can function as easy release on aqueous coatings because when dry they become very brittle and perform better than latex- or oil-based easy-release glue.

Temperature and humidity conditions can greatly affect the performance of glued products. For example, an upper Midwest bindery shipped a trailer load of latex easy-release-glued products to Texas. Shortly thereafter, the client reported that the job was unacceptable because fiber was tearing. Although time-pull production samples functioned perfectly, the problem was apparent after observing samples. A bindery

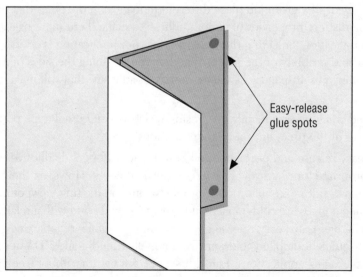

An example of easy-release glue being used with a three-gatefold (also known as a "double gate") product.

Easy-release glue spots

- Easy-release glue is an economical and attractive substitute for wafer sealing. (Properly manufactured products work great in the U.S. mail.)
- It keeps foldouts and gatefolds from unraveling during binding operations.
- It holds products together so that they can be automatically inserted (i.e., consumer product instruction sheets into bottles or boxes).
- It is great for pharmaceutical and/or miniature folded products.

Common uses for easy-release glue.

representative was sent to Texas and discovered that the 2-in. (50.8-mm) Mylar tape used to seal the shipping cartons had blistered. The tape manufacturer explained that blistering occurs with the Mylar tape when it is exposed to a temperature higher than 120°F (49°C). The due diligence process next revealed that the truck had remained outside during an intensely hot weekend prior to delivery. Interestingly, the fiber-tearing product was only in the cartons on the external layer of the skids, not in the more protected internal cartons. Clearly, extreme heat caused further reaction in the curing of the easy-release glue.

When planning a project for fugitive gluing, avoid placing glue over areas of heavy ink coverage. Ink may transfer to the glue when panels are separated.

Permanent Seam Glue

Permanent gluing problems do occur but are infrequent. For best results, select a paper with a porous surface, and position the glue away from ink and coatings. Permanent glue needs to bite into paper, so the harder the surface, the more difficult it is to penetrate the sheet and create good adhesion. Knock out ink, varnish, UV, and aqueous coatings wherever you place permanent glue because glue tends to rest on top of coatings and cannot penetrate and grip fiber. Permanent resin glue spreads on stocks and coatings with a high barrier to penetration and can result in a poor bond or sloppy glue coverage. Absorbent and porous paper will allow glue to penetrate paper fibers and produce a strong bond. If gluing must occur over ink coverage, use wax-free ink. When stuck with a difficult permanent gluing job with aqueous coating, as a last resort, try using ammonia-based latex easy-release glue instead of permanent. It might just work.

Because water-based resin glues spread, projects with critical glue registration require constant monitoring and sample pulls during production. Take special care when applying resin glue in a trim-out area. If glue reaches the paper's edge, sheets will stick together. Conversely, if glue spreads too far into the piece, it will not be removed during the final trimming process. If the trim-out area is shorter than ⅜ in.

An assortment of products that have been glued.

(9.5 mm), consider using easy-release instead of permanent glue because the negative consequences of excess glue spread are less.

When gluing sheets that are 8-pt. or thicker, paper memory can cause puckering at the fold. Hot-melt oil-based permanent glues perform well with thick stock because its open (setting) time is much shorter than that of cold-applied resin glue. Resin and latex easy-release glues work by evaporation and have three or more minutes of open time. Hot-melt sets as soon as its temperature drops below 250°F (120°C), which is nearly instantaneous once the fold is made. When applying permanent glue in conjunction with remoistenable glue, be careful that water-based glues don't come in contact with the backside of the remoistenable-glue strip. Moisture seepage might migrate through the sheet and activate the remoistenable-glue strip.

Unfortunately, hot-melt can be hard to apply. Contamination problems occur more frequently in jobs requiring small applicator orifices. For example, if the glue pot overheats, it creates char that, in turn, clogs the orifices. Because a hot-melt unit has a working temperature in excess of 300°F (150°C), it is difficult to fix a problem while in operating condition. Hot-melt contamination usually requires a time-consuming system flush that wastes a lot of expensive glue. One method of reducing hot-melt glue waste is to clean contaminated applicator heads with hot vegetable oil.

Machinery Issues

Prior to the 1970s, gluing wasn't widely viable, but the last three decades have seen vast advances. Now, electronic systems that sense the presence of a sheet, wait a specified period of time, and then apply glue have made gluing practical. Most systems on the market now have pretty good electronics, but the next big advance in gluing technology is almost here.

Today's air-activated noncontact permanent gluing systems are extremely accurate and remarkably trouble-free. The capability to apply permanent glue from the bottom of a sheet is useful. No doubt many binderies would replace all of their gluing machines with air-activated units if only they performed well with easy-release glue.

Developing a Good Relationship with a Glue Supplier

If your company does gluing, be in frequent contact with your glue suppliers. Because most glue has a short shelf life, purchase and use glue biweekly to ensure good adhesive properties.

Often jobs require custom-made glues for special situations. For example, you may need glue to penetrate a tough aqueous coating, work in high humidity, hold in freezing and thawing situations, or bind folded plastic while in a washing machine. A responsive supplier can save you hours of fruitless experimentation and help you meet deadlines. Good suppliers know government regulations, too. For example, when uncertain of FDA requirements, call a trusted supplier and have them fax back applicable regulatory code.

*   *   *

The Final Word...

A myriad of production and end-use factors come into play on bindery jobs that involve glue. Warehouse, shipping, and destination climates; packing details; ink and paper chemistry; size and weight of the finished project; and even government regulations all need to be considered before a drop of glue is placed on the paper.

Contributors:

- *Fred Daubert, The Riverside Group, Rochester, New York*
  www.riversidegroup.com

- *Russ Haines, Rapid Bind, Inc., Portland, Oregon*
  www.rapidbind.com

- *Jack Rickard, Rickard Bindery, Chicago, Illinois*
  www.rickardbindery.com

29 Remoistenable Glue

Until the 1990s, sheetfed printers had little opportunity to sell products with remoistenable glue. Today, short-run remoistenable-glue jobs are practical because the current machines yield high-quality jobs at good production rates. Both sheetfed and non-heatset web printers now can produce products with direct-response reply devices and participate in profitable direct-mail campaigns.

What You Will Learn

- Hot-melt vs. cold-applied remoistenable glues
- In-line solutions
- Layout considerations

Remoistenable glues are designed to be activated by an end user, making them ideal for applications such as envelopes and other reply devices. One of the main advantages of remoistenable glue is that it dries almost instantly, a characteristic that permits it to be applied economically in-line with other finishing operations such as folding and perfing, as well as permanent or easy-release glue application. In-line production greatly reduces turnaround times and cost, making nonheatset web and sheetfed companies competitive on a wider range jobs, including profitable direct mail applications.

There are primarily two ways of applying remoistenable glue. The older technology—cold application of water-soluble remoistenable glue—works by transferring glue to paper by either a wheel or a blanket. This process has two main advantages. First, heat by itself doesn't activate it, which means it is downstream laser-compatible. Second, glue application pads come in different sizes and run in various directions, which allows the efficient manufacturing of products such as three-sided "U" bar reply devices (reply envelopes that have remoistenable glue applied on three non-parallel lines) and stamps (a glued area wider than a typical remoistenable-glue application head).

Unfortunately, there are some significant drawbacks with cold-applied glue. First, it has to be run through hot dryers, which frequently cause excessive paper curling and cracking. Second, cold adhesives tend to be thicker right at the beginning of the glue strip. Sometimes this thick buildup takes longer to dry and forces operators to choose between having either brittle paper or semi-wet remoistenable glue that may stick to neighboring sheets. And third, a potential fire hazard is created when paper is left in the oven when conveyors stop.

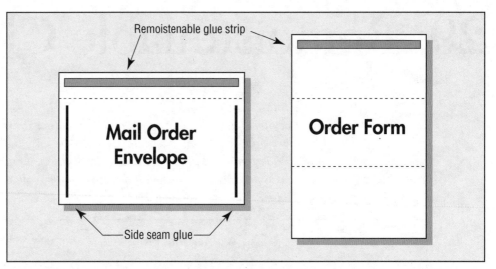

On mailpiece designs such as these, remoistable glue placement must meet postal requirements to avoid costly penalties

Extruded Glue

Hot-melt extrusion is the other way to apply remoistenable glue. These machines give operators more control over the placement and appearance of glue strips as they're being applied to the paper. Computer-controlled solenoids allow operators to precisely start and stop glue flow wherever necessary. For example, if a two-up piece is being glued on an 8½-in. (215.9-mm) side, an extrusion machine will detect the presence of paper and begin the glue flow ¼ in. (6.4 mm) away from the paper edge. Then, it will apply glue for 8 in. (203.2 mm), stop for ½ in. (12.7 mm), apply glue for another 8 in. and finally stop the flow ¼ in. away from the trailing edge.

Water-soluble glue applied on a pattern gluer can do this, too, but because pattern gluers rely on timed entry rather than motion sensors, its application isn't as precise. In addition, hot-melt extrusion glues rarely curl paper and generally have a professional appearance, while cold-applied glues look duller, may have raggedy edges, and tend to curl because moisture is being added to only one side of the sheet.

A potential drawback of extrusion machines is that they can only apply remoistenable glue in parallel lines. This means that glue laid down in the shape of a "U" either needs two passes or two machines running at right angles to each other.

In-Line Application

Many trade binderies can perform remoistenable gluing in-line with other binding processes. For example, they may apply remoistenable glue, stop-perforate the sheet, apply seam glue to form a pocket, fold it, apply wafer seals, slit it, and keep the job in mail-sort order—all in-line. Needless to say, in-line production greatly reduces turnaround times and cost, making non-heatset web and sheetfed companies competitive on many jobs. Whether the piece is a self-mailer or bound into another product, in-line production is a good value.

Extrusion remoistenable-glue jobs can be fed from cut sheets, fan packs, or rolls. It's not uncommon for a bindery to receive frantic calls from web printers whose remoistenable-glue didn't work for some reason. Many binderies have reported that they were able to save huge jobs for companies that ran them off without noticing that the glue strips were missing.

The Key Factors

The five key factors of successful remoistenable-glue application are paper, glue, ink, coatings, and atmospheric conditions. Let's take these one at a time.

Paper. Knowing the characteristics of your paper is important. Remoistenable glue rests on the surface of enamel stock yet is able to create a good bond when moisture-activated. Uncoated stock also generally works fine but will normally require a heavier line of glue because the glue tends to seep into the porous sheet.

Glue. Understanding the difference between water-soluble and hot-melt glue is important. Ask your bindery which glue they intend to use on your project and why.

Ink. Generally, remoistenable glue can be applied over ink with fine results, but problems may occur when activated glue needs to adhere to paper with 100% ink coverage. Be safe and plan your artwork so that remoistenable glue doesn't require adhesion to heavy ink solids.

Coatings. Remoistenable glue doesn't adhere to paper coatings such as varnish. If you're planning on flood-varnishing a sheet, change the design to spot and knock out varnish from where the remoistenable-glue strip is to be applied and to where it will be adhered.

Atmospheric conditions. In high humidity areas, it's essential to apply water-soluble remoistenable glue in a climate-controlled environment. Regardless of glue type, be safe and include a moisture-absorbing packet in each box. These packets draw moisture out of contained areas and prevent remoistenable glue from unintentionally bonding. Even perfectly manufactured remoistenable-glue products sometimes will unintentionally bond inside a hot truck.

Layout Considerations

If you have a form with side-by-side envelopes, don't have the glue strips rest against each other as they're coming off the machines. Unintentional adhesion can occur when glue strips are directly in contact with each other face to face, especially during shipping. Staggering designs so that glue strips avoid contact with each other is much better.

Avoid flatbed trimming after a remoistenable glue application because it may cause a series of three problems. First, productivity will decline because sheets will

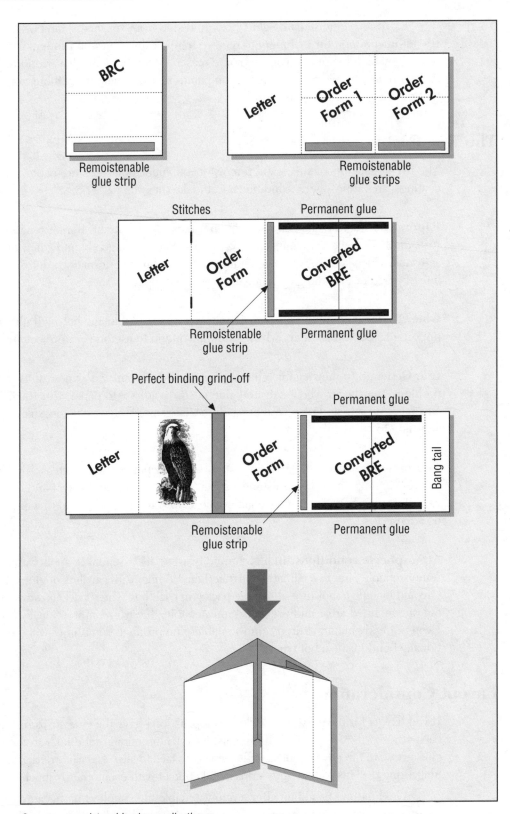

Common remoistenable glue applications.

have to be cut in very small lifts in order to clamp properly and not tear due to inadequate clamp pressure. Second, glue bulk will raise a bump in each lift resulting in the top sheets being longer than the bottom ones after trimming. Third, cutting through remoistenable glue wreaks havoc on knives, especially those super-hardened for long life.

* * *

The Final Word...

Remoistenable glue makes many direct-mail programs better. Printed pieces with easy ways to respond are more effective than those without. In summary, remoistenable glue makes response mechanisms easy and quick to use.

Contributor:

• *Jack Rickard, Rickard Bindery, Chicago, Illinois*
  www.rickardbindery.com

30 Loose-Leaf Ring Binders

Loose-leaf ring binders are popular for a broad variety of uses, ranging from in-house-produced employee-training handbooks to professionally published software manuals. This perennial favorite is versatile, easy to use, and permits frequent updating.

What You Will Learn

- Available options
- Ring sizes and shapes
- Planning considerations

In the age of high-tech wizardry, loose-leaf ring binders are refreshingly simple. However, self-evident as they may seem, ring binders are not without their own particular rules and guidelines. Ring-binder jobs still require good planning.

Binder Basics

The end user determines decoration options for binder material. For instance, vinyl binders, made from two pieces of vinyl heat-sealed around either a stiff or slightly flexible board, are popular choices because they're sturdy, durable, and stand up by themselves on a shelf. Typical uses for such binders include cookbooks, software manuals, seminar and presentation literature, inventory lists, and reference materials. Molded plastic trays for holding products like audiocassettes and videocassettes or computer disks may be mounted inside a vinyl binder. With or without rings, these products allow for a range of applications, such as self-instructional language courses or small-business software packages.

Vinyl binders come in a wide array of colors and textures and may be silk-screened, foil-stamped, or appliquéd. Adding a full-size plastic pocket to the outside front, back, and spine can allow a vinyl binder to accept printed inserts. Slipping artwork underneath the plastic is an inexpensive way to give the binder a fancy cover and spine.

Polyethylene (i.e., "poly" or "cut-flush") binders are a more durable and less costly alternative to vinyl. Because they are made of virtually indestructible polyolefin, this type of binder can withstand frequent handling and abuse. It's well suited for workshops, construction sites, and other rough-and-tumble settings. If you're going to the North Pole or the Sahara Desert, this is the binder to take because it withstands

Vinyl and "poly" binders.

temperatures ranging from –150°F (–100°C) to a scorching 150°F (66°C) without cracking, fading, tearing, or losing its shape.

Like vinyl, poly binders can be silk-screened or decorated with halftone or even four-color printing. Both vinyl and poly binders can be constructed with an extra flap so that when opened, they stand like an easel during tabletop presentations.

Paper board binders are typically on 18- to 24-point stock and can be offset or screen-printed, foil stamped, embossed, or debossed. Paper binders are diecut and run through a straight-line gluing machine; the edges of these binders are folded up and glued and then ring mechanisms are riveted in. For added strength and protection, paper binders should be film-laminated or at least UV-coated.

Turned-edge binders can be made from paper, synthetic paper, cloth, or leather. The edges of these binders are "turned" from the outside to the inside cover, hence the product's name. On the inside cover, a liner sheet seals the turned edges underneath it. While the process is expensive, it is considered the deluxe style of ring binder.

Sheet Size

Once you've decided which material is appropriate for your binder, consider the size of the sheets your binder must accommodate. The most common binder size holds 8½×11-in. (215.9×279.4-mm) sheets, but 5½×8½-in. (139.7×215.9-mm) and 6×9-in. (152.4×228.6-mm) formats are also popular for products such as software manuals, employee directories, and cookbooks. There are binders designed for legal-sized sheets as well.

Capacity

Once you've determined the sheet size of your binder, consider your capacity requirements. Keep in mind that a binder's capacity is determined by the inside diameter of the rings, not the width of the spine. Standard ring diameters range from ½ in. (12.7 mm) to 3 in. (76.2 mm), but other sizes may be specially ordered. Select your size based on the weight of the stock to be used. The accompanying chart provides rough capacity guidelines, but when in doubt, construct a bulking dummy with the actual stock and base your capacity decisions on it.

Ring size	16-lb. bond or 40-lb. offset	20-lb. bond or 50-lb. offset	24-lb. bond or 60-lb. offset
1 in. (25.4 mm)	200	175	170
1½ in. (38.1 mm)	300	265	254
2 in. (50.8 mm)	400	350	340

Binder capacity—approximate number of sheets that will fit into binders of various ring sizes.

Ring Shapes

Binder rings come in four primary shapes: round, oval, D, and angle-D. Round and oval rings work well for most applications. The D or angle-D rings permit pages to lay perfectly jogged along the hole-punched edge and are typically found in large-capacity binders. These rings are shaped like a backwards D and hold up to 30% more than round rings of the same diameter. For example, a 2-in. (50.8-mm) angle-D holds one-third more than a 2-in. round ring. If your project has mixed stocks (e.g., cover stock for tabbed pages and regular text) or an unusual paper weight, construct a bulking dummy or consult with your finishing house during planning.

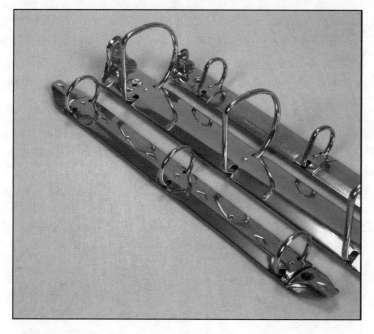

Common ring styles.

Binder Decoration

Binders can be enhanced and customized with certain finishing processes. For instance, images can be silk-screened, offset printed in multiple colors, appliquéd, or foil stamped nearly anywhere on the binder case. Most finishing houses require camera-ready art that conforms to certain specifications. Because vinyl isn't as porous

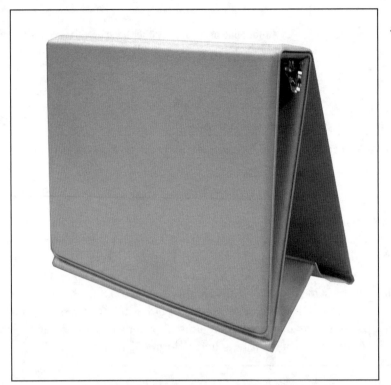

Vinyl binder with self-standing easel.

as paper and inks readily bleed, artwork for silk-screening should have a 65-line/in. (2.6-line/mm) screen.

Graphics or lines should be at least 1 pt. thick and type should be 10 pt. or larger. Avoid printing pale colors on dark vinyl or poly because silk-screening inks are not opaque. If artwork is to be printed on the spine, design it so that letters or images are at least ¼ in. (6.4 mm) from edges and rivets. If necessary, your binder can be constructed so that the rivets are either concealed or located on the back cover to provide more room for art on the spine.

When preparing artwork for either foil stamping or appliquéing, avoid fine lines, halftones, and screens. If the designs are not kept within a 24-sq.-in. (approximately 127×127-mm) area, more than one die will be needed, raising the costs of the project. If the design contains reverse type, use a boldface font so letters don't fill in when stamped.

*   *   *

The Final Word...

The loose-leaf binding world is wide open. There are many jobs that take advantage of exotic binder materials, such as rings with unusual spacing and beautiful multi-colored cover decorations. Even the choosiest designer has many tools from which to work.

Contributors:

- *Marty Anson, Bindagraphics, Inc., Baltimore, Maryland*
  www.bindagraphics.com

- *Jerry Bridges, Vulcan Information Packaging, Vincent, Alabama*
  www.Vulcan-Online.com

- *Chris Eckhart, Eckhart & Company, Indianapolis, Indiana*
  www.eckhartandco.com

31 Catalog Binders

When it comes to binders, most people think of the classic three-ring vinyl variety. That's not surprising because for small capacities of paper, they are functional, easy to use, and plentiful in the marketplace. However, for larger capacities, the ring mechanisms may not hold the weight of the paper satisfactorily. In addition, the pages won't turn as easily and will sometimes tear. If you are looking for a functional, versatile, and durable solution to house large amounts of paper, a catalog binder built like a fortress is an unbeatable alternative.

What You Will Learn

- Market uses
- Available construction materials
- Tabs and other components

So-called "catalog" binders are ruggedly constructed, good-looking, heavy-duty, long-lasting, and often expandable. They come in a variety of styles and sizes and generally are made from either thick-gauge polyethylene ("poly") or durable "turned-edge" materials stretched over and adhered to a thick board stock and finished on the inside with a lining sheet. Board materials range in thickness from 120 to 200 points and provide a solid, durable, and warp-resistant foundation.

Because the cover material must be super strong, it usually is made from heavy cloth, bonded leather, artificial leather, or 75-gauge poly. These options are stronger and have a longer useful life than vinyl or other less-durable materials. If a "normal" vinyl binder lasts two to three years, a comparable heavy-duty binder should function beautifully for ten to twelve years.

Since catalog binders are designed to withstand heavy use in rough environments, options such as stainless steel "rims" and metal "piano hinges" add extra durability. Rims fitted around the outside edges of a cover consist of molded tube-like pieces of stainless steel, which provide protection against bending and ripping. Piano hinges allow binders to open easily and provide for greater durability in this high-stress area.

A strong backbone is essential for binder durability and longevity. Because it resists rust, steel is preferred for backbones, as well as for hinges and posts. Inside angles also are made of 50- to 55-gauge steel shaped on a forming machine. Before these metal parts are finished, they should be vapor-degreased and cleaned prior to painting or plating. All paint should have a scratch-resistant finish. Painted steel spines are a popular alternative to cloth-covered ones. The glues used to hold binders together must be at least as reliable as the other components.

The most popular catalog binder is the expandable-post binder, which boosts capacity up to 150% of its minimum. Also available are fixed-capacity binders, which "relax" or spread, allowing better readability, especially close to the spine. And there are fixed-capacity binders that won't stretch or expand. Catalog binders are generally available in two-, three-, four-, and five-inch pre-expansion capacities and have three posts. Although some binders still are made with four posts, today most conform to the common three-hole "loose-leaf" standard.

After binder materials are chosen, it's time to think about decoration. Binders can be screen printed or foil stamped with company logos, personal messages, organizational data, or other information. Cover embossing, debossing, foil stamping, and screen printing on whole-grain leather or heavy-gauge poly are options that add a sophisticated look. It may be desirable for operating instructions or other information to be printed on the inside-lining sheets.

To help identify binder contents, clear label holders can be attached to the spine or front cover, regardless of style. Windows can be diecut out of or spot-welded onto metal spines. Pockets and business card holders can be added, usually on the inside front cover.

Tabs and Indexes

Another way to make the finished products even more usable is to include index tabs, custom-printed on 90- or 110-lb. white, manila, or colored index stock. Tabs are generally printed in black ink, but PMS colors are available. Body printing on tab sheets is also possible. Other options include reinforcing the binding edge with clear Mylar and coating the tabs themselves with clear or colored Mylar to prevent post holes from tearing.

For the ultimate in durability, heavy-duty metal index tabs attached to 16-gauge black poly sheets turn normal catalog binders into pillars of strength and beauty. These "insertable" tabs, made from aluminum, feature clear Mylar windows for paper inserts and are secured by eyelets to a poly sheet. They come in two styles: a 1⅝-in. opening with four tabs per bank and a ⅝-in. opening with ten tabs per bank. Both styles include white tab paper for writing. (For more on tabs and indexing, see Chapters 44 and 45.)

Universally punched flyleaves made from 16-gauge black poly also can be added to protect catalog materials on both sides of each sheet-holder section. A handle of hand-sewn leather or riveted plastic that can be secured with a snap-style grip flap makes binders easier to carry and prevents unintentional opening.

*   *   *

The Final Word...

It's best to consult with a manufacturer or other expert before starting a binder project. Heavy-duty catalog binders are not appropriate for every project—for instance, when bound materials will be added and removed regularly. But when clients need tough, attractive, large-capacity binders, there's no better defense against the ravages of time and abuse than a catalog binder built like a fortress.

Contributors:

- *Chris Eckhart, Eckhart & Company, Indianapolis, Indiana*
  www.eckhartandco.com
- *Peggy Rhodes, Sperry Graphic Inc, Folcroft, Pennsylvania*
  www.sperrygraphic.com
- *Rod Rothermel, formerly of Buchan Industries, Clifton Heights, Pennsylvania*

32 Managing Digitally Printed Materials

It wasn't all that long ago that digital printing was something of a curiosity rather than a viable production option. Especially for color applications, digital print quality was suspect, and digital production times were only sluggishly competitive with offset. The combination of factors relegated digital printing to only very short runs of the simplest applications.

What You Will Learn

- Digital printing is growing rapidly
- How to handle toner vs. ink
- Layout considerations for binding and finishing

What a difference a few years make! Digital print quality now approaches—and in many instances is nearly indistinguishable from—offset. Production speed has vastly improved, along with the range of substrates that can be used for digital applications. These improvements have made digital printing an attractive option for a broad range of products.

From a binding and finishing standpoint, however, there are significant differences between digital and offset printing. We'll cover some of those differences here and offer planning tips to keep in mind when designing for digital printing.

Toner vs. Ink

The most significant difference between digital and offset printing is what's being applied to the paper. Digital toners have a different chemistry than standard offset inks. Toners are dry when they're laid on the sheet. Paper and toner are then fused using heat and "fuser oil," which helps bond the toner to the paper surface. By contrast, ink is balanced with water, enabling the ink to dry as it seeps into the sheet.

It is important for a finisher to keep in mind the differences in the reaction between toner and paper and ink and paper, as these can affect the quality of certain applications. For example, many laminating films used on offset-printed pieces are not aggressive enough to bond properly with toner. The presence of fuser oil also can become a production challenge further down the line. Many finishers have found that the presence of substantial fuser oil on a sheet compromises the adhesion of both glues and UV coating.

The choice of paper also may have a bearing on whether toner will flake. Flake-resistant uncoated sheets and matte finishes are ideal for digital applications. On the other hand, sheets with a glossy finish will not permit toner to fuse properly, making these papers more susceptible to flaking.

Binding and Finishing Considerations

In the world of digital printing, layouts can have an even greater impact on postpress costs, largely because the range of available sheet sizes is so limited. Since most digital products are printed one-up, your layout should strive for the most efficient use of paper. In any case, thoughtful job planning will help you design projects that are compatible with any postpress processes your project requires. Here are a few things to keep in mind:

Folding. The digital printing process involves heating the sheets to fuse the toner to the paper. That heat tends to dry the paper out, which also contributes to cracking. To combat cracking, you may want to consider scoring prior to folding, especially if your projects have dense blocks of color or are on sheets thicker than 80 lbs.

Grain direction. Whenever possible, lay out book projects so that the grain of the sheet runs parallel to the spine and parallel to any folds. Because toner sits on the surface of the sheet, it is more susceptible to cracking during folding than ink on paper, especially if the fold occurs cross-grain.

Location on the sheet. Many digitally printed sheets are laid out so the image area is in the center of the sheet. This can cost you both time and money once your project reaches the postpress stage. For example, a 6×9-in. image placed in the center of an 8½×11-in. sheet would have to be trimmed on all four sides. Placing the image in one of the top corners, however, necessitates only two-sided trimming, reducing both cost and production time (unless there are bleeds on opposite sides of the image, in which case trimming all four sides will be unavoidable).

Laminating. Coating digitally printed sheets—especially those with a substantial amount of toner—will help protect them during cutting or packaging. Be careful how you protect those sheets. Single-sided lamination may not be the best solution for sheets printed on both sides, due to the effects of friction on the opposite (non-laminated) side of the sheet, which may cause the toner to flake off as the sheet moves through the laminating process.

Saddle stitching. Saddle stitching is a popular binding option for many digital printing applications, especially thinner book projects like guides, brochures, and newsletters.

One reason stitching is so economical is that it can be done in-line with a variety of ancillary functions. A postpress services provider that can gather sheets, stitch, fold, and face trim in-line will be able to offer the tight turnaround times that digital print applications demand.

Mechanical binding. Leave ample punching margins between your copy and the spine edge when planning a mechanical-binding project.

Perfect binding. Incorporate the proper trim margins. In addition to a ⅛-in. grind-off margin at the spine, be sure to also leave at least a ⅛-in. trim margin on the other three sides. In addition, a –¼-in. glue trap at the foot of your covers will help prevent glue from seeping onto subsequent covers during binding. This may require you to print covers with bleeds on a different size stock than the text sheets.

Adhesive case binding. Believe it or not, this can be a viable option for digital printing applications. Normally, the cost and production time associated with case binding are not compatible with the short-run applications typical of digital printing. However, many case-bound book applications would benefit from containing digitally printed text sheets, cost and turnaround time permitting. One of our clients has created an inventory of pre-formed cases in a variety of colors, styles, and formats commonly used in digital printing. This practice makes adhesive case-binding a realistic option for a range of digitally printed products.

Preproduction samples (dummies). With digitally printed products, it is especially important to have your finisher provide a printed sample on the exact stock to be used for the actual production run. Many design programs that enable you to factor book bulk by calculating paper weight and the number of sheets to be bound don't account for the minute increase in thickness caused by the presence of toner on the surface of the sheet. Multiplied over dozens of pages, that extra bulk will render those computer-generated calculations useless. A sample printed on the exact production stock you plan to use enables your postpress services provider to take an accurate book thickness measurement and suggest an appropriate binding wire size.

*   *   *

The Final Word...

In terms of both quality and speed, digital printing is now an attractive option for a broad range of applications, most of which require some form of binding or finishing work. Keep in mind, however, that while many postpress functions are applicable to digital printing projects, not all postpress providers can handle digitally printed materials. Find a provider with the range of equipment, production capacity, and experience to meet both your needs and the needs of your customers.

Contributors:

- *Fred Daubert, The Riverside Group, Rochester, New York*
  www.riversidegroup.com
- *Sylvia Konkel, EU Services, Rockville, Maryland*
  www.euservices.com
- *Chuck Manthey, Sentinel Printing Company, St. Cloud, Minnesota*
  www.sentinelprinting.com
- *Frank Shear, Seaboard Bindery, Woburn, Massachusetts*
  www.seaboardbindery.com
- *John Snyder, HBP, Hagerstown, Maryland*
  www.hbp.com

Section III
Finishing Processes

33 UV and Press-Applied Coatings

Do your printed products need to pack a powerful visual punch? Don't "gloss over" varnishes and coatings. Do you want your images to jump off the page and be protected at the same time? Look no further than UV coating for a terrific solution.

What You Will Learn

- Coating features
- Environmental impact
- Do's and Don'ts

Press varnishes, aqueous coatings, and ultraviolet (UV) coatings are common finishing options used to seal the surface of paper while enhancing the overall aesthetic appeal of the printed design. Each of these processes can be combined with other finishing techniques, such as foil stamping and embossing, to create a truly beautiful product.

Press-Applied Varnish and Aqueous Coatings

Press varnishes and aqueous coatings are usually applied in-line during the printing process. Both afford protection and some gloss, but unlike aqueous, varnish is solvent-based, which raises concern about negative environmental impact. In addition, varnishes require longer drying times than aqueous and UV coatings.

Aqueous coatings are water-based and are generally regarded as safer for the environment than varnishes, although some do contain formaldehyde. These coatings, however, do not provide as high a gloss and are neither as hard nor as durable as UV coatings. Aqueous coatings, like UV, can be spot-applied.

UV for High Gloss

Although UV technology has been available for a long time, its use has ballooned since the mid-1980s. Highly durable and scratch-resistant UV coating is much glossier than either water- or solvent-based coatings and does not present the pollution and flammability problems of the latter. There has been some controversy about the recyclability of paper with UV coating, but several mills have found ways to repulp such materials.

An added advantage of UV coating is its rapid drying time. Passed under short-wavelength ultraviolet light (hence the name), UV coating cures in seconds, which dramatically reduces production time. With a UV curing unit, approximately 70% of the energy is heat, which may make this radiation curing method unsuitable for heat-sensitive substrates.

UV coating is applied in one of two ways. If the entire surface of the sheet is to be covered, roller coating is the preferred method because it is faster and involves less setup time than silk-screen coating. For UV spot coating, screen printing with its thick application is the most common method. UV spot coating has recently gained popularity among graphic designers as a way to draw attention to photos or other elements of a design.

Nearly 85% of all paperback retail titles are UV-coated. Other common applications include trading and greeting cards, posters, magazine covers, brochures, catalog covers, calendars, currency, wine labels, folders, menus, direct mail pieces, and other promotional materials.

Regardless of the manner in which it's applied or the product on which it's used, UV coating, like other finishing methods, has limitations and special considerations. For example, UV coating is generally more expensive than traditional coatings. And, as of the late 1990s, it has not been FDA-approved for use on materials that come in direct contact with food.

Ink and UV

Applying a UV coating over a conventional ink may prove problematic. If conventional ink does not have twenty-four hours to dry, gloss-back, a decrease in the surface gloss, often occurs. If you're using conventional inks, make sure they're free of waxes, anti-oxidants, and mineral oils. If not, the UV coating will have an "orange peel" appearance and adhesive problems, and its scuff resistance will be reduced. When in doubt, call your ink manufacturer and request inks that are specially formulated for use with UV coating.

Use reflex blue, rhodamine red, and PANTONE purple inks cautiously because their high alkaline content will cause fading when UV coating is applied. If you're printing with one of these inks, have your finisher conduct an ink fade test before running the job through the UV coater. Also consider the wax content of the ink you plan to use. A high wax level will cause poor adhesion between the ink and the UV coating. The uneven coverage that results is known as **reticulation.** In addition, be aware that the UV coating's deep, mirrorlike finish shows fingerprints when applied over dark solid colors.

Substrates

Clay- or enamel-coated stocks are the best paper surfaces for UV coating. Uncoated stock will yellow and absorb the coating, resulting in a greatly diminished high-gloss effect. UV-coated stocks that are lighter than 60-lb. cover tend to curl and may also crack when folded, depending on the thickness of the coating. Stock weights between 60-lb. and 50-pt. cover generally accept UV coating well. Also, other substrates with coated surfaces, such as cardboard and vinyl, are good candidates for UV coating.

Paper porosity is another factor in the success of UV coating. Highly porous paper absorbs UV coating and prevents the curing process. The result is low gloss and poor abrasion resistance. On the other hand, papers that are poorly calendered will yield deceptively acceptable results…at first. Eventually, however, the UV coating will flake off if scratched. This phenomenon, called **candling** or **shelling,** is caused by poor coating and adhesion.

*   *   *

The Final Word…

Consult with your finishing house, particularly if UV coatings will be combined with other finishing methods, such as scoring, stamping, or embossing. When used properly, UV coating returns a glossy, high-quality look and offers significant scuff and scratch protection to your printed products.

Contributors:

- *Marty Anson, Bindagraphics, Inc., Baltimore, Maryland*
  www.bindagraphics.com
- *Fred Daubert, The Riverside Group, Rochester, New York*
  www.riversidegroup.com

34 Film Laminating

Top-quality lamination increases the value of printed products. Educating yourself and your customers about the benefits of laminating will increase not only the value you bring to the selling process but also the demand for your laminated products. It will also boost your profits. Products that are frequently used and/or roughly handled— such as automotive shop manuals—need protection against abuse. Lamination is the most durable of paper coatings. To ensure the longevity of products that must perform under the roughest conditions, there is no substitute.

What You Will Learn

- Laminate materials
- Appropriate applications
- Reduce laminate gauge

Laminating improves a printing product's appearance. With laminating film that exaggerates light refraction, your printing appears to jump off the paper. For a more readable piece, an application of glare-reducing laminate is suggested. Frequently handled paper products will have their useful life and durability extended with laminating. Products that are exposed to high humidity or direct moisture should always be laminated.

Manufacturing Considerations

Because wax-based inks melt under the heat of lamination and produce imperfect seals, their use should be avoided. Before going to press, make sure your ink is wax-free. Output from color copiers usually contains wax and therefore does not laminate well.

Top-quality laminating companies have virtually eliminated silvering problems caused by trapped air pockets and poorly melted opaque glue that hasn't turned clear. Silvering results from running sheets too fast, not applying enough nip pressure, or using nonaggressive adhesive glue. Laminating professionals carefully choose the glues they use on their film, have cooling units on their machines, and know the right amount of pressure and heat to use during the laminating process.

Laminate shelf life is important. Most laminate glues chemically deteriorate within six months. If you have light-duty laminating equipment, don't let your laminating stock age because old film can spoil a job. Quality commercial laminating companies usually turn their laminate supplies in thirty days but never longer than sixty. Another downside of light-duty laminating equipment is that it has slow operating speeds, increased likelihood of curl, limited raw material purchasing power, and no in-line trimming.

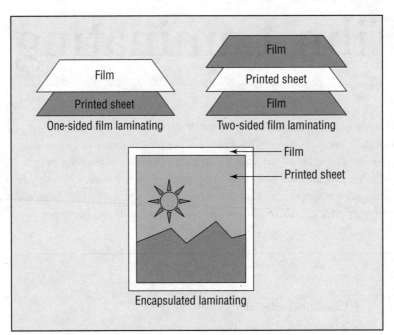

Types of lamination.

Types of Laminate Film

Following are a few of the most common types of laminate film:

- *Clear polyester.* Provides high gloss, durability, and scratch resistance.
- *Satin polyester.* Has a medium gloss, with excellent color consistency.
- *Matte-finish polyester.* A low-gloss, durable laminate that is great for readability.
- *Nylon-based laminate.* Counteracts moisture that causes curl.
- *Animal-glueable stampable laminate.* A laminate that is compatible with foil stamping and other processes using animal-based glues.
- *Polypropylene.* A softer high-gloss film that folds easily but is prone to scratching. Although it is a lower-cost film, it is not recommended for two-sided laminating because of its lack of rigidity.

Trends in Laminated Products

The following is a short list of growing markets for laminated products:

- *Ad specialties and premiums.* Lamination greatly enhances the promotional appeal of advertising pieces. Laminated guides, reference charts, and handy tip sheets are applicable to virtually any industry. Promotional items only work if they are durable, kept, and used. In short, lamination is an effective weapon in any marketer's arsenal.
- *Book covers.* Mechanically bound (e.g., Wire-O®, plastic coil, GBC, spiral wire) products will greatly improve their attractiveness and utility for a small increase in cost if laminated.
- *Easel-backed flip charts.*

Examples of laminated products.

- *Educational and sales presentation pieces.*
- *Map books, flip books.*
- *Reference manuals.*
- *Customer service reference cards.* For example, many large companies with extensive telephone customer service departments now print, laminate, and distribute telephone courtesy reminders to their customer service telephone representatives.
- *Government books.* During the late 1990s, the Government Printing Office (GPO) significantly increased its laminating quoting activity.
- *Business cards.*
- *Diecut laminated products.* Diecutting really adds value and excitement to tabletop advertising.
- *Menus.* Lamination makes menus waterproof and durable. Restaurants concerned about their image needn't worry about grape jelly or syrup damaging laminated paper products.
- *Plotter prints.* Directional, political, and real estate signage and point-of-purchase (POP) easel-backed consumer product displays all have increased functionality and longer life with laminating.

Money-Saving Tips

The following are a few money-saving tips that you can pass on to your customers in savings.

1. If you have a customer who is sold on laminating but isn't sold on the cost, there's one trick that might reduce the price and make you a hero. If you double or triple the weight of your paper and reduce your laminate gauge, you should achieve nearly the same rigidity, strength, and utility while decreasing your customer's cost as much as 35%.

2. On some jobs, quick printers can reduce their customers' costs by converting a job from coated to uncoated stock (assuming printing on uncoated is acceptable).

3. When producing a business card order, ask the customer if he or she would like the job laminated. If the job is properly imposed with at least eight cards up, your laminating costs will be small.

Partial Book Lamination

If you need the benefits of lamination on every page of a book but believe the cost will be prohibitive, consider laminating only a portion of your job. Partial book lamination will earn you more money while you better service your customers' product needs.

Changing job specifications can make full book lamination even more attractive. If you're used to running the text portion of a job on 80-lb. cover because some users beat up the product, consider reducing your paper to text-weight stock and double-side-laminate each page for only the heavy users. This will give heavy-use books the best protection available without affecting light users' product functionality. You will save your client money. In addition, laminating a partial quantity won't require you to do anything different in your prepress and press departments. As always, consult your laminating services provider first.

An Example

This example job has the following specifications: 2,500 quantity, 32 pages plus cover, 4/4 color, 8½×11 in. (215.9×279.4 mm), plastic coil binding, and 10% of the job needing full-page lamination. It might sell for $10,500 if the text pages are run on 80-lb. cover. If you change the 32 pages to 80-lb. text, your paper cost should drop by more

	Scenario A	Scenario B
Percentage of job laminated	0%	10%
Nonlaminated quantity	2,500	2,250
Laminated quantity	0	250
Prep work	Normal	Normal
Pages	32	32
Size	8½×11 in.	8½×11 in.
Binding	Plastic coil	Plastic coil
Text weight (4/4 color, #1 sheet, gloss)	80-lb. cover	80-lb. text
Cover paper and printing cost, 4/4 colors, #1 sheet	100-lb. cover	100-lb. cover
Total selling price	$10,500	$9,800
Please note: your costs may vary.		

Economics of partial book lamination.

than $1,000. The bottom line is simple. The selling price to your client should fall even after laminating 10% of the job (see the table on the preceding page). By making these changes, you will have provided your customer with a better solution, reduced the price, and increased his or her loyalty to you.

Industry Improvements

In the past, laminating trimmed-flush products was risky because of laminate separation. Nowadays, however, improved laminate glues with low-melt copolymer adhesives, increased nip pressure and machine heat, and automatic cooling systems have virtually removed the risk of laminate separation. Your laminating services company should use commercial thermal film laminates with top-quality glues.

Laminating equipment has made strides toward reducing offset powder problems. This is in contrast to UV coating—which still experiences rough results from excessive offset powder. Also, unlike UV coating, film laminating won't show cracking.

*   *   *

The Final Word...

Turnaround times have greatly decreased in the laminating industry. Competitive laminating service companies routinely offer very short turnaround times in addition to ancillary services such as shrink-wrapping, collating, mechanical binding, scoring, easel-backing, and eyeletting.

Contributors:

- *Fred Daubert, The Riverside Group, Rochester, New York*
  www.riversidegroup.com
- *Brian Hills, Nationwide Laminating, Lorton, Virginia*
  www.nationwidelaminating.com
- *Frank Shear, Seaboard Bindery, Woburn, Massachusetts*
  www.seaboardbindery.com

35 Embossing and Debossing

How can designers produce products that capture attention in a world where people are distracted and have very little time to absorb information? One answer is to incorporate embossing and/or debossing into your printing because these processes add emphasis and snap.

What You Will Learn

- Die materials
- Beveled edges
- Paper considerations

Embossing refers to the process of raising the paper surface using heat and force. This is accomplished by pressing the paper between a heated, etched female die and matching male counter-die. The heat allows the paper fibers to stretch more easily, while the force created between the dies "molds" the paper into the etched area. When this process is used to indent the paper rather than raise it, it's referred to as **debossing.**

People notice height. Mountains, tall people, and embossing command attention. Raised images on an otherwise flat sheet of paper will catch a busy reader's eyes and force a closer look at the intended message. People like to run their fingers over embossing because it adds a third (tactile) dimension to two-dimensional printing.

Embossing and debossing techniques create peaks and valleys that give printing depth, make images pop out, and engage readers' attention in fresh new ways. Embossing creates raised images, while debossing introduces sunken ones. **Blind embossing** refers to impressions that don't register to previously printed images. Obviously, if you're embossing over printed elements, registration is important because embossing a printed image is like adding another ink color. Misregistered embossing results in unusable products.

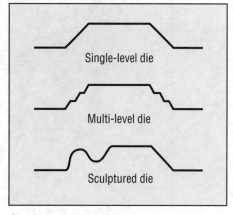

Popular embossing die styles.

The intricacy of the embossed pattern is directly related to the level of detail etched onto the die. A simple single-level die can be created to render a flat image with a 30° beveled edge. For the finest detail, multi-level dies can be sculpted into a nearly limitless range of patterns and designs.

The Die-Making Process

Foil stamping and embossing dies can be formed from several different materials. The level of detail a die can contain—and the lifespan of the die itself—is dependent upon the die material and the process used to etch it.

Magnesium is a soft metal that does not conduct heat very well, which is why magnesium dies are used primarily for stamping applications with quantities of a few hundred and are not recommended for embossing. The softness of the metal also limits its lifespan. Magnesium dies are usually acid etched, which is a process that uses a chemical solution to create the desired patterns or images.

Copper dies have sufficient strength and heat conductivity for both foil stamping and embossing applications. Although copper dies are usually used for single-level embossing, they are able to be double-etched for multiple levels. Like dies made from magnesium, copper dies are usually manufactured with acid etching. With a correct makeready, copper dies will yield many impressions, making them sufficient for high-volume projects that call for a few thousand impressions per month.

Brass dies are the best and most versatile foil stamping and embossing dies available. Although they can be acid etched, brass dies are typically machine milled, a process that grinds off unwanted metal. For projects that call for the most exquisite detail, brass dies can be hand sculpted. This involves a die maker carving the die to

Embossing on board.

exacting detail. Hand sculpting is often necessary for intricate, multi-level dies. Brass dies conduct heat the best and last the longest. With a proper makeready, these dies can be used regularly for many years.

Perhaps the only negative to a brass die is its cost. Although they last a very long time, they can be expensive to create. For that reason, you may want to have die duplicates created from brass masters. Duplicates are particularly useful for regularly repeating projects or those that are printed multiple-up.

There are three main materials used to create duplicates: Bakelite, fiberglass resin, and nickel. Bakelite is a hard plastic material that's inexpensive and easy to produce; however, the heating and cooling associated with embossing limit its lifespan. Fiberglass resin is slightly more expensive than Bakelite, but will last longer. Nickel is a little more costly than Bakelite and fiberglass resin but is more durable and suitable for multi-level embossing or combination dies. Nickel duplicates are generally used for embossing and combination applications from brass master dies.

There are a few things to keep in mind to determine if a die is becoming worn. First, compare a piece from early in the run (or one from a previous run using the same die) to one from the end of the current production run. Reduced depth or clarity of the embossed or stamped image is a sign that the die is dull. Also, check the die itself for dull, rounded edges. Perform these checks after each production run if you plan to keep the die for a future run, and consider replacement at the first signs of wear.

Die Depth

The depth of embossing and debossing dies range from 0.006 in. (0.15 mm) to 0.025 in. (0.64 mm). Very deep dies (0.020–0.025 in., 0.51–0.64 mm) must have beveled edges so that they don't cut through the paper. **Bevel** refers to the way the edge of the die is angled. The wider the angle, the more three-dimensional the resulting image. You can specify bevels to be from 30° to 60°. They can even go as high as 80°.

Job quantity, function, and appearance all should be considered when specifying the material from which a die is crafted. For long-run jobs or those that are expected to be reprinted several times, dies should be made from either copper or brass, both of which are very durable. Inexpensive magnesium dies, commonly referred to as "mag" dies, tend to smash out or break down fairly quickly. If the design is very detailed or you're embossing heavy, textured stock, use either copper or brass dies.

Artwork Preparation

There are a few guidelines regarding preparation of artwork for die-makers. In stark contrast to the increasingly digitized world of lithography, die-makers still work from paper or film. For single-level dies, prepare either film or good-resolution black-and-white mechanicals. The artwork for multi-level dies should have a tissue overlay for each level. In general, designs should be slightly oversized, with lines and fine points heavier than if they were going to be printed.

A variety of products that have been embossed.

Rules should be at least 2 pt. wide or the paper may not press into the lines in the die. Wide kerning (extra space between letters in a word) should be the norm, and tiny or highly intricate designs should be avoided. The designer must indicate whether the die should have a rounded or beveled edge, keeping in mind that only copper and brass dies can be tooled for beveled edges. Advise your customers that beveled edges play an optical trick by making images appear smaller than their actual size.

Paper Choices

Paper stock is an important consideration. Soft papers are easier to emboss than laid bond and other hard stocks. Uncoated sheets are best for deep embossing. Embossing and debossing involves both heat and pressure, which smooth out textured stock. While the contrast between the smooth, embossed image and the rest of the page is striking and often desired, be safe and let your customers know in advance that this will happen.

*   *   *

The Final Word...

If you're unsure about selecting an appropriate paper for your project, get advice from your finishing house in advance. A brief meeting held between the end customer, designer, printer, and finisher would save everybody a lot of time, money, and aggravation.

Contributors:

- *Marty Anson, Bindagraphics, Inc., Baltimore, Maryland*
  www.bindagraphics.com
- *Fred Daubert, The Riverside Group, Rochester, New York*
  www.riversidegroup.com
- *Bob Windler, Diecrafters, Inc., Chicago, Illinois*
  www.diecrafters.com

36 Foil Stamping

Few printed pieces shout, "Look at me!" as powerfully as those with foil stamping. Foil irresistibly draws the eye and commands attention. Foil-stamped images add punch to promotional mailers, a festive air to brochures and invitations, and a dazzling touch to wrapping paper, stationery, packaging, menus, and presentation folders.

What You Will Learn

- Ink and coating impact
- Foil characteristics
- Design issues

Customers can choose among various colored metallic foils; patterned foils, such as wood grain and marble; and more than 200 pastel and matte colors. Increasingly, there are more rainbow, prismatic, and holographic foils available, too. Transparent, tinted, and partially opaque foils (i.e., smoke and clear) are also common.

In foil stamping, hot dies press a micro-thin plastic film containing metals or pigment against a sheet of paper. A foil stamp can either be flat or combined with embossing or debossing. Because nearly anything that can withstand heat or pressure can be foil-stamped, the applications are virtually endless—limited only by substrates, inks, varnishes, laminates, and creativity.

Coated paper allows metallic foils to really shine, whereas uncoated sheets absorb some of the foil's brightness. Uncoated, heavily textured sheets, however, really work for metallic foil embossing because the embossing smooths the surface of the paper where the foil is applied.

When applied over inks and varnishes that contain waxes or silicone, foil tends to blister or bubble because gases are released during the heat of the stamping process. Blistering also occurs when the foil-stamped image area is too large. Unfortunately, there are no good rules of thumb for what determines too large of an image area for foil stamping. Be safe. Consult your finisher first. Additionally, foil stamping over UV coatings, lacquers, and some film laminations can be challenging. Unless stampable laminate is used, the foil should be applied first.

Design Options

Ink, paper, and color selection can all be used to create unique and exquisite foil-stamped pieces. There are several additional treatments and techniques that can be used to alter the paper surface to give pieces a highly customized appearance:

- **Refractive engraving.** This treatment creates a series of cross-hatched lines on a flat foil-stamped surface, resulting in added texture and dimension, especially when used with metallic foils on coated stocks.
- **Foil over foil.** This process uses a second pass through the stamping process to create a wider range of color options and effects.
- **Gloss embossing.** A method that combines a deep, clear foil with blind embossing to produce a high-gloss embossed image.
- **Textured embossing.** The use of patterned foils lends a unique quality to an embossed or foil-stamped piece. Popular textures include woodgrain, leather, and snakeskin. Contact your finisher for a complete range of textured foils.

Be aware of makeready and scheduling realities: When planning a foil-stamping (or embossing) project, it's important to understand that these are not "same-day" processes. Die creation can take up to several days for a hand-sculpted, finely detailed brass die. Although some projects require dies with this level of intricacy, slight alterations in project design may drastically reduce makeready times on foil-stamping and embossing projects. Involve your finisher early in the project planning process to see if alterations can be made to reduce turnaround times for your application.

Examples of foil-stamped products.

Managing the Foil-Stamping Process

The following checklist can help you manage your foil-stamping process better.

1. Play a consultative role with your customer. Keep in mind that minor adjustments in product design may result in great savings. For example, reducing a two-pass job to a one-pass job may be easier than you think. Customers appreciate time- and money-saving alternatives, and if you are the one who brings fresh options to them, your value to their organization will increase.

2. Communicate with your finisher to make sure that your customers' foil selections (e.g., metallic, pigment, pastel) will work with the chosen paper stock. Also, verify that foil coverage areas aren't too large.

3. Check the opacity of your foil. Many pigment and pearl translucent foils appear differently after adhesion to colored stocks.

4. Because dry stocks diffuse reflected light, choose dry, textured stocks for foil stamping to prevent dulling.

5. Ultraviolet (UV) coating with high silicone content, lacquers, and some film laminates are difficult surfaces upon which to stamp. Be safe and test foil adhesion prior to applying a coating to your printing.

6. Designs that simultaneously incorporate large solid areas and fine intricate spaces may require two foil-stamping passes. To determine if both can be done in a single pass, consider the following factors:

   ☞ *Foil stamping equipment.* Because solids require more pressure, choosing a cylinder press is generally a good idea. Less tonnage on the solid areas mean that there's also less pressure on intricate areas, reducing the chance of foil fill-in. Other equipment factors to consider include whether the press has different heating zones, foil pull directions, and multiple foil webs.

   ☞ *Foil type.* Even if the press can run two foil webs, a single web may have to be used if the designs are spaced too closely together. If only one foil is being used, it should have a moderate release and medium-to-heavy coverage capabilities.

   ☞ *Stock.* For foil stamping applications, stocks that are too porous may cause the foil to push too deeply into the sheet. The result may be color that appears washed out or metallic foils with an uneven surface. Deep embossing onto a foil stock may cause the stock to split, although this depends on the size and depth of the image. Before a project is printed, let your finisher help select a stock that will yield the best stamping and embossing results.

7. Foil-stamped letterhead for downstream use in laser printers should be tested prior to running a job. The heat from a laser printer may be too high for certain combinations of foils and coatings. Any foil that goes through a high-speed laser printer should be tested when the laser printer is hot (after it has been running a long time).

8. As a rule of thumb, the space between the lines in an intricately detailed design should be no less than half the thickness of the stock. And as previously mentioned, coated and smooth stocks work best.

9. Avoid wet trapping (overprinting ink or varnish over a wet ink film) varnish because it can result in gassing (trapped air) after foil application.

10. If foil is to be stamped over ink, be sure to choose an ink with a low wax content. Petroleum-based inks can be used, but they require the use of specially formulated foils.

11. Avoid silicone anti-setoff spray powder because sheets contaminated with silicone cannot be successfully foil stamped. When coatings are applied over spray powder, the sheet will feel like fine sandpaper. Also, make sure silicone spray isn't used on folding, gluing, or diecutting equipment.

Create Proper Electronic Die Files for Foil Stamping and Embossing

Eliminate all print-related information. Electronic files should not contain any information that you don't want foil stamped or embossed. This includes all color information, masks, and screens.

Convert fonts to outlines only. The outline of a font is all that's necessary when creating dies for foil stamping and embossing. In Adobe Illustrator, select the Create Outline option for every font in the file. To avoid problems, also include key information about each font, such as point size and font name.

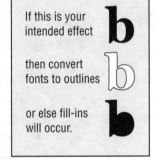

If this is your intended effect

then convert fonts to outlines

or else fill-ins will occur.

All scans should be high-resolution. If the file will include scanned artwork, it should be no less than 600-dpi resolution. A lower resolution may result in blurry, inaccurate lines and edges. Make sure all images are sent in black and white only; color or grayscale images may compromise quality and turnaround times.

Send files in the appropriate format. Save files at 100% scale and indicate right-reading.

Enclose hard copy proofs. This step verifies electronic file accuracy and prevents surprises.

These tips will help you create electronic foil stamping and embossing die files that are easier and faster to use.

*   *   *

The Final Word...

When specifying foil, consider the following characteristics: scuff resistance, stamping speed, the ratio of fine lines to large solid areas in your artwork, fading resistance (to chemicals or light), water and humidity resistance, price, and availability.

Contributors:

- *Marty Anson, Bindagraphics, Inc., Baltimore, Maryland*
  www.bindagraphics.com
- *Fred Daubert, The Riverside Group, Rochester, New York*
  www.riversidegroup.com
- *Bob Windler, Diecrafters, Inc., Chicago, Illinois*
  www.diecrafters.com

37 Diecutting

A beautifully printed piece can be breathtaking, but the impact of ink on paper alone simply isn't enough for some projects. That's where the formidable alliance of high-quality printing and creative diecutting can work wonders.

What You Will Learn

- The three Gs
- Registration
- Importance of consistency

The strength of diecutting lies in its versatility. It can be used to create business card slits and windows on a simple portfolio or an entire three-dimensional product from a flat sheet. Puzzle pieces, video boxes, self-standing point-of-purchase displays, CD slots, iron-cross folds, sliding-scale cards, and pop-up books are just a few examples.

Like other processes that help define the graphic arts industry, successful diecutting depends on good planning and clear communication. Nobody can help a designer plan jobs better than an experienced diecutting partner, so let this person be you! Detailed information about diecutting needs to be shared among all involved in downstream manufacturing operations. For example, if a diecut project will be perfect bound or saddle stitched, the bindery should be informed of diecutting decisions so that the job ultimately will work as a whole.

When your design is complete, a preproduction sample or "dummy" that includes gripper, guide, and grain markings should be sent to your diecutting services company well in advance of the job itself. Your diecutting specialist will be able to help catch and correct any problems at this point. It is also important that your diecutter constantly monitor the progress of your job during production. Critical factors like press tonnage or paper bulk may vary, changing score depths and rendering ill-conceived products useless. For this reason, frequent visual comparisons with the preproduction sample should be made throughout the run.

Paper

Paper affects diecutting in many ways. Stock thickness, grain direction, and moisture content all play important roles in diecutting production. Reduce production spoilage and improve turnaround times by considering these factors early in the planning stage.

A variety of diecut products.

Paper thickness. Variation in stock thickness requires diecutters to accommodate the thickest stock in a production run. This can cause a chain reaction of undesirable effects: First, thinner stock will be cut too hard, which causes sheets to fall apart. To compensate, machine operators may need to add small marks or nicks to hold the sheets together. This, in turn, has the undesirable effect of adding to many unsightly rough edges (after stripping). Therefore, never mix paper weights, brands, or lots—at least without telling your finisher first.

Grain direction. If the grain runs the wrong way, sheets will tend to be too weak, again requiring more nicks than necessary.

Moisture content. Brittle, dry stock tends to fall apart. This requires more nicks. Controlling heat and moisture during the printing process will help. In addition, dry stock negatively affects scoring quality because paper fibers in dry paper aren't as pliable as necessary and therefore are more susceptible to cracking as the ink lays upon its surface. Controlling heat and moisture during the printing process will help.

Uncoated stock. Uncoated stock tends to run better and requires fewer nicks than coated stock.

Paper finishes. Some paper finishes are more difficult to work with than others. For example, laid stock often will appear to crack, even after steel rule scores are applied. Knowing this up front can prevent unexpected disappointment.

Layout Considerations

The "three Gs" of diecutting—clearly marked grippers, guides, and grain—are essential to the success of any diecutting job. As a rule of thumb, diecutting can be performed much more quickly and accurately if your finisher is able to work with uncut press sheets. Cutting sheets down before diecutting is a common mistake made by many printers who do it reflexively, causing problems for diecutters. Working on uncut sheets makes it much easier for your diecutter to match registration and control quality because printer grippers and side guides are more consistent than trimmed paper edges.

Most diecutters require margins of approximately ⅜ in. (9.5 mm) for both gripper and side guides, so be sure to plan your layouts accordingly. (If you need to squeak by with less, ask your diecutter first.) Do your diecutter and yourself a favor by clearly indicating the grain direction, as it can make a big difference in quality. Grain is readily apparent on most papers, but it is better to know for sure than to have to guess. When cross-grain scores are made improperly on recycled stock, downstream operations may produce cracking—even after channel scoring. Save yourself a lot of unnecessary telephone time and reduce your risk of production problems by marking the "three Gs" clearly ahead of time.

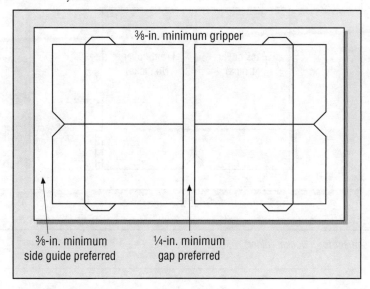

Two-up pocket folder layout.

Register marks also will help your finisher create accurate, attractive diecut pieces. These marks enable your finisher to get your sheets in registration quickly, without "eyeballing" it. Whenever possible, place register marks in trim-off areas. If the image area happens to take up the entire sheet (exclusive of gripper and guide margins), locate register marks where they will be covered by a glue tab or otherwise obscured.

Nicks

In order for pieces to move through diecutting equipment, your finisher may need to place small marks or "nicks" on the sheet. These nicks must be factored into your design to minimize their visibility on the finished product. Pocket folders, for example, should be laid out so that nicks will be placed on pocket glue tabs, where they will be hidden once the pockets are formed.

On some projects, however, nicks are too difficult to hide. Circular pieces with little or no waste area likely will show finishing nicks. Be sure to involve your finisher as early as possible in the project's design phase to be sure it is laid out to minimize the appearance of finishing nicks.

If you need to add nicks for any reason, your finisher can minimize project appearance problems by allowing for a re-trim area. However, this may add cost and time. Another solution may be to sand away the nicks after the diecutting process has been completed, but this, too, will add production cost and time.

One of the keys to accurate diecutting is ensuring that your diecutter has both a sample product and either a film positive or die line file that can be used to create dies. A "film positive" is a sheet of Mylar—usually output by the printer—showing

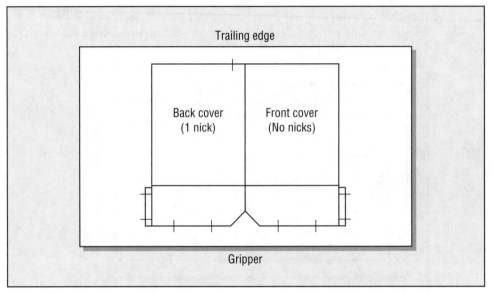

Diecut nick placement for a pocket folder.

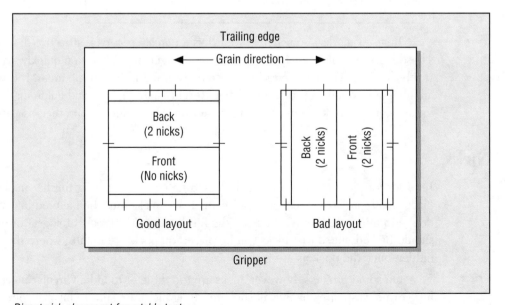

Diecut nick placement for a table tent.

the outline of the project and the area to be diecut. One alternative is to send the die maker a computer file of the project. Typically, such a file can be output from the same file used to print the job. It should be free of all images and copy, leaving just an outline of the diecut area.

And More...

Diecutting registration marks. As in printing, hairline register marks improve diecut registration. If your image uses up all the paper, excluding gripper and guide margins, it can be impossible to place register marks in waste areas located in the body of the sheet. Using these marks—and letting your diecutter know about them in advance—means that diecutting operators no longer have to scan whole sheets during production. This, in turn, reduces turnaround time and increases registration accuracy.

Crossovers. Precision crossover images in stitched products should be carefully planned. For on-the-money registration, the bead of the scores of each form must nest into those directly behind it. Work-and-turn and work-and-tumble print formats cannot be properly scored unless they are cut apart first.

Cartons. All major scores should run against the paper grain, such that the carton remains square after conversion. If the scores run in the wrong direction, cartons tend to bulge in the middle. In this case, poor aesthetics is the least of your worries, because bulges may cause a real problem downstream. If videotapes are to be machine-inserted, for example, cartons with the wrong folding scores can cause major fulfillment problems.

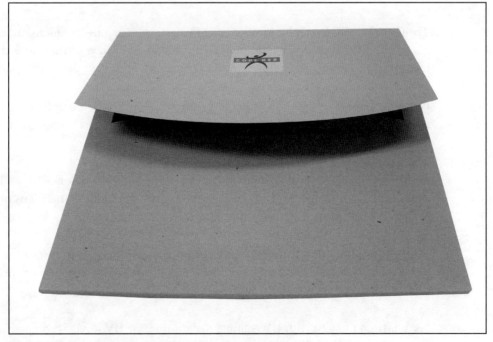

Dimensional pocket folder with three-color hot foil stamping.

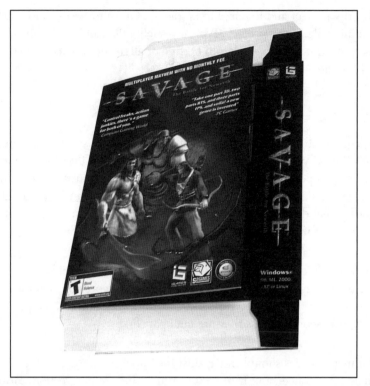

Diecut multimedia box.

Creep (pushout). When diecutting stitched signatures, make a dummy on the actual stock so that you can accurately plan for "creep." This is especially important for jobs that feature tab banks. It can be dangerous to rely on standard creep-adjusting formulas (i.e., ⅟₃₂ in.), especially on thicker books.

Thin stocks. These can be problematic. Diecut window jobs on onionskin can give rise to production waste on a dramatic scale. Carefully plan your thin stock diecut jobs. Start by getting advice about waste allowances from your diecutting partner.

Gripper area. Diecutters usually can get by with less gripper area than a printer; nevertheless, a common print-stripping mistake is failing to leave enough of a gripper on projects with ink-free, diecut grippers.

Scuffing. Some new coatings provide better protection than older coatings, but experienced diecutters also know how to pass paper through the machines properly to minimize stray marks.

Multiple paper lots. If you use more than one paper lot during a pressrun, be sure to mark clearly where the paper lots change on the skid. This will prevent problems, such as scores not being deep enough.

UV coating. On jobs with UV coating, make sure your UV services company monitors paper curling. This will prevent downstream diecutting problems.

Laminated sheets. When diecutting laminated sheets, keep excess lamination away from the gripper and guide edges.

Encourage your customers to stay flexible and open-minded about their diecutting options. Experienced diecutters may be able to suggest changes to a job's design and/or specifications that will save them both time and money. In one case we recall, the project called for a diecut wheel grommeted onto a base. The design called for significant paper waste during printing, an inordinate amount of handwork, and it ran poorly downstream in production. When the diecutter suggested changing the design to highlight a free-spinning but completely entrapped wheel, the change yielded a 35% savings in paper cost, a 15% reduction in diecutting cost, and additional time and money savings during later bindery operations. The lesson? The lines of communication should always be open between diecutter and customer.

*   *   *

The Final Word...

Whether the diecutting process will be used to enhance a finely printed piece or to create an entire product from flat sheets, successful diecutting depends upon competent execution of the basics. Especially important are the "three Gs" as they relate to proofs, mock-ups, and properly marked-up press sheets. Doing these well will help your projects succeed, regardless of how many hands are involved. In terms of pre-planning and quality control, diecutting does not mean cutting corners.

Contributors:

- *Mark Beard, Finishbinders, Inc., Des Moines, Iowa*
  www.finishbinders.com
- *Fred Daubert, The Riverside Group, Rochester, New York*
  www.riversidegroup.com
- *Russ Haines, Rapid Bind, Inc., Portland, Oregon*
  www.rapidbind.com
- *Tony Hoholik, The John Roberts Company, Minneapolis, Minnesota*
  www.johnroberts.com
- *Bruce Sanderson, Springfield Printing Corporation, Springfield, Vermont*
  www.springfieldprinting.com
- *Bill Seidl, Seidl's Bindery, Houston, Texas*
  www.seidlsbindery.com
- *Joe Sferlazza, formerly of S&F Die Cutting Co., Inc., Clifton, NJ*
- *Frank Shear, Seaboard Bindery, Woburn, Massachusetts*
  www.seaboardbindery.com
- *Bob Windler, Diecrafters, Inc., Chicago, Illinois*
  www.diecrafters.com

38 Diecutting Die File Creation

Technology offers a tremendous opportunity to streamline the process of making diecutting dies, saving valuable time and effort. Years ago, your finisher was required to wait for press sheets and art boards. Today, this can all be accomplished electronically, and finishers that do so offer several production advantages.

What You Will Learn

- Choose a file format that works with your finisher
- Remove extraneous text
- Save time and money

Here are some key guidelines to bear in mind when creating and sending electronic files for diecutting dies:

- **Send an appropriate file format.** Many die makers import your die line file directly into a CAD program, which needs to "read" the information to reproduce the die line. Certain formats work better than others for this purpose. For creating diecutting die files, programs such as Quark are not conducive to manipulation and therefore should be avoided.

- **"Strip" the file of print-related information.** In order for die makers to produce an accurate die, the source file needs to be "stripped down" of the information needed to print the job. Color information, masks, and screens can obstruct the exact dimensions of the die line.

- **Be sure to remove any "hidden" elements.** Occasionally, files are sent with "hidden" or embedded lines. Though these lines aren't always visible on-screen, the die maker's CAD program will read them. This will cause the laser to execute repeated burns, rendering the die useless. This may not be caught until the die is on press, which will cause production delays. Be sure to check for any hidden layers in your file.

- **Send text instructions in a separate file.** Designers often color-code die lines to distinguish different cuts, such as perfs and scores. These colors can be misinterpreted without clarification. A separate file containing written instructions that serve as a guide will eliminate confusion.

By keeping these tips in mind as you create your diecutting die line files, you'll be sure to avoid costly production delays.

*   *   *

The Final Word...

In addition to getting your job done right, proper die file creation reduces extraneous messenger fees, lost production time, and other valuable resources that need to be conserved. As an added benefit, potential problems are identified sooner, which certainly saves time and money.

Contributor:

• *Bob Windler, Diecrafters, Inc., Chicago, Illinois*
  www.diecrafters.com

39 Rotary Scoring

Here's a question. You're bidding on a beautiful six-color job on a heavy enamel sheet. It has color breaks on folds and a T-perforated business reply card. It is just the kind of printing you're looking for. Before sending off your bid, you call your local diecutter for a price on channel scoring and perforating, right? Not necessarily.

What You Will Learn

- Why rotary scoring?
- Flexibility and quality
- Common applications

Don't ignore the many benefits of today's high-speed, versatile rotary scoring machinery. If you plan to die-score jobs that should run on rotary scorers, you probably will lose these bids. Assume your competition knows that rotary scoring technology saves both time and money on many types of scoring and perforating projects.

If you're concerned about quality of rotary scoring, don't be. You sacrifice nothing with rotary scoring. In some cases, you'll even gain in quality over traditional letterpress die scoring. Here's why:

- **Speed.** Rotary scoring is fast. When you outsource letterpress work, you immediately lose time waiting for the die to be made. Then, once the job is on press, die scoring run speeds are significantly slower. For many jobs, rotary scorers outperform letterpresses by a factor of two or three.

- **Cost.** Faster rotary-scoring production speeds yield lower manufacturing costs. In addition, setup charges are less because rotary scoring eliminates the need for letterpress dies, which typically cost between $150 and $300 apiece.

- **"Opposing" scores.** Most letterpress systems need to run these types of jobs in two passes, which is slow, inefficient, and costly. Worse, scoring accuracy may suffer because the raised score of the first pass can cause feeding variation during the second. One-pass rotary scoring assures the best quality, lowest cost, and fastest turnaround. Scoring jobs with color breaks and tight registration are better produced on rotary scorers because operators can run them using a sheet's true press guide and gripper. Furthermore, rotary scorers don't need sheets cut prior to production, again enabling the operator to use the press guide and gripper.

- **T-perfs.** With the help of sophisticated stop/start timing devices, late-model rotary machines can swiftly and precisely cut T-perfs into a wide range of

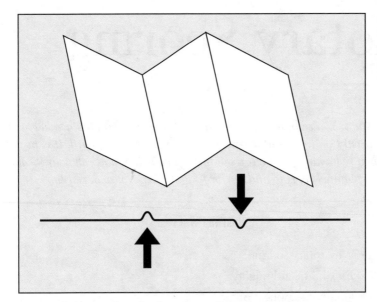

Rotary scoring allows for the placement of opposing scores in one pass, making it ideal for Z-folding applications.

direct mail and other printed products. Since T-perfing equipment doesn't require letterpress dies and runs at high rates of speed, products with T-perfs typically cost less when produced on rotary scoring machines.

- *"Difficult" stocks.* If your project needs cross-grain scoring or contains heavy enamel coatings, clay fillers, or brittle fibers, rotary scoring also may be your best choice. Unlike one-pass die-scoring letterpresses, dual-shaft rotary scorers can attack difficult projects with an in-line, two-pass approach. The dual-shaft design enables a "soft" score to be applied as sheets pass through the first shaft. This prepares or "softens" the sheet for the final "hard" score as the sheet passes through the second shaft. The result is a beautiful, cost-effective, efficiently produced project with minimal cracking (or no cracking at all) on even the most difficult folds.

Common Applications

The uses for rotary scoring machines are virtually unlimited. Common applications include book covers, brochures, promotional materials, coupon books, multiple-up BRCs, tear-off cards, perforated pages, book inserts, crack-and-peel labels, and more. Look for binderies with rotary scoring machines so you can one-stop-shop for integrated applications involving mechanical binding, perfect binding, index tabbing, collating, folding, and fulfillment.

Some rotary scorers have stop/start, solenoid-driven, timed perforating wheels. For example, the use of a timed-perf feature on a 16-page signature that needs one page perforated close to the binding gutter will cause the job to be produced much faster, and at a lower cost, than if the job had been run on a less efficient letterpress. When your job needs both continuous and timed perfs, think of rotary scoring first.

Another useful feature of rotary scorers is their micro-perfing abilities. If you need to micro-perf sheets for downstream use in laser printers, the last place you should look for a solution is on a die letterpress. Rotary scorers handle these types of jobs with ease.

Most rotary scoring machines are able to convert stock as thick as 28 points and as light as 16 lb. Run speeds on some scoring machines can exceed ten thousand sheets per hour, easily netting between six thousand and eight thousand sheets per hour. In addition to being versatile enough to convert stocks as difficult as synthetics, other rotary scoring machines can process sheets as large as 41 in. One feature many rotary scorers and letterpresses share is a highly accurate top-loading paper feeding mechanism.

Other Considerations

- When planning multi-panel projects with complicated folding sequences, make sure to size your panels appropriately. The laws of physics still apply. Allow for creep and pushout. For example, a roll-folded project with equal-sized panels will suffer from wrinkling and bend-overs, regardless of how perfect the scores are.

- Even if you're not used to outsourcing finishing services at a bindery, rest easy. Rotary scorers are more like folding machines than die presses. In fact, with minimal training many folder operators can run rotary scoring machines because so many of the core skills are the same. Die presses require very different operational skills.

- To be fair, however, some projects still need to run on traditional die letterpresses. If your job features shapes, patterns, curves, cutouts, or kiss cuts, plan on diecutting.

*   *   *

The Final Word...

If you need to have scoring done, don't hesitate to investigate the benefits of rotary scoring machines. In the cutthroat graphic arts market, extra turnaround time or a few additional cents can result in work lost to the competition. Knowledge of high-speed rotary scoring machinery may be one of those small advantages that could put more profit in your pocket today.

Contributors:

- *Sue Hein, Rapid Bind, Inc., Portland, Oregon*
  www.rapidbind.com
- *Kevin Rickard, Rickard Bindery, Chicago, Illinois*
  www.rickardbindery.com
- *Brenda Slacum, formerly of Freedom Finishing Solutions, Baltimore, Maryland*

40 Mounting

The next time you walk into a store, take a look at the various displays that are hanging from the ceiling or standing near the register. Many of them utilize the process of mounting to make them sturdier and more noticeable.

What You Will Learn

• The mounting process
• Tolerance guidelines
• Drying time

Mounting refers to the process of gluing one substrate onto another, such as a printed sheet onto a thicker backing. Chipboard is the most common backing material, while products like Fome-Cor® and corrugated board are used for projects that require extra strength. Although board thickness may vary, 50-pt. board is a popular size.

Plan your diecuts carefully. Due to the inherent lack of precision in the mounting process, diecutting and foil stamping with tight registration can be difficult. When planning a project that will be mounted, allow at least ¹⁄₃₂-in. tolerance on all sides. For that reason, blind registration for diecutting and foil stamping projects is recommended.

Fluctuations in humidity will cause different materials to contract and expand at different rates once glue is applied between them, so choose material combinations carefully. For example, an enamel-coated sheet mounted to chipboard may result in wrinkling, warping, or delamination as the drying glue causes the materials to shrink at different rates. For projects where warping is a major concern, Fome-Cor® may be a better solution since it isn't nearly as porous as chipboard.

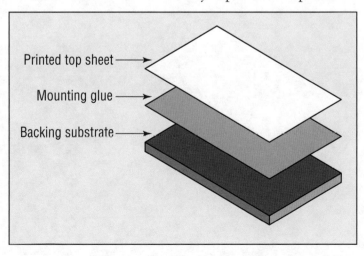

The three ingredients of mounting.

Printed top sheet ⟶

Mounting glue ⟶

Backing substrate ⟶

Failing to give a mounting project ample time to dry can cause a host of adhesion and registration problems. In general, try to allow at least five days in your production cycle for proper drying.

*   *   *

The Final Word...

You can combine mounting with in-house diecutting and foil-stamping capabilities to create eye-catching, customized point-of-purchase displays.

Contributor:

- *Bob Windler, Diecrafters, Inc., Chicago, Illinois*
  www.diecrafters.com

41 Double-Sided Taping

Do you have projects that are ideal for remoistenable gluing but need a little more strength? What about items that need to be applied to surfaces such as glass or fabric? Double-sided, "peel 'n stick," or Kleenstik™ taping is an attractive solution that can fill those needs. Kleenstik is a double-sided adhesive tape that includes a plastic strip on one side, allowing it to be sealed by the end user.

What You Will Learn

- Double-sided taping uses
- Stronger than remoistenable glue
- Knock out coatings

Popular Uses

Kleenstik taping can be used in place of remoistenable glue to form pockets or seal envelopes on applications such as direct mailers and point-of-purchase displays. One of the key benefits of Kleenstik taping is its strength relative to remoistenable gluing. That makes it ideal for use on products such as two-way CD carriers, which require a sturdy closure to keep items intact.

An Example

A client of ours regularly converts a pocket folder job that has Kleenstik tape running along the face of the outside back cover. If these pocket folders arrive in any format other than flat sheets, applying tape flush to the cover's face is nearly impossible. However, this customer involved our client during the project's infancy, and together they worked out a manufacturing process that has endured. Prior to diecutting the job, they apply the

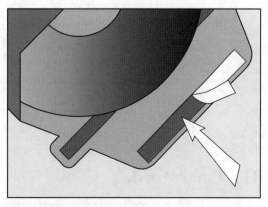

Kleenstik tape can be used to seal products such as disc mailers, which require a sturdier closure than remoistenable glue.

Diecut shelf talker with Kleenstik™.

tape to flat sheets so there's a side-guide that provides an adequate margin for accurate tape placement. Once the tape is applied, the product is diecut and converted to its final form. Since our client has modified the feeding sections on their diecutting machines to handle this pre-taped product, their production is now highly automated. Production efficiencies have driven costs down.

Helpful Planning Tip

Knock out inks and coatings. As with fugitive and other gluing applications, make sure inks and coatings are knocked out of the area to which Kleenstik tape will be applied. This allows the adhesive to form the best bond possible. If you're unsure of the adhesion quality of your products, let your finisher test a printed sample. Kleenstik tape can be used to seal products such as disc mailers, which require a sturdier closure than remoistenable glue.

＊　　＊　　＊

The Final Word...

Kleenstik can be used to form either a permanent or reusable seal, depending on the nature of the application. It can also be applied to a wide range of surfaces, including plastic, synthetic papers, and glass.

Contributors:

- *Mark Beard, Finishbinders, Inc., Des Moines, Iowa*
  www.finishbinders.com
- *Russ Haines, Rapid Bind, Inc., Portland, Oregon*
  www.rapidbind.com
- *Bob Windler, Diecrafters, Inc., Chicago, Illinois*
  www.diecrafters.com

42 Media/Information Packaging

As information that needs to be packaged changes, so do the packages themselves. When information packaging needs to hold more than just paper, a regular old pocket folder may not do the job. Multi-dimensional information and media packaging can be designed to hold anything from perfect-bound or saddle-stitched books to product samples, VHS and audiocassettes, CDs and DVDs.

What You Will Learn

- Information packaging market opportunities
- Media-package design
- Self-mailers

There are many factors that must be considered when planning a media package. Before a design is finalized, consider the end use of the product, and ask yourself a few questions about it: Will more information be added to it over time? Will it hold only paper, CD-ROM media, or product samples—or a mix of all three?

As digital media products such as CD and DVD continue to augment printed materials as a means of exchanging information, it's important to find efficient, cost-effective ways to distribute them. Whether you need to distribute your discs individually or with complementary products, there are dozens of packaging solutions that will fit your needs.

Media packaging can be designed either for complete assembly by the manufacturer or for assembly by end users. This second option defers assembly costs to

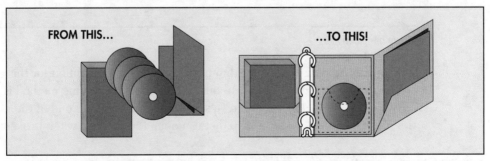

When your customers have several products that need to be consolidated and organized (left), help them create an information packaging design that's both attractive and practical.

the field, while also allowing the products to be shipped flat for an additional cost savings.

The booming software and entertainment industries continually demand innovative packaging that can house both media and literature. Here are a few media packaging design options available:

Single- and double-pocket mailers. Most CD self-mailers involve gluing a pocket into one panel on a two-panel, folded piece. When folded, the facing panel encloses the disc, and the open end is then sealed with a spot of fugitive glue or a wafer seal. If two discs need to be mailed, a second pocket can be formed on the other panel to accommodate it. The second pocket could also hold a booklet or other literature that

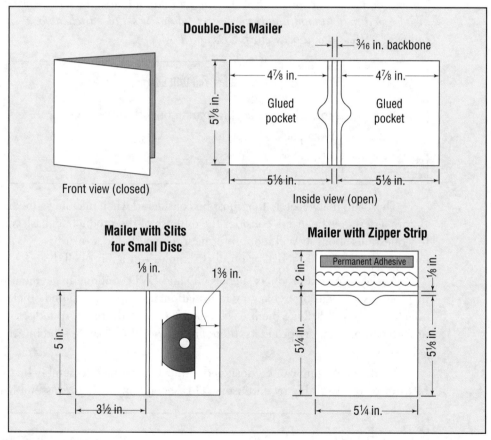

A variety of disc mailers.

will accompany the disc. A diecut thumb notch is a common option for this design, as it can be clumsy to remove discs without it. An alternative sealing method is a zipper strip, which involves gluing or taping a short flap over the open end of the mailer. A series of perforations creates a strip that can open the package when broken.

Miniature-disc mailers. As convenient as CD and DVD discs are, they're still not small enough for some applications. Credit-card-size discs are popular for distributing

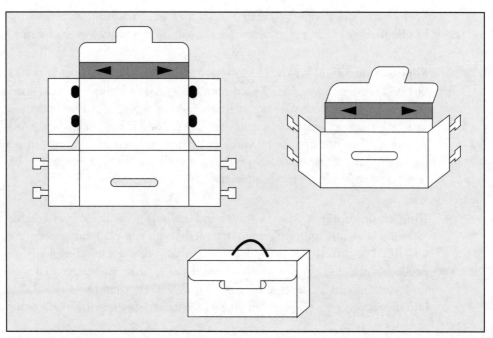

Self-assembled media briefcase.

brief video presentations or as a "virtual" business card. A pair of slits rather than a pocket are used to secure the discs and display them prominently.

Foam or vacuum-formed trays. CD-ROM and DVD-ROM discs require packaging that displays as it protects. In a foam disc package, a bare disc is pressed onto a foam "button" that holds it firmly in place. Vacuum-formed plastic trays can be designed to

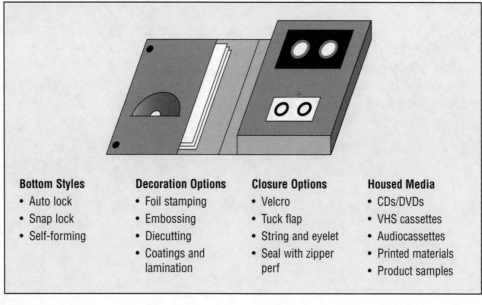

Bottom Styles	Decoration Options	Closure Options	Housed Media
• Auto lock	• Foil stamping	• Velcro	• CDs/DVDs
• Snap lock	• Embossing	• Tuck flap	• VHS cassettes
• Self-forming	• Diecutting	• String and eyelet	• Audiocassettes
	• Coatings and lamination	• Seal with zipper perf	• Printed materials
			• Product samples

Media holder.

hold a bare disc, jewel case, VHS or cassette tape. Foam and vacuum-formed trays can be used as either a standalone package or on the inside cover of a ring binder.

Slipcases and slant cases. Do you have a set of software discs that need organizing or DVD movies that need to be prominently displayed? Slipcases and slant cases can be customized for your specific application. A wide range of turned-edge construction materials (such as laminated paper, vinyl, cloth, and imitation leather) are available. Additional finishing options let you create truly customized slipcase and slant-case packaging. For example, a slipcase that houses a set of DVD movies can be diecut to register to an image on the front of the DVD package itself.

Ring binder options. Many software and business information packaging applications call for a large amount of paper to be housed with complementary software on either CD-ROM or diskette. Ring binders are a great solution and offer plenty of media packaging options. For discs without jewel cases, clear vinyl pages that are punched for insertion onto the rings allow easy storing and viewing. Discs can also be tucked into diecut slits on a polyethylene page or into heat-sealed vinyl pockets formed on the inside cover.

*   *   *

The Final Word...

Learn about media packaging because the market opportunity is large and growing. Good postpress services companies help their customers create customized packaging solutions to fit any budget and manufacturing time constraint.

Contributors:

- *Chris Eckhart, Eckhart & Company, Indianapolis, Indiana*
  www.eckhartandco.com
- *Bob Windler, Diecrafters, Inc., Chicago, Illinois*
  www.diecrafters.com

43 Point-of-Purchase Displays

There are many types of point-of-purchase (POP) applications, ranging from simple wall posters to elaborate retail displays. Complicated projects may be printed on unusual substrates, then coated, diecut, glued, and hung on special support mechanisms. Since there are so many POP end uses, printing and finishing options are plentiful.

What You Will Learn

- Substrates, coatings, and glue
- Specialized equipment
- Fulfillment issues

When considering printing and finishing techniques for a POP project, look no further than its end use. Select paper, ink, coatings, backings, substrates, laminates, and glues for appropriate environmental and usage needs. For example, a POP display destined for a fast-food restaurant may require a laminate rather than a UV coating because it will be exposed to grease and cleaning chemicals. Perhaps another project will be displayed near bright lights and would benefit from a glare-reducing, clear matte coating for enhanced readability. These are just a couple of the options to consider when working with POP displays.

Substrates

Select the right backing for each POP project. For example, a piece that will be vacuum-formed, drilled, diecut, embossed, and glued will require one type of backing, whereas a piece that's intended for hanging, easel display, or mounting to a wire display rack will need another kind of substrate.

Glues

Since POP projects usually require some type of gluing, carefully consider your substrates and their reactions to glue. For example, glass, metal, paper, and plastic require very different adhesives. Also, depending on the equipment used, glue can be applied to either the sheet or the backing, as long as it's the smaller surface of the two.

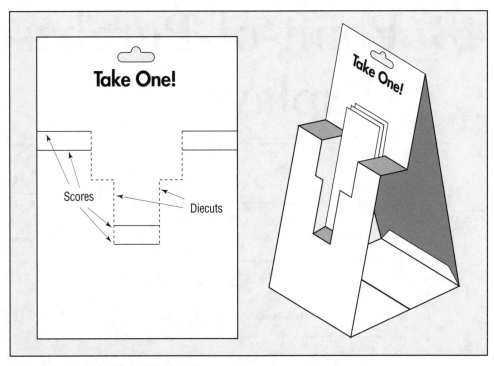

Take-one holder with self-contained easel.

One category of glue bonds the paper to the substrate. Another affixes mounted displays onto walls, display racks, or even windows. Pressure-sensitive tapes, which themselves use a range of adhesives, are another widely used method of attaching components (i.e., pads, coupons, or booklets) to main displays. Some postpress companies have machines that automatically attach the D-tape (double-sided pressure-sensitive tape) to coupon books, instruction sheets, tear-off pads, and wire-bound booklets. These products are then affixed onto the base unit. Double-sided tape is widely used on plastics. Heavier displays may require pad backing (a large pad of the pressure-sensitive adhesive applied to the base surface).

Inks and Coatings

Printers that regularly work with the POP market are well versed as to how inks and coatings interact with glues. For example, heavy top coats, including varnishes and UV coatings, can penetrate the printed stock and may result in the sheet not properly adhering to the base when glue is applied. One way to avoid this undesirable result is to use a heavier stock such as 80-lb. to 100-lb. If notified early enough, clients often will accept an extra charge of 10–15% for paper if the heavier paper stock will ensure success at the finishing stage. Also, your finisher may be able to recommend alternative glues that will perform better.

Proper ink selection is important for good-quality diecut POP projects. Printers familiar with the POP market know that some inks cut cleanly without chipping, while others don't.

Point-of-purchase (POP) displays.

Equipment

Your finishing house's equipment plays a role in successful and cost-efficient POP production. For instance, if a job requires mounting and laminating a lightweight printed sheet onto a rigid backing, such as corrugated, foam-core, or chipboard, look for a POP company that can automatically apply the sheet to decrease production time and costs. While most machines manufactured in the last ten to fifteen years can apply a wide range of paper stocks, many shops still run older equipment that has difficulty handling lightweight or coated two-sides (C2S) paper.

Because diecutting is one of the more essential POP processes, your finisher should have equipment that can cut cleanly through many substrates in a wide range of sizes—from life-size cutouts to board stock "slips" in which samples are displayed.

Fulfillment

Retail POPs often involve substantial fulfillment requirements. Sometimes these projects are manufactured by many different vendors and then shipped elsewhere for fulfillment operations. Many projects involve a large number of pieces such as banners, counter-top displays, toys, "take-one" coupons, and assembly and marketing instructions.

POP displays often are timed with holiday and other event-based promotions. For example, McDonald's often launches campaigns that tie in with an upcoming animated movie release. Franchisees might receive fulfilled packages that include interior hanging cardboard cutouts of the animated characters, cash register displays, outdoor signage, and posters. These diverse elements must be collected, packaged, and distributed by a fixed deadline. Once again, appropriate equipment can help ensure that costs are kept down and jobs get out on time. For instance, there's specialized equipment that can automatically insert posters into tubes, thereby eliminating the need for expensive handwork.

$$* \qquad * \qquad *$$

The Final Word...

While on-time deliveries are important for virtually every graphic arts job, a missed deadline for a POP display can easily mean the loss of sales for the end-user company.

Contributors:

- *Marty Anson, Bindagraphics, Inc., Baltimore, Maryland*
  www.bindagraphics.com
- *Bob Windler, Diecrafters, Inc., Chicago, Illinois*
  www.diecrafters.com

44 Tabbing

Tabs are not as common in the United States as they are in Europe, but there is a noticeable trend toward using them here. These modest, commonplace devices help end-users organize their printed material for ready access.

What You Will Learn

- Standard sizes and coatings
- Tab positioning
- Indexing options

Tabs are often taken for granted. Their simple appearance is deceiving and gives no hint of the planning that goes into their design and production. Tabs and indexes may be small, but they are some of the most enduringly practical ways to make loose-leaf binders, reference books, and directories easy to use.

Diecut tabs are commonly found in three-ring binders and are frequently used in training and seminar manuals. They also appear in mechanically bound cookbooks, directories, instructional texts, and some software manuals. Adhesive-bound books may contain tabs, which are usually folded in on themselves so that the signatures can be trimmed to final size. The end user later unfolds the tabs to extend beyond the face of the book.

Common Sizes

What tab size do you need? Tab indexing can be produced in sizes as small as a notebook or as large as accounting ledgers, although the majority of products fall somewhere in between. Before venturing too far into odd stock sizes, get some advice about product cost. Consider how your products will be bound and whether they require other downstream manufacturing operations, like punching and drilling. Just because your intended size fits one machine doesn't mean it will fit all others.

Although tabs and indexes come in various shapes and sizes, the most common style has rounded corners and extends ½ in. (12.7 mm) beyond the other pages. Other standard sizes include those that extend ¼, ⅜, or ⅝ in. (6.4, 9.5, or 15.9 mm) beyond the page size. The length of a tab (its vertical dimension) is referred to as "the cut" and can range from ½ in. to 10 in. (254 mm).

Planning is necessary to determine the correct tab length for a given project. Look for a tabbing partner that offers templates to make your planning easier, but recognize that discovering the best solution is not that difficult. For example, if there

Common products with tabs.

are ten sections in a 7×9-in. (177.8×228.6-mm) book, you will need ten tabs that can be arranged in one or more separate rows—each called a ***bank.*** To compute the maximum allowable length per tab in a bank, subtract 1 in. (25.4 mm) from 9 in. (for tabs, you must indent ½ in. [12.7 mm] from the top and bottom of the page), then divide the answer by the number of tabs in the bank. Let's say you want only one bank of tabs. In this example, you'd divide 8 in. (the length of the sheet after subtracting 1 in. for the top and bottom indents) by 10 (the number of tabs), resulting in 0.8 in. (the maximum length of each tab).

Conversely, the minimum length is dictated by the amount of copy on the tab. For instance, if each will carry two lines of 10-pt. type, the minimum length per tab is about ½ in. (12.7 mm). Let's say that the tabs in our 7×9-in. (177.8×228.6-mm) book have to be at least 1 in. long (25.4 mm) to carry additional type. You would then need to create two banks of five tabs each, with each tab measuring 1.6 in. (8 in. ÷ 5).

Location

Planning tab positions for loose-leaf projects is easy, but the same task can be challenging in adhesive-bound books because it affects page counts and signature formats. The production process can vary greatly depending upon whether the tabs fall within or between signatures. Again, consult with your bindery in advance when planning the production of a book that contains tabs. With the bindery's help, you can reduce or even eliminate the need for handwork, bring down production costs, and gain a competitive advantage in bidding on a job.

Reinforcement

Particularly recommended for loose-leaf binding applications that will experience heavy usage, binding-edge reinforcement can add years to the lifespan of your materials.

Example of products with step indexing.

Reinforcing substantially increases strength and durability, eliminates the expense and bulk of heavy-weight stock and provides better protection for your indexing investment. The most common type of reinforcement material is Mylar.

Tab reinforcement eliminates dog-earing, protects the printed title, and increases the useful life of your indexes. Colored reinforcement is an inexpensive way to dramatically increase the impact and effectiveness of your presentation. Tab reinforcement material is approximately three millimeters thick in clear (colors are a bit thicker).

More about Mylar

- Mylar is a sturdy transparent or colored polyester film applied to tabs to give them improved strength. It is applied using 330° heat and a pressure process that fuses the film to the sheet. This is an important consideration when selecting ink and paper stock. Non-heat-resistant ink will smear and leave you with unreadable tabs.

- When reinforcing tabs with Mylar, select a porous stock such as uncoated 110-lb. index stock for dependable results. Coated stocks can trap air when the Mylar is applied, creating bubbles that ruin the appearance of the tabs. As with many other finishing and binding processes, it's important to consult with your bindery expert well in advance to avoid production glitches.

- Binding-edge reinforcement is clear in color and approximately 1 mil thick. Although the standard width is $9/16$ in., other widths are available to accommodate a variety of binding methods. Binding-edge reinforcement is not recommended for use with plastic comb binding.

✳   ✳   ✳

The Final Word...

Traditional tabs look great, but they can be overshadowed by step indexing. The advantages of step indexing over tabbing are obvious: less handwork, faster setup, and no protruding elements to be torn or bent. Indexing is a viable and user-friendly solution for printing customers who are turned off by the special considerations associated with the use of tabs in adhesive-bound books.

Contributors:

- *Marty Anson, Bindagraphics, Inc., Baltimore, Maryland*
  www.bindagraphics.com
- *Sue Hein, Rapid Bind, Inc., Portland, Oregon*
  www.rapidbind.com
- *Jim Shear, Seaboard Bindery, Woburn, Massachusetts*
  www.seaboardbindery.com

45 Indexing

Whether your project is a thick directory or an eight-page pamphlet, there is an indexing style that will make it easier to use, easier to recognize, and easier to sell.

What You Will Learn

- Indexing options
- Automated production
- Job planning

Thumb Cut Indexing

This style involves half-moon cuts made into the book. Numbered or lettered tabs of the same size can be applied, or descriptions can be printed directly onto the page. Both single- and double-bank styles are available in sizes from ⅜ in. to ¾ in. Popular uses for thumb cut indexing include bibles, dictionaries, and reference manuals.

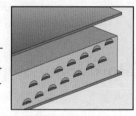
Double-back thumb cutting.

European Thumb Cut Indexing

This is a unique variation on thumb cut indexing. Instead of a thumb-size cut in the book edge, a radius is cut from the cover down to the specific page. The front cover can either be trimmed to expose the cuts, or stay flush with the back cover. European thumb cut indexing is available in widths from 12 mm to 24 mm, or ½ in. to ¹⁵⁄₁₆ in. Tab options are the same as for standard thumb indexing.

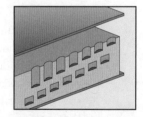
European thumb cut.

Step Indexing

There are several different varieties of step indexing. Steps can be cut with 90°, 110°, double-radius, or straight cutting dies. In addition to single- and double-bank styles, step indexing can be produced with either corner steps or full-cut front edge steps. Step indexing can be used for everything from annual reports to trade directories.

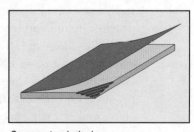
Corner step indexing.

Step-indexed catalog (left) and three-hole-drilled catalog with corner step indexing (right).

All of these indexing options are page-specific. This means indexes are placed at exact pages rather than page intervals. In addition, all indexing is done with trimmed and bound books. You don't have to alter your production workflow to have your projects indexed. If it's a spiral-bound or Wire-O book, it can be indexed as either a book block or a fully finished product.

More about Step Indexing

Historically step indexing was performed manually. The productivity of step indexing improved, however, with the introduction of step indexing machines. Today, a micro-processor-controlled machine is used for electronically supported indexing. With equipment that can be programmed for many separate steps, step indexing is a quick and cost-effective way to divide and organize a book.

There are three main options when it comes to index tab shape. Straight-cut tabs can be cut at either 90° or 110° angles, and a double-radius cut is available for a unique, rounded look. Step indexing can also be performed as a full front-edge cut or as a corner step in either the top or bottom right corners of the book.

All of these step indexing options can be produced on fully or semiautomatic machinery. In the case of a fully automatic production process, bound and trimmed books are fed auto-matically where an infrared photo lens scans each book to ensure 100% accuracy with each cut. It then counts the exact number of pages required for each tab (up to 28 tabs are avail-able), makes a page-specific cut, and applies a tab label to it.

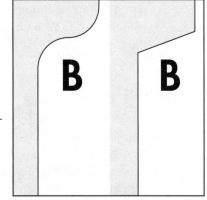

Tab cut styles: double-radius cut (left) and 110° straight cut (right).

Front cover: flush or trimmed? There are two cover options available for step indexed softcover books. The cover can remain flush with the book block to hide the indexing until the book is opened, or it can be trimmed with the first (top) index to display the index descriptions. The choice is yours.

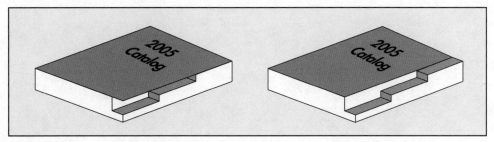

Softcover books can be indexed with the cover flush with the book block (left), or trimmed to reveal the indexing.

Step Indexing Production Tips

Allow for extra margins. To ensure that the step indexing process goes smoothly, allow extra margins from the face trim to the copy or image area. Since step indexing machines can be programmed for cuts of any depth, communicate the details of your project before the project is printed so that proper margins can be determined.

*   *   *

The Final Word...

Don't forget locator marks! Locator marks ensure greater accuracy during the step indexing process. They should be printed on the lefthand page below the tab, where they will be removed during the indexing process. Locator marks are not necessary if you choose to print tab descriptions as part of the text or to use different paper or colors to define each step. If you do opt to print descriptions, be sure to leave extra room between the tabs to be sure everything lines up properly.

Contributor:

- *Tom Ross, Ross Gage, Inc., Indianapolis, Indiana*
  www.rossgage.com

46 Attaching

Inserted products are a great way to make many printed pieces more attractive and functional. However, it can be annoying to open a piece of mail and have an item fall out of it onto the floor or to pry an envelope out of a stitched booklet only to wind up tearing it. Wouldn't it be nice if these items were somehow affixed to the piece, yet easy to remove?

What You Will Learn

- Items that can be attached
- Glues used in attaching
- Manufacturing concerns

Attaching (*a k a* "placement") can be an ideal solution for products that will include inserts. In addition to direct mail applications, attaching can be used to augment point-of-purchase displays, trade show directories, product inserts, information packaging, and more.

Attaching involves affixing an item to a backing substrate—the "carrier"—using either fugitive (removable) or seam (permanent) glue. Fugitive glue allows the items to be removed by the end user without tearing either the attachment or the carrier. Once the item is attached, the carrier is folded. The size of the attachment usually determines which folding style will be used. Typically, projects that include cards and other flat attachments are buckle-folded, while thicker attachments such as product sample packets are usually gatefolded.

Attaching can be performed in-line with many other processes, including folding, perfing, and gluing. It is also easily integrated with subsequent offline production techniques such as saddle stitching, mechanical and perfect binding, diecutting, index tabbing, film laminating, and more.

The versatility of attaching enables it to be performed on a variety of substrates, including

This direct mail piece includes a plastic membership card attached using removable glue. The piece is then folded and sealed with seam glue to make sure the card stays inside the carrier.

text, cover, and card stocks, as well as chipboard and plastic. The chemistry of the adhesive, carrier, and attachment are the only real limitations, so be sure to involve your postpress services provider early in the design process to be sure all materials are properly prepared for attaching.

Applications

The beauty of attaching is that almost anything (within reason) can be affixed to a carrier. Plastic cards, postcards, business reply cards, envelopes, and pharmaceutical inserts are all popular attachments. But some out-of-the-ordinary products such as product sample packets and electronic media make attachments with significant eye appeal.

Direct mail applications are an increasingly popular market for attached products. Many newsletters include attached business reply cards and envelopes for contributions and other correspondence. Objects such as paper or plastic membership cards, rigid or flexible phone cards, business cards, currency, and magnets are also popular attachments on direct mail campaigns as they draw attention to your customer's marketing message and help them build rapport with their customers.

Digital media is becoming more portable and economical to produce. Several Internet service providers attach their installation disks inside magazines, in direct mail pieces, and on in-store displays. Electronic media also can be attached inside a perfect-bound or saddle-stitched instruction book.

Planning Tips

Pay attention to placement tolerances. When designing your carrier, leave a small margin between your copy and the placement target. Although attaching placement is very accurate, it is a high-speed process that involves some variation. Most applications have a placement tolerance of ⅛ in. to ³⁄₁₆ in., so leave at least ³⁄₁₆-in. clearance around your target placement area to be sure adjacent copy isn't obscured.

Know your envelope placement options. For applications that will include attached envelopes, determine how you would like the envelope to be placed. Typically, envelopes are placed address-side up, which allows the recipient to see where their response will be sent. Envelopes also can be attached flap-side up, if you prefer. Regardless of which side you choose to show, keep in mind that the folded edge of the envelope must be placed at the lead edge of the sheet to prevent the piece from catching on folding and other equipment.

Use a carrier of sufficient weight. Attached items can place additional stress on a carrier piece during folding and other operations. That's why it is important that the carrier piece—especially if it is paper—be thick enough to support that stress. Most card- and cover-weight stocks are fine; for stocks thinner than this, we recommend no less than a 50-lb. sheet as a carrier.

Avoid center spreads for stitched products. For saddle-stitching applications such as newsletters and other booklets, an attached envelope or business reply card is preferable to a bind-in because it does not require the end user to tear the items from the stitches. When attaching items to stitched products, avoid placing them at the center spread, where they're likely to catch on the stitching equipment. Even a single sheet between the attachment and the saddle is sufficient to move the piece through the stitching process properly.

*   *   *

The Final Word...

There are many variables that need to be accounted for early in the process of job preplanning. Involve your finisher early to prevent costly—and usually avoidable—problems, especially when unique postpress processes such as attaching are involved.

Contributors:

- *Jim Egan, Rickard Bindery, Chicago, Illinois*
  www.rickardbindery.com
- *Russ Haines, Rapid Bind, Inc., Portland, Oregon*
  www.rapidbind.com
- *Bill Seidl, Seidl's Bindery, Houston, Texas*
  www.seidlsbindery.com

47 Magazine Inserts

Magazine inserts are an effective way to distribute information to a wide array of customers. They can be used to introduce a new product, publicize a special promotion, create awareness about a pertinent issue, or kick off a new advertising campaign. Because magazine insert programs are often scheduled for placement in a variety of publications, the print production process can be complex. A typical production run could be in the millions, with each publication having its own set of production specifications. The following tips are intended to help you plan magazine insert programs and business response vehicles that maximize production efficiency and minimize headaches.

What You Will Learn

- Why inserts?
- Design options
- Placing inserts in multiple publications

Marketers place greater emphasis on the versatility of their programs as they search for and develop vehicles that will give them the most for their marketing dollars. A single marketing vehicle that can be tailored to provide high response rates, customer data, and maximum marketplace awareness will keep costs down without compromising effectiveness. This is where magazine inserts come in.

Why an Insert?

Versatile inserts are suitable for a wide range of uses and marketing messages. Whether you're a small non-profit organization or a major corporation, an insert can help you reach large, targeted segments of the population with an eye-catching vehicle. Inserts attract the attention of readers because a trusted friend delivers them: the publication for which the reader has a particular interest.

Here are some of the benefits:

- ***Pass-along factor.*** A key benefit of magazine inserts is the "pass-along" readership they generate. The lifespan of a magazine is much longer than that of a piece of mail, meaning that several people often will see a single magazine. Although a particular publication may not be of interest to every member of a household or office, the potential for "pass-along" readership is much higher for a magazine insert than for direct mail.

- **Consistency.** For many companies, the highest priority with any outbound marketing message is control over the quality of the finished piece. A standard run-of-book magazine page takes quality control out of your hands and places it in the hands of the publication and the printer. Consistency is especially difficult to achieve if your message will appear in several publications. Inserts, on the other hand, permit control over the exact color, size, and quality of the printed image. The quality of inserts is also consistent, regardless of how many publications they appear in. That's especially important when marketing food or consumer products such as cosmetics or furniture, which rely heavily on an accurate visual representation for their appeal.

- **Differentiation.** One of the main uses for magazine inserts is to differentiate a message from the rest of the pages of the magazine. Inserts are printed on thicker, higher-quality stock than the magazine and are placed between signatures. Magazines naturally "break" to inserts when opened, giving them optimum visibility.

- **Involvement devices.** Do you want readers to remember your message? Inserts that include tabs or tear-outs encourage recipients to interact with the insert, leading to higher retention of and response to the information.

- **Carriers.** Inserts are a great way to introduce readers to new products. Inserts like scented fragrance strips and tipped-on product sample packets create a multi-sensory experience for the reader.

- **Retention.** Retention devices such as removable information cards and coupons allow the reader to save something from the publication for later use. One popular use for a retention device is to provide a link for additional information on a corresponding website.

- **Image.** An insert presents an impressive image that creates a higher perceived value to the reader compared with a standard book page. Diecut pop-ups, fold-outs, and tipped-on product samples build a buzz around information in the insert. As direct marketers know, attracting the attention of readers is one thing, but holding their attention is far more difficult. A detachable information card, coupon, or product sample packet helps boost retention by giving readers something to save for use later.

Design Options

The design of an insert should reflect the intended function of the piece. For example, an insert that will introduce a new product—complete with a tipped-on simulated product sample—will serve a much different purpose than the standard four-page insert that is intended to raise awareness for a charitable cause.

The weight and finish of an insert play an important role in how it is likely to be perceived. Paper stock quality and coating selection should mirror the message of the insert. While an information sheet for a new prescription medicine may be simple, straightforward, and require a low- to mid-range weight and paper quality, the launch of a new automobile model will likely require a heavier, high-gloss, higher-quality paper to draw attention.

An insert that includes a business reply device requires a paper stock that's both attractive and practical. A recipe card may benefit from a thick, glossy stock that resists staining and highlights the vibrant colors of food images. A reply device that asks users to write information on it may require an uncoated stock (for writability) that's at least 7 points thick (for mailability).

Production Tips

Get specifications and production details for each publication before you design and print an insert. An insert that's created for a perfect-bound magazine typically is not compatible with a saddle-stitched publication. An insert that will be placed in multiple publications with different binding types typically will need separate formats for each method.

Although inserts can be produced in a wide range of sizes, they can never exceed the final trim size of the publication itself. When an insert is going to bind into several publications of varying sizes, care must be taken to make sure the insert will fit the specifications of each publication. For example, an insert designed for a publication with a final trim size of 8×10½ in. shouldn't be used for a publication with a 7⅞×10¼-in. trim size. An insert that's too large for a publication will have to be sent to a bindery for trimming by the publisher (at substantial cost) and may be refused altogether.

An insert that's smaller than the full-size page—such as a business reply device— usually will be positioned to the head or foot of the publication. Make sure you know the binding direction of each publication, as this will need to be factored into the insert production process. Some titles have stock weight and finish guidelines designed to match inserts closely with the rest of the magazine. The same insert may need to be run on several different stocks to accommodate the requirements of each publication.

Use a preproduction dummy. It's a good idea to have your printer provide a preproduction dummy to aid in planning before submitting an insert to a publication. A dummy should include all images and text, have all trim and fold locations clearly marked, and be run on the exact stock to be used during production. If images or text cross over a foldout or gutter, be sure everything lines up properly. This is especially true for complex gatefold pieces, which may have copy or a single image crossing over three separate panels. Be sure any diecuts that register to print are aligned properly.

Of critical importance is to verify that business-reply cards and envelopes meet all postal requirements. In addition to maintaining proper size and weight requirements, mail pieces must have the proper barcodes, indicia, and address information. A complete insert production resource can help you design reply devices that conform to all postal regulations.

*   *   *

The Final Word...

Look for an insert production resource that understands your creative intent and can offer suggestions designed to help you reach that goal. A wider range of production options means greater efficiency, as well as time and money savings.

Contributor:

- *Mike Conlon, Meredith Print Advantage, Des Moines, Iowa www.meredithprintadvantage.com*

48 Poly-Bagging

When you land a great print job, whether it is a perfect-bound magazine, saddle-stitched book, or other promotional piece, ask yourself, "How am I going to get this project safely through the mail?" Paper envelopes are expensive, hide the product, and are subject to damage. Synthetic envelopes cost even more. The answer? Poly-bagging.

What You Will Learn

- Design and cost
- Typical applications
- Printed poly

Nothing will get your printed pieces through the mail more safely, attractively, and inexpensively than poly-bagging. You can bundle companion pieces together, big or small, thin or thick, in virtually any order, and maintain the proper mail order sequence. Newspaper inserts with free samples, magazines packaged with accompanying pieces, computer magazines with free software, piggy-backed periodicals, atlases with maps, sewing magazines with patterns, and building plans with architectural drawings: all can, and should, be poly-bagged. Subscription renewal notices, brochures, statements, and invoices are poly-bagged inexpensively every day.

Poly-bagging isn't complicated. The poly-bag is formed over stacked product and heat-sealed on the front, back, and top as it travels down a conveyor belt.

Today's high-speed poly-bagging lines are very versatile. In addition to handling a wide variety of printed material, they can bag products as diverse as sample shampoo packets, small detergent boxes, CDs and other multimedia, pens, magnets, and more.

Poly-bagged products.

Poly-bagging is at the beginning of its U.S. growth curve. In Europe, where magazines have been poly-bagged for years, newspapers also are being poly-bagged because the economics are so attractive. How many products consistently save you money, look better, and run faster than the alternative?

Whereas excessive moisture and jostling wreaks havoc on traditional packaging, poly-bagging protects its contents. The most common poly-bag films are between 1 and 2 mils thick, but up to 4-mil film can be used. One of our clients once enclosed poly bags with sacks of fertilizer. Try that with paper envelopes!

Only for Long Runs?

While many people think of poly-bagging for long runs, it needn't be so. Poly-bagging can also be a low-cost protective solution for shorter runs. Of course, if you spread a makeready over a couple of hundred pieces, poly-bagging will be costly on a per-unit basis. Then again, so is everything else in the graphic arts. Poly-bagging starts to make economic sense at about two thousand pieces. Beyond ten thousand pieces, where mechanically inserting materials into paper envelopes makes little sense, poly-bagging is economically very attractive.

What about when compared to shrink-wrapping? First of all, double-layered shrink-wrapping film is expensive. Moreover, most automatic shrink-wrapping machines have a maximum running speed of just two thousand pieces per hour. Not only is poly-bag film cheaper by comparison, but high-speed poly-bagging machinery runs at speeds up to twenty thousand per hour. Poly-bagging also has a neat, clean look and will never "scrunch" thin sheets.

More Features and Benefits

Poly-bagging has a lot going for it, including:

- *Clear packaging.* Let the beauty of your printed work show through your packaging. Paper envelopes cost more and hide the package's contents. Sometimes this is good, but often it isn't.

- *Eye appeal.* A lot of direct mail gets poly-bagged. So do annual reports, coffee table-quality perfect-bound books, mechanically bound products, ledgers, diaries, manuals, loose-leaf packages, single sheets (don't try shrink-wrapping these), and loose-leaf binders.

- *Poly printing.* Printing on poly-bag film looks great. You've undoubtedly received magazines and other materials wrapped in great-looking printed poly film. But is it practical? In a word: Yes. The economics of printing on polyurethane are similar to those of printing on paper. Likewise, short-run, four-color poly-printing jobs are also expensive, but per-unit printing costs also decrease as run lengths increase. Halftones, PMS colors, metallic inks, you name it—it all looks great on polyurethane. If security is an issue, opaque inks with knocked-out mailing areas ensure that poly-bagging is as safe as paper envelopes. Proxy statements, financial information, and other projects that require security are well served by poly-bagging technology. Today's ink registration is terrific. The use of register-marking systems, machine clutches, and servomotors guarantee that your message will appear at the same place on each bag.

- **Automation compatibility.** Some poly film is approved by the U.S. Postal Service to receive full postal discounts. No longer do you need to sacrifice postal savings to reap the many benefits of poly-bagging.

- **Downstream automation.** At the end of the poly-bagging line, automatic sorting, stacking, and strapping makes for easy entry into the mail stream.

- **User-friendliness.** Easy-to-open perforated seams make it easy for end users to open the bags.

- **Technology.** Spot glue that keeps pieces in place, blow-ins, selective pockets, and inkjet imaging are all widely available.

- **Thick bundles.** Your total poly-bag thickness can be well over 2 in.

- **100% recyclable poly is good for the environment.**

Production Issues

Since a poly bag is built over stacked product, you have much more flexibility when midstream job changes occur. For example, if your project requires the addition of a thick "onsert," or if a project's "footprint" changes, you or your client may be stuck with the cost of prepurchased envelopes. However, if you've chosen poly-bagging, a minor setup tweak of a machine may be all that is needed. Also, since shuttle feeders and loading pockets accommodate a wide variety of object shapes and sizes, many

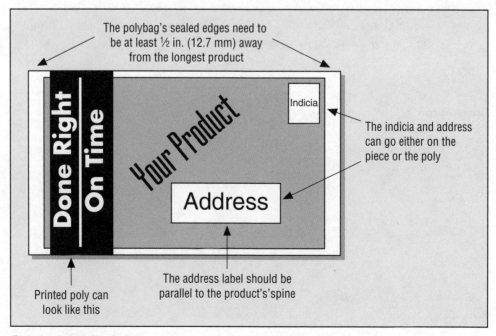

Typical poly-bagging design.

consumer products can be fed automatically. Unlike some inserters, your spine or folding edge no longer needs to run parallel with the poly-bag seam.

Here are some other factors to keep in mind:

- Before printing the address panel, remember that indicia and address label positioning usually are parallel to the spine edge of normal-sized mailings, not perpendicular to them.

- While this is not mandatory, try to have your carrier (bottom) piece be the largest and sturdiest of the package.

- The poly-bag seam is usually between 1 in. and 2 in. wide. For aesthetic purposes, it can be positioned to suit your needs, but there are limitations, especially when printed polyurethane is involved. Design your piece appropriately.

- Insist that your poly-bagging services company test adhesive strength before applying paper labels directly to the poly bag. Poly film is a petroleum-based product that often has complicated glue-adhesion properties.

- Keep metallic inks away from sealed edges on printed poly.

- If your mailing project is unusual or atypical in any way, exercise caution. Get a preproduction sample approved by your local postmaster.

*　　*　　*

The Final Word...

Take advantage of the opportunity to educate your print-buying customers about this great product. If you're still skeptical about poly-bagging, you can verify its power for yourself. Go to your local post office and watch people interact with their mail. Notice a lot of unopened envelopes getting tossed? Sure. But poly-bagged products? They get opened—almost every time.

Contributor:

- *Mark Beard, Finishbinders, Inc., Des Moines, Iowa*
  www.finishbinders.com

49 Handwork and Assembly

We live in a technologically advanced age. Machines help us do a multitude of ordinary tasks automatically: withdraw money from the bank, pay tolls on the highway, and even start your car while you're still inside the house. With so many high-tech options at our disposal, it is easy to discount the virtues of doing things by hand. This is particularly true of the graphic arts. Although almost any project from prepress separations to bookbinding can be designed for automated production, automation simply isn't feasible from a cost or scheduling standpoint for every application. Many operations are still best performed by hand.

What You Will Learn

- When to specify handwork
- Handwork presents job-winning opportunity
- Analyze scheduling impact prior to production

When Is Handwork Needed?

Occasionally, in-line production is not the best solution, even for processes that are normally automated. In addition, there are a number of production functions that are best performed—or that can only be performed—by hand. A lengthy makeready also may offset the cost and scheduling advantages of automation, especially for shorter-run projects.

A project that involves several complex operations may take more time to set up on a machine than to do the actual job by hand. Ultimately, the design of a piece determines whether fully automated production is feasible or desirable. This is where a quality finisher can be a real asset. Since so many handwork projects are actually "hybrid" pieces that involve both automated and manual production, a knowledgeable finisher can help you determine if handwork is a viable alternative to automation.

Prime candidates for handwork include projects that require extensive kitting; insertion of multiple product samples into a portfolio; placement of a CD and instruction book inside a binder; and tucking a pamphlet into a diecut slit inside a book cover. Projects that incorporate mixed media are becoming more popular. Being able to offer a "tour" via CD-ROM, for example, impresses customers and wins their loyalty. Another advantage of handwork is that it permits greater design flexibility, including use of materials. A folder can be "stuffed" with a shampoo sample, diecut picture—almost anything you can think of.

Handwork represents an opportunity to offer yours customer time-saving assistance. This not only makes your clients' lives easier; it also brings in additional revenue. Does a project require extensive kitting? Ask the customer how it plans to accomplish this step. Companies that design a project often count on doing the necessary handwork in-house, straining their internal resources. They may need to be reminded that a handwork production facility also can handle assembly services efficiently. In this way, not only can designers create products that stand apart from the competition, but also a trusted finisher still can produce such hybrid products.

Analyze, Prioritize

There are many factors that enter into a determination of whether certain functions should be performed automatically or by hand. Keep these considerations in mind when planning your next project:

Impossible to automate. A bindery recently completed a three-panel pocket folder project that included a tuck-in cover with a pamphlet and business card placed inside. Although automatic folding was requested, the cover tuck, pamphlet insertion, and business card insertion already were to be performed manually, so the addition of hand folding had little impact in terms of production speed, given that all three manual operations could be performed at once. As a result, the piece was completed in nearly the same time as that required for machine folding. Most important, however, the finished quality of the piece was higher because of the softer hand fold.

Cost and scheduling. Before you determine that automation is your preferred methodology, look at the total production time needed. A folding and gluing project may take three hours to complete automatically and six hours to assemble by hand. However some complex projects involve a makeready longer than the production run itself. If the makeready on this project is double its production time, handwork may be a less expensive and faster choice.

Spoilage. Many low-quantity projects are quoted with few "overs." However, a complex project that involves several finishing processes likely will produce considerable spoilage, compared with the total production. That's because lengthy makereadies— which can be the cause of scheduling difficulties—use up a good deal of product. To calculate the number of "overs" required for a given project, your finisher must calculate the spoilage produced during makeready and production for each. A project that will be folded, trimmed, glued, diecut, and Wire-O-bound, for example, is likely to require a significant number of "overs" to compensate for the spoilage incurred during each process. That, in turn, will have an impact on your cost, because you must ensure that the print run is sufficient to cover both spoilage and production.

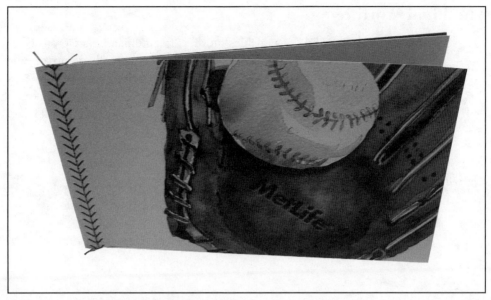

A side-sewn oblong booklet, an example of a project requiring handwork.

A quality finisher with a staff experienced in handwork can minimize spoilage on some of those processes while still offering competitive turnaround times. The exact savings in spoilage (and time) will vary by project, however, so consult with your finisher to see if manual production makes sense for your application.

Full-Service Advantages

Just as all finishing facilities are not the same, handwork facilities have varying levels of expertise. By selecting a company that is unfamiliar with the graphic arts industry, you sacrifice that expertise. Handwork typically is performed in conjunction with several other postpress processes. A provider that can perform all of them under one roof offers clear cost and turnaround advantages.

For example, if a saddle-stitched booklet and shrink-wrapped software set will be inserted into the capacity pocket of a portfolio, look for a postpress services provider that can perform both the handwork and the automated functions—saddle stitching, folding, gluing, trimming, diecutting and more—under one roof. By choosing a facility that can process both the finishing details of a project as well as the handwork, you not only will achieve greater peace of mind, but the finisher will know more about the project and more likely be able to help you if complications arise. If, to cite another example, the project is a folder that will be stuffed with shrink-wrapped CDs and a brochure, you can have the finisher score the project and fold it in-line, then stuff the CDs and brochures by hand. This combination of automated and manual processes would provide the fastest turnaround while holding down costs.

✳   ✳   ✳

The Final Word...

Although today's technology enables finishers to automate many projects, handwork may sometimes be the best option, due to run size, materials, setup, or other specifications that vary from project to project. Combining other finishing services with handwork saves time and eliminates extra steps. Planning ahead is important. If you think your project may require handwork, get all the specifics and ask your finisher.

Contributors:

- *Sue Hein, Rapid Bind, Inc., Portland, Oregon*
  www.rapidbind.com
- *Kevin Rickard, Rickard Bindery, Chicago, Illinois*
  www.rickardbindery.com

50 Prevent Transit Marking

Have you ever had customers complain about receiving jobs with stray marks such as small white splotches where ink was rubbed away? Or extraneous marks where ink shouldn't be? Or scratching? If you've experienced any of these problems, then you know that "transit marking" can be a nightmare.

What You Will Learn

- Predictive indicators
- Testing
- Prevention

The most discouraging thing about transit marking is that it happens after jobs have been beautifully produced. Transit marking is just as its name implies: unwanted marking that occurs during shipping. Unless preventive measures are undertaken, abrasive paper surfaces may rub against each other while being jostled around in trucks, causing stray marks. The presence of microscopic grit, such as press powder or carton debris, may cause unattractive scratches in a paper's surface.

Transit marking happens on many types of printed products, but it is especially prevalent in books. Although there is no way to know for certain which jobs will experience transit marking, preventive steps can and should be undertaken to minimize the likelihood of problems.

Predictive Indicators

First, determine if your book job is a candidate for transit marking. If the book's cover has moderate or heavy ink coverage and lacks any coatings such as varnish, aqueous, UV, or laminate, then it should be considered "likely" to mark. Before bindery operations begin for jobs in this category, check for wet ink by running your hand across sheets, searching for tackiness. Unfortunately, even if your ink is dry and the job has been flood-varnished, there is still no guarantee that transit marking won't happen—especially if dull varnish has been used. Generally speaking, you're less likely to have marking problems if varnish is applied "dry trap" (during a separate pressrun) instead of "wet trap" (during the same pressrun as the ink).

For book products, consider the physical characteristics of the book itself. High-gloss enamel stock reduces ink penetration and causes ink to rest high on the paper's surface where it easily can be scratched or chipped off. Heavy books with unvarnished enamel covers are highly susceptible to transit marking. If the book has areas diecut out of the cover or has any other uneven surface levels (i.e., pockets on the inside cover), marking may form along the raised edges due to uneven friction—much like a brass rubbing. Also, colored paper, especially gray stock, is likely to mark.

Be careful of books with heavy ink coverage on the outside front cover and light coverage on the back. Any time heavy ink rests against light ink after packing, the chances of marking increase. If reflex blue ink is present, then the problem is worse because it dries so slowly. Other inks to be careful of include red, purple, and metallics. If your job is wire-bound, beware of using uncoated tin wire because it marks very easily.

General weather conditions are also significant factors. High humidity is dangerous because it can hinder the drying process of both ink and varnish. Also, high heat can cause problems because it may moisten ink, making it more prone to scratching. Even if weather conditions are good in your area, consider where the job is to be shipped. If you're located in the north, expect marking problems for work being shipped to the south during the summer. As the distance of the final destination increases, so does the likelihood of transit marking.

Unfortunately, books that have shipped flawlessly in previous runs still need to be carefully monitored. Even though success may have been achieved before, every repeat job is different and could go wrong.

Testing

There is no foolproof way to guarantee the prevention of transit marking. A simple first testing step is to rub covers together with moderate pressure and look for ink either flaking off or transferring to the opposing sheet. If this happens, the odds are high that you'll experience shipping problems, unless counteracted in advance.

For a better test, bind and pack enough books to completely fill a box and place it in a jogger for a while. Afterwards, if there isn't any sign of transit marking, your job will probably be OK. For those truly faint of heart, with the luxury of time, place a couple of properly packed boxes in your car trunk, drive around normally for a few days, and then examine the contents to see if marking has occurred.

Prevention

The first step in avoiding transit marking is to choose the proper carton size. Printed products should fit snugly without corners being damaged and filled to the top of the box. Loosely packed books slide around in cartons and mark easily. If gaps within boxes are unavoidable, your bindery should add packing or filler materials to remove the voids. Fortunately, there are a lot of ways to protect your products from transit marking, including:

- ***Dry trap varnish.*** Protecting your covers with varnish is an inexpensive way of reducing the chances of unwanted marking. As long as varnish is applied dry-trap, it's usually quite effective.

- ***Aqueous, UV coating, and laminating.*** The general rule of thumb is that aqueous offers more protection than varnish, UV more than aqueous, and laminating most of all. If your covers have already been cut to size and no longer have a gripper, then UV coating will be your best coating option.

- ***Slip-sheeting books.*** Slip-sheets absorb excess friction and significantly help prevent marking. Unfortunately, slip-sheeting is expensive because additional packers are needed at the end of binding lines. If slip-sheets are used, make sure that they are exactly the same size as the finished product.

- ***Packing perfect-bound books spine-to-spine.*** Packing books spine-to-spine and separating lifts with nonabrasive foam prevents transit marking better than slip-sheeting but is more expensive.

- ***Stagger-stacking books.*** Stagger-stacking (alternating each book) Wire-O, plastic spiral, GBC, and spiral-wire-bound books prevents binding elements from coming in contact with each other. Stagger-stacking perfect-bound books makes sense if the glue has caused a "nail-head" spine thicker than the face. Nail-head spines are common in notch perfect-bound books.

- ***Shrink-wrapping.*** Shrink-wrapping is the best way to prevent books from marking, but it is quite costly. Individual shrink-wrapped products almost never mark, unless the ink on the cover is grossly wet. Group shrink-wrapping also offers excellent protection because contents within properly shrink-wrapped bundles don't shift.

- ***Skid wrapping.*** It is important to keep cartons secure on skids during shipment. If products can be banded tightly enough so that nothing moves as trucks start and stop and make sharp turns, transit marking shouldn't occur.

*   *   *

The Final Word...

The best way to prevent transit marking is to take the time to predict which jobs are the most likely to mark and then develop a plan to combat the problem once identified. Choose a binding partner knowledgeable about transit marking problems, and work together to adopt preventive measures on a job-to-job basis. With a good game plan, your customers won't be rubbed the wrong way.

Contributors:

- *Kevin Rickard, Rickard Bindery, Chicago, Illinois www.rickardbindery.com*
- *Frank Shear, Seaboard Bindery, Woburn, Massachusetts www.seaboardbindery.com*

Section IV
Mailing

51 Mailing: A Historical Overview

In the search for better and faster ways of conducting business, new technologies have reached every corner of our industry, including the realm of print production. Today, a print project can be handled entirely in the digital realm, and your extensive customer data can be used to create truly personalized marketing communications. Yet, top-quality prepress, printing, binding, and finishing services don't make a bit of difference unless the final printed product gets into the hands of the appropriate target audience. For this reason, mailing is a natural extension of the graphic arts industry. Because print now must compete with the Internet and electronic media for its share of audience dollars, the direct mail stakes are higher than ever.

What You Will Learn

- Direct mail processing
- Mail preparation
- Back-end postal discounting

To better manage the direct mail process, it's useful to understand how this seemingly complicated mailing environment runs.

Direct Mail Processing

In the late 1960s the computer found its way into list maintenance. At this point, the direct mail industry rapidly changed from metal plate addressing to data card addressing to computerized label generation. With computers, maintaining mailing files became significantly easier and making record "selection" (targeted mailings) became feasible. Although most databases were developed and maintained by individual companies, the end product was generally four-up Cheshire labels printed in ZIP code order.

The United States Postal Service (USPS) attempted postal cost reduction by encouraging large-volume mailers to prepare their mailings in a fashion that would minimize postal handling. In 1977, the USPS offered a discount for Carrier Route Presort, which reduced postage costs for mail prepared by individual carrier route. By giving mail bundles directly to mail carriers, the USPS eliminated a number of sorting steps and costs went down. Appending carrier route information to data files

Direct mail samples.

while simultaneously pursuing the postal discount qualification process caused many mailers to abandon homegrown software in favor of standard presort programs.

Throughout much of the 1980s, mail presorting was primarily done on mainframe computers with expensive software. In the 1990s and the 2000s, this software became widely available on PCs, offering a large number of individual users the capability of preparing their own mailing files. The output of these presorting programs slowly changed from Cheshire labels to an electronic medium capable of driving high-speed inkjet and laser printers. Today, presorted files frequently have to factor in drop-shipment consolidation (the consolidation of several companies' drop-shipped mail) and commingling (the pooling of several companies' mail together) of mail to achieve the maximum postal discounts. To give you an idea of how quickly the direct mail industry has changed, the USPS has made more changes in its last ten years than in its first two hundred years.

Mail Preparation

Mail-preparation equipment has evolved from slow, simple machines requiring a lot of workers to fast, automated, one-operator units. Today, high-speed imaging devices have largely replaced Cheshire labels. While there are many imaging techniques available, the direct mail industry is dominated by laser and inkjet printing. Customers seeking high quality and large image areas generally prefer laser printing. If personalization is required on only a small portion of the printed product (e.g., name and address), inkjet printing is more attractive.

Recently, great strides have been made toward bridging the quality gap between inkjet and laser printing. Today, there are inkjet units that not only produce images as large as laser printer output (with the same font selection), but they also do so faster and cheaper. The resolution standard for inkjet printing is now 240×240 dpi while laser printing is 300×300 dpi. After imaging, more online or offline postpress processes can be done, or the job can directly enter the mail stream. Generally, laser-printed forms

Example of products that have been laser imaged or inkjet printed.

are personalized box to box or roll to roll, then converted, folded, and glue-sealed, tab-sealed, or inserted into an envelope. A lot of time and money can be saved when inkjet printing is done in-line with other paper conversion processes.

The final step is to correctly package the mail to maximize postal discounts. Mailbags, like Cheshire labels, are all but dead. Non-letter mail palletization qualification has been reduced to a 250-lb. (114-kg) minimum, enabling mail bundling by proper qualification level. Mail bundles are placed on pallets with destination placards affixed to each pallet. Postal trays, which protect and maintain proper mail orientation, can be used for both first class and bulk letter mail.

Back-End Postal Discounting

Until 1993, a mailing job ended after USPS verification. Now, the USPS encourages more cost-saving steps including commingling of mail and drop shipments. Commingling reduces postage expense by creating larger ZIP strings. It also means that a lot of mail that previously would have traveled at basic rates is lowered to three-digit rates, while much of the three-digit mail is now charged at five-digit mail rates. Based on 2002 postal rates, these changes result in postage reductions of $21–29 per thousand pieces of standard mail.

The USPS rate structure is based on how finely mail is presorted when it is deposited into the mail stream. When all mail is sorted to a five-digit level (first five digits in a ZIP code), USPS can eliminate two sorts, saving USPS time and money—hence the discount. When mail is sorted to a three-digit rate (first three digits in a ZIP code), only one sort is eliminated—hence the discount over the basic rate, but not as good as the five-digit rate.

Since presort machines commingle jobs at thirty thousand to forty thousand pieces per hour, large mailing companies can offer postage savings far in excess of additional processing costs. Needless to say, this is a classic win-win-win situation because customers incur less postage costs, mailers make more money, and the USPS reduces processing time. Unfortunately, presort machines are very expensive and generally only found at the largest high-volume mailers.

The USPS allows drop-shipment discounts for mail delivered directly to bulk mail centers (BMCs) and an even larger discount for mail transported directly to destination section center facilities (SCFs). Large-volume mailers are often able to consolidate several customers on one truck and return more than 50% of the increased postal discount to their clients. Smaller mailers that don't have the consistent high volume that is necessary to support an in-house consolidation program can use consolidators (a company that pools the mail to ship it all together for a discount) for this purpose. With a consolidator, small-volume mailers may still be able to return as much as 25% of the gross savings to the client.

*   *   *

The Final Word...

Direct mail has changed immensely. Over the years the emphasis has shifted from mechanical efficiency to electronic wizardry. In addition, keeping abreast of the changing postal climate is more important now than ever. Investing the time to find the right mailing partner will save you a lot of money.

Contributors:

- *Ken Boone, Boone Consulting, Baltimore, Maryland*
- *Art Simpson, EU Services, Rockville, Maryland*
  www.euservices.com

52 Direct Mail Planning

The careful integration of information and design is the key to a winning direct mail campaign. It all starts with a comprehensive database that includes information about the intended recipients, from updated addresses to specific personalized data—or does it? The fact is, you'll be unable to utilize the full potential of that data and ensure sky-high response rates unless you also have an attractive and functional design for each piece of your mail package.

What You Will Learn

- Direct mail design
- USPS automation compliance
- Self-mailers and envelopes

The design of a direct mail program needs to accomplish two important objectives: get to the recipient at the least possible cost, and attract the recipient's attention once it gets there. Creating mail pieces that do both requires careful planning and—unless you want your customer to spend a mint on postage—adherence to strict USPS automation regulations.

First Things First

Before ink is laid to paper, the production priorities of the mail campaign should be clarified. A full-service mail services provider can help customers identify their options and plan a mail program that meets their needs. Among the most important considerations are:

- ***Budget.*** Customers working under a tight budget may look for the most efficient production and distribution plan possible. Clients looking for the highest "mailbox appeal" may want a design that attracts attention, regardless of cost.

- ***Scheduling.*** Does the piece need to be printed yesterday, or is it a showpiece that will be in the works for a while? The answer will affect the many ensuing production choices.

- **Aesthetic objectives.** What mood are you trying to set with the printed piece? Consider whether the tone will be corporate, "fun," or something in between. What message is the piece designed to deliver?

- **Functional objectives.** How long is the piece expected to last? Will it be read and discarded or kept for reference?

- **Automation compatibility.** If reducing postage costs is a top priority (and it almost always is!), mail-piece design should qualify for automation-compatibility discounts.

Unfortunately, it's relatively common for expectations to exceed results. Developing direct mail programs that qualify for the maximum levels of postal discounts can be more complex than most people realize. There are many guidelines that need to be followed, and they cover everything from the dimensions of the mail piece to the placement of barcodes.

Major direct mail campaigns are complex. Successful campaigns unite content, design, and database into a seamless whole, whose foundation has been laid, brick by carefully selected brick, well ahead of time. A typical characteristic of budget busters is that you don't realize their cost until the project is already produced. This is especially true in the case of mail pieces that fail to qualify for lower, automation-compatible postage rates. Nothing will cause your costs—and your blood pressure—to rise faster than finding out after a mailing is sent that it was hit with a surcharge because something wasn't in accordance with compatibility guidelines.

Automation compatibility is an essential brick in the well-designed campaign, as well as the reason a mail piece should qualify for every applicable postal discount. The latest postal rate increases include hefty non-machinable surcharges for disqualified pieces. The non-machinable surcharge, which replaces the previous nonstandard surcharge, has a much broader application than the nonstandard surcharge it replaces, affecting a larger percentage of direct mail projects.

Knowing U.S. Postal Service requirements can cut postage costs by many thousands of dollars. Start by:

- **Reviewing the latest USPS rates and regulations.** Postal rates and regulations change constantly. Familiarize yourself with the key rate changes that recently went into effect, and take note of the ones that apply to the types of mailings you typically send.

- **Cleaning databases.** How "clean" is your client's data? Their databases probably aren't as mailable as they think. A "dirty" database is one of the biggest budget busters around. Every undeliverable piece wastes both postage and production costs, but the real cost of a dirty database is even higher. For example, a misspelled name is a sure way to get your piece thrown in the trash.

- **Choosing the right mailing endorsements.** Endorsements are instructions printed directly on the address side of your mail piece that tell the Postal Service how to handle undeliverable mail and how to notify you of the results. Endorsements can be a great tool. The response you receive can help you maintain an accurate database.

Automation Rate Compliance

It's definitely worth your while to have your mail processor verify the technical details prior to production. Endear your customers to you by helping them avoid typical production and design errors that lead to automation rate disqualification.

Improper printing and placement of barcodes and FIMs (facing identification marks) are two of the most common direct mail mistakes. Barcodes need to adhere to strict postal guidelines. Designers will occasionally create barcodes with regular graphic design programs. While it is possible to create a useable barcode this way, it's much easier—and more accurate—to use one of several available programs that automatically create barcodes with the proper thickness, height, and spacing required by the USPS.

Barcodes also must be placed in one of four locations: below the city, state, and ZIP line; above the address line containing the recipient's name; above or below the keyline information; or above or below the optional endorsement line. Regulations also require at least $\frac{1}{25}$ in. of clearance between the barcode and any information line above or below it, as well as $\frac{1}{8}$ in. of space between the left and right edges and any adjacent printing. Placement of the barcode in any other location could negate the use of automated handling, causing postage costs to skyrocket.

Similarly, get your indicia right. Indicia are the printed postage markings used in lieu of an actual postage stamp. First class, presorted, standard, and nonprofit mail all require different indicia. Be sure the indicia on your mailing matches the appropriate postal class. Incorrect indicia can cause your mailing to be charged significantly more than the actual rate for which it should have qualified.

Reflectance

In order for a barcode or FIM to be read, it must contrast with the background of the envelope or mailer. The level of contrast the background provides is called *reflectance.* Reflectance caused from ink contrasting with paper color can render the postal service's equipment unable to read the barcodes.

Many designs or printed graphics offer too much reflectance, which will cause your piece to lose automation discounts. For the most part, common sense will do when determining proper paper colors. Dark colors, of course, are out. Though screens and pastel colors of less than 5% usually provide satisfactory reflectance, a pure white background is the safest bet since reflectance cannot be accurately measured until the piece is printed.

It's important to note the difference between reflectance and barcode clear zones. While reflectance standards are stringent, clear zones are much less so. The area extending $\frac{1}{16}$ in. from the top and bottom and $\frac{1}{8}$ in. from the left and right of the barcode must be free of any printing. That's a very small quantity and leaves plenty of room for teaser copy and high-quality graphics.

More Regulations

Here are some other postal regulations to keep in mind:

Improper aspect ratio. Are you looking to generate more visibility for your mail piece by using either a square or a long and thin format? If so, there's a good chance it doesn't conform to USPS limits on aspect ratio, which is defined as the length of the envelope divided by height. To qualify for automation rates, the aspect ratio of a piece must be between 1.3 and 2.5. That still leaves plenty of room for creative design.

Exceeding the thickness range. To qualify for automation discounts, mailings must fit within minimum and maximum thickness guidelines. For postcards, select a stock that's at least 0.007 in. thick. Letter-size pieces, including single-sheet self-mailers, must be at least 0.009 in. thick.

Overweight. Even if you've done it five times since last week, weigh your mail piece again just before production begins. If possible, use a digital scale. Check the placement of tabs and wafer seals.

Do the "tap test." All components in a mailing need to fit together properly to qualify for automated rates. The tap test is a quick way to ensure that any information that is read through a window in the envelope actually shows through that window, no matter where in the envelope it settles. There should be at least ⅛ in. of clear space around all sides of the printed address. When the envelope is stuffed, tap it on all four sides to check the movement of the text within the window. If part of it disappears at any angle, it may not make its way through the postal system.

Ask about further discounts. Postal discounts are not limited to size and weight requirements. Your database can be conditioned to qualify your mailing for further discounts. Planet codes, carrier route codes, NCOA processing, and ZIP+4 assigning all can be used to condition your list and qualify your project for additional discounts.

Have a response management plan in place. Once the mail campaign has dropped, your client needs to have a plan in place to handle all responses. Response management varies by project but can include fielding inquiries by telephone, mail, and email; processing order requests; and handling list maintenance.

Choose the Right Paper

One of the most confusing aspects of any print program can be selecting the proper paper stock. Basis weight, type of coating, quality grade, and brightness are just a few of the details you need to consider. Never mind that there are many paper varieties to choose from; just knowing what to ask for can be confusing enough! Here are a few tips to keep in mind when selecting paper for your next project:

Paper thickness. Pay attention to thickness if the piece will be mailed. Paper thickness can play a role in both the production and mailing costs for direct mail pieces. For example, depending on the size of a reply card, the paper stock must be either 0.007 in. or 0.009 in. thick to be accepted by the United States Postal Service. In addition, mail pieces that weigh more than 3.3 ounces are charged increased postage. Selecting the proper paper for your mail pieces will eliminate the chance of incurring a postage penalty.

Coated or uncoated? The decision to use a coated or uncoated sheet should be based on the end use of your project. A coated sheet will offer improved clarity over an uncoated sheet, making it appropriate for applications that demand high quality. The increased dot gain of uncoated sheets makes them less suitable for applications with a lot of sharp graphics. This makes uncoated sheets preferable for applications where quantity is more important than quality.

Look beyond the numbers. Paper selection entails much more than just coatings and basis weights. There are typically several paper options within any given paper grade and/or weight, which means not all "60-lb. coated" sheets are the same. The papers may vary by opacity, gloss, and/or brightness. To be sure you select the right paper for your project, look for a printing resource that can provide several options and offer plenty of information about each one.

Self-Mailers

Self-mailing pieces are a creative alternative to standard inserted mailing packages. Since they consist of just one printed piece, production is reduced from printing multiple mailing components to printing just one. Self-mailers can be designed as single-sheet cards (like oversized postcards) or with multiple folds and panels. In this way, a compelling message can be revealed piece by piece, in the context of substantial design creativity. Each panel can include full-color printing, and there will be plenty of space available for inkjet personalization. Each of these designs also can be processed for USPS automation discounts.

The self-mailers described in the following paragraphs put a premium on attractiveness and functionality without a premium production cost. These designs are highly customizable, enabling you to mix-and-match variable data segments to create personalized messages.

Cross-folded self-mailer. This design involves four panels that fold in sequence over a center panel. Each panel builds intrigue as the message of the piece is revealed little by little. The creative possibilities are nearly limitless with this design. Panels can be diecut to give the piece a unique look or perfed to include a detachable reply card.

Six-panel gatefold. Six printed panels provide plenty of space for a detailed message. Two of the panels contain areas for inkjet personalization, which can be done in a single

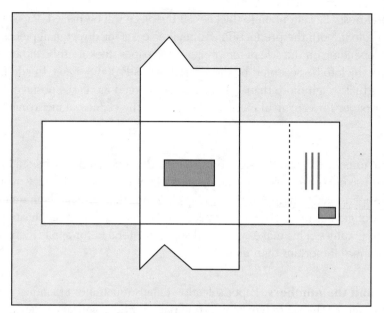

This cross-folded self-mailer includes diecut panels, a perfed reply card, and an attached membership card.

pass when the printing on the panels is oriented correctly. The "end" panel can be perfed for easy detachment as a reply card, and one side of it can even be designed to contain a personalized message or exclusive offer.

Eight-panel roll fold. Do you want the look of a diecut address window, without the additional cost? This eight-panel design features a colored front panel with an address area knocked out to white, creating the look of a diecut window. This piece also can be designed to accommodate single-pass inkjet personalization on two panels. The short fold on a piece like this can act as a flap to close the mail piece with the use of wafer seals or tabs. Creative uses for the flap and underlying area include conveying a two-part message that's gradually revealed as the piece is opened. The other end of the sheet can be perfed to create a business reply card.

Eight-panel roll fold with straight-cut flap. This unique design is similar to an eight-panel roll fold but features a trimmed end panel that simulates the look of a diecut piece, even though it's easily created with a diagonal straight cut. When sealed, the fold-over gives the piece the look of an envelope. There's still plenty of space for inkjet personalization, as well as placement options for a reply card.

Insert Packages

Insert packages offer a lot of flexibility and creativity. Inserts can range from a simple, single sheet to a variety of items that are personalized for specific segments of a given database. The following insert package options ensure that your next mail campaign will take full advantage of personalized data. You'll reap increased response rates, but you won't break your budget to get them.

Lift-up envelopes. Surprise recipients with a small, tipped-on sheet that pops up as soon as the envelope flap is lifted. Lift-up sheets can be printed in a variety of colors and sizes for maximum impact and can be inserted automatically to keep costs down.

Large envelopes. Consider larger envelopes and inserts. For example, a No. 14 envelope (5×11½ in.) is a larger-than-standard business envelope that qualifies for letter-rate postage, meaning that the added impact won't add postage costs. In addition, larger inserts leave more room for you to be creative with your message by adding graphics, a reply card, and more.

The more inserts, the better. Make customers feel as if you have tailored their mail piece just for them. Employ a variety of insert styles to create dozens of different packages tailored to specific recipient segments. Tipped-on notes, for example, are a great way to draw attention to an insert sheet. If your company has been in the news lately, a reprint of the corresponding article will generate increased interest in your message. Your inserts don't even have to be printed on paper. Coins, stickers, bookmarks, and pins all can be inserted to create a true one-to-one marketing solution that will leave a lasting impression. Most of these items won't even disqualify the pieces for automation-compatibility discounts.

Envelopes

Don't ignore what the recipient sees first. The envelope gives the recipient a first impression about the piece, and often determines whether the piece is opened in the first place. Unless your goal is to waste a lot of money, nothing is more important than getting your envelope opened. Significant mail performance and revenue implications hang in the balance. If your message involves an affinity relationship of some kind, put it right on the envelope. Just do it in a way that makes recipients feel compelled to open the piece.

Envelopes have two fronts. You can't control which side someone looks at first. Don't let any space go to waste. Consider adding teaser copy to both sides and don't shy away from making an offer. If there's something free inside, i.e., an exceptional guarantee or special financing, call attention to it on the outside, too.

Include attention-grabbing creative copy. Consider putting copy on the envelope that makes the contents seem so valuable that a gatekeeper cannot in good conscience throw it away. The use of boldly printed copy—"Important: Do Not Bend"; "The information you requested is enclosed"; or "185mm × 85mm print inside"—will frequently do the trick. Just make sure the inside lives up to the hype.

Know your recipients. Avoid misspellings at all costs, especially in salutations. Let recipients know you know them without invading their privacy). For example, addressing a piece to "Leslie Smith, MIS Director" is much better than simply "MIS Director," which is too impersonal.

Full-face envelopes. This type of envelope features a see-through window across the entire face, with only a ½-in. border on all sides. This provides a measure of security by making it easy to see the envelope's contents. And it does show off those beautifully printed inserts.

Oversize and undersize envelopes. Full-color printing isn't the only way to make your envelope stand out from the crowd. There are a wide range of envelope sizes that will make your piece unique and stay within USPS automation guidelines.

Indicia. How you send your mail is important. Preprinted indicia can save a few dollars in processing costs, but both metering and pre-cancelled stamps out-pull indicia in terms of response rates. A significant swing in response rates (sometimes as much as 15%) is at stake when selecting how to apply postage.

Mailing Endorsements

Not all endorsements are created equal. While the service on some endorsements is free, a few involve per-piece surcharges. On a first-class mailing, for example, an endorsement of "Return Service Requested" will result in the return of any undeliverable pieces with the new address (or other reason for nondelivery) indicated, free of charge. On the other hand, an endorsement of "Address Service Requested" tells the Postal Service to forward the piece to the correct address within twelve months of the original mailing date.

Issuance of a separate notice bearing the new address carries a fee. You have to choose whether to have all undeliverable mail sent back to you with the new address free of charge or have it forwarded automatically and pay for separate notification of those new addresses. If it's your first time mailing to a new database, it may be worth it to pay for the address service. (Of course, you'll be charged that fee before you place the endorsement.) Keep in mind that the exact quantity of the charges—and the time period for which they apply—will vary depending on the endorsement, mail class, and the quantity of undeliverable mail (see "Cleaning Databases," earlier). To avoid paying surcharges needlessly, let your mail services provider help you place the proper endorsements according to how your want your mail handled. The options include the following:

Forwarding Service Requested. When instructed with this endorsement, Priority and First Class mail will be forwarded to the recipient's new address at no charge within the first twelve months of the original mailing date. In months thirteen through eighteen, the pieces are returned with the new address, again at no charge. After eighteen months, or if the piece is deemed undeliverable, it will be returned with the postal service's reason for non-delivery at no charge. For Standard Mail-class pieces, the action is the same for the first twelve months. After a year, however, there are some "weighted" fees involved. These fees can run to $2.00 or more per piece, which is why we don't recommend using an endorsement that carries a weight-based fee for Standard Mail.

Address Service Requested. After twelve months, this endorsement is identical to the Forwarding Service endorsement outlined above. Within the first year, however, the USPS will send a notice bearing the recipient's new address (for both First Class and Standard Mail classes). These notices make the Address Service endorsement valuable for updating your database. This endorsement also carries an address correction fee.

Change Service Requested. With this endorsement, the Postal Service will issue a separate notice with either the new address or reason for non-delivery. An address correction fee will be charged, and the piece will be destroyed. This endorsement is the same for all mail classes but is only available if you request electronic Address Change Service (ACS).

Return Service Requested. When instructed with this endorsement, Priority and First Class mail will be returned to the sender with the new address or reason for non-delivery attached to the piece itself. For First Class pieces, there is no charge for this endorsement. However, Standard Mail-class pieces will be charged return postage at either First Class or Priority Mail rates as applicable for the weight of the piece charged.

Personalization

Personalization is a great way to create impact with your mail campaign. Recipients associate a high level of value with a mail piece that includes elements tailored to their specific interests.

Not long ago, "sophisticated personalization" was confined to basic elements such as name, address, and salutation. Today's computing technology allows personalization to extend far into even the most complex databases. Laser-printed variable content can produce a mail campaign that's pertinent to the needs of individual recipients, greatly increasing the relevance of your direct mail piece on a one-to-one basis. Consider including valuable information about buying preferences or history, contributions, family size, geographical considerations, and much more. Personalization is limited only by the amount of information available in your database.

Data processing and personalization must be planned carefully in order to integrate seamlessly with production of the piece. The following tips will help you get the most out of data processing and personalization:

Consider a single, pre-printed "shell." As your database expands, so do your customized marketing options. Today's computing technology allows personalization to extend far beyond the basic elements of name, address and salutation. Today's laser printing technology offers the flexibility to create multiple versions of a direct mail program from a single pre-printed shell. Variable data printing is a great way to create marketing materials with a personalized look. This shell must contain only the elements common to all versions, such as a company logo or high-quality image.

Full-service mail services providers are able to laser-print copy changes—including black-and-white and some color graphics—for all versions in a single run.

Flexible laser imaging technology allows you to create many versions from a single template during the personalization process. Widely available software solutions allow black-and-white copy and digital image changes on the fly between versions. The flexibility of this software means that all versions of a carefully planned project can be produced in a single run while preserving mail sort order and all postal discounts. Some of the options for this content include valuable information about buying preferences, contributions, purchase dates, or other areas of special interest. Personalization is limited only by the amount of information available in your database.

Mailing Drop Dates

Be careful when mailing during historically busy times or when people have other things on their mind. Think twice before scheduling a mail drop around major holidays, national political elections, and the April 15 income tax deadline. Take into account the selling cycle of your own product or service and your program goals.

*   *   *

The Final Word...

Outside and in, package variety can help you take advantage of an information-packed database, giving you the opportunity to tailor a compelling message for each segment of your mailing list. Consult your direct mail services provider for a complete range of self-mailer, insert, and envelope designs that maximize response rates while minimizing costs—and don't overlook your return address label options.

Contributors:

- *Ken Boone, Boone Consulting, Baltimore, Maryland*
- *Mike Conlon, Meredith Print Advantage, Des Moines, Iowa*
  www.meredithprintadvantage.com
- *Tony Hoholik, The John Roberts Company, Minneapolis, Minnesota*
  www.johnroberts.com
- *Sylvia Konkel, EU Services, Rockville, Maryland*
  www.euservices.com
- *John Leonard, SMR/Tytrek, Toronto, Ontario*
  www.smrtytrek.com
- *Bill Seidl, Seidl's Bindery, Houston, Texas*
  www.seidlsbindery.com

53 Data-Processing Management

The future of direct mail has never been brighter. While technological advances have changed the competitive landscape in the data-processing industry, however, successful direct mail programs still start with basics: by-the-numbers data management. Campaigns achieve the right results only when myriad production elements come together perfectly. What good is the most beautiful customized piece if it isn't delivered?

What You Will Learn

- Data cleansing
- Merge/purge
- Reducing postal charges

Project lead times seem to shrink every year. Effective data controls will increase the speed of your data processing and get your materials in the mail stream faster. Cost is also very important these days. Front-end data management will decrease data production time and save you money. Mailings that use multiple lists will benefit from back-end data analysis so future mailings can be smaller yet achieve the same number of responses.

Key Ingredients for Successful Programs

The first step in any direct mail program should be the identification of your target market and desired results. Many project designs would run better and cheaper if minor adjustments were made at the beginning of creative development. Therefore, a direct marketing technical team, with data processing and response management, imaging, binding/finishing, and lettershop expertise, should be present at all program development meetings. Next, establish a realistic critical path. Once a project's goals have been agreed upon, clearly communicate them to all appropriate people. Unless your internal and external business partners know your project's goals, their ability to help you is limited.

Make sure your data file structure is uniform and use industry standard media formats. Prior to handing off the project to your data house, create a data-file layout. Without this, your supplier will need to decipher one, which takes time and increases your chance of error. A data-file layout includes elements such as name and address components, list identifier codes, telephone numbers (for tandem telemarketing), account numbers, and various other demographic and psychographic information. Then, provide your supplier with detailed instructions (data specification logic) that enables programmers to clean up your database exactly the way you want.

Data Cleansing

Companies that manage your data also manage your future success. Fully service your data needs by selecting a data-processing provider with a wealth of direct-mail industry knowledge. Experienced data partners will help you avoid pitfalls and costly errors while allowing you to get a restful night's sleep. After verifying your instructions and requirements, an experienced data house will:

- Ensure that your data files contain all required components, match the data-file layout, and are otherwise error-free.
- Build cleansing processes in a logical manner to ensure accurate data output.
- Extract a representative record dump to test the cleansing processes prior to full production. This test will reduce the likelihood of logic errors and unnecessary multiple cleanup runs.
- Verify key fields such as state and province codes. For example, in Quebec, "PQ" and "QU" are frequently used instead of the correct Canada Post abbreviation "QC."
- Check that apartment and suite numbers are located in a standardized position within an address field or are placed in a field of their own. Incorrect placement will reduce your project's chances for proper delivery.
- Ensure that proper recipient names are used. Up to 60% of the general population prefers to be addressed by a different salutation than the one used on most of their mail. Using a salutation field instead of a parsed first name field may boost your response rate. Properly place and punctuate name components such as honorific, first name, middle initial, last name, and suffix. Initial names such as "J.R. Ewing" often are truncated to "Dear J." unless a separate salutation field is used.
- Develop and update your house lists. Require a salutation field. Verify that each record has properly spelled name components (e.g., Claire, Clair, Clare), gender codes (e.g., Pat, Francis, Robin), casing (e.g., DeLane, Delane, deLane), and punctuation (e.g., L'Argent, Largent).

Merge/Purge

A "match-code" merge/purge requires that duplicate records be typed in exactly the same. If there is a slight variation, such as "Tom Destree" and "Tom Destrie," both at the same address, neither record would be purged—and the real Tom Destree would receive two pieces of mail. For large mailing projects, this can be very costly. Therefore, avoid match-code merge/purges because they cannot compensate for key field character variation and may cause an underkill situation. Unfortunately, they can also overkill records. In Canada, mail addressed to "General Delivery" in rural areas and records without apartment and suite numbers can be wrongfully purged.

Instead of using match codes, perform "weighted-value" merge/purges and determine for yourself which fields and record lengths are most appropriate for your project. A weighted-value merge/purge is more forgiving of different spellings of the same record. When multiple lists are combined, there will be duplicate records spelled slightly differently. Some software programs allow a weighted-value; for example if 80% of the characters match in certain fields, the records would be considered duplicates and one would be eliminated. "Loosely" weighted values tend to overkill records and are desirable in situations when there are to be absolutely no duplicate pieces of mail sent. "Tightly" weighted values tend to underkill records and should be used when the cost of duplicate mailings isn't very high.

Sophisticated weighted-value merge/purge algorithms enable you to skirt variances within name and address components and reduce your overkill/underkill error frequency. For example, a properly constructed weighted-value merge/purge program will detect three variants of the following "Dave Loudon" records and eliminate two:

1. Dave Loudon   649 N. Horners Ln.   (301) 424-3300

2. David Loudon   694 N. Horners Ln.   (301) 424-3300

3. D. Louden   649 N. Horners Ln.   (301) 424-3330

Most merge/purges are based upon data files being sorted first by postal code in ascending sequence. Grouping records together (address verification/correction) prior to merge/purge is usually recommended.

NCOA

Nothing is more frustrating than discovering a high incidence of "undeliverables" in your mailing database. Although there's no such thing as a "perfect" list, verifying your house files and membership lists regularly against a National Change of Address (NCOA) file will help eliminate bad or outdated addresses. No database is too small to benefit from the comparison. Most mail and data-processing vendors can make arrangements to provide this service through a licensed NCOA provider.

Some Design and Production Issues

During a mailing project's conceptual stage, develop a detailed checklist. Common problem areas include, but by no means are limited to:

- *Window positioning line-up.* Careful planning of mastheads, logos, address field positions, and other preprinted page parts will prevent many downstream postal problems.
- *Registration.* Rather than registering personalized fields into preprinted image areas, full-sheet laser imaging maintains a more consistent appearance.

With today's technology, fitting personalization into preprinted boxes and underscores often is unnecessary.

- **Ink selection.** For your offset printing, specify laser friendly wax-free inks for any job that is to be laser-personalized.

- **Paper stock selection.** Involve your lasering partner (laser printing services supplier) prior to selecting your paper. Although the latest generation of commercial lasers can process a wide variety of paper stocks, it's still wise to discuss stock weight, grain direction, and paper coating.

- **Multiple imaging.** Running two or more images up on a sheet usually saves significant time and money.

- **Duplex imaging.** Duplexing allows variable imaging on either or both sides of a sheet and maintains a piece's consistent look and feel. In addition to fighting offset printing dot gain, laser toner never looks the same as offset ink. In short, duplex imaging offers you far more image consistency and flexibility than simplex imaging.

- **Data transfer.** Although the information superhighway is getting better every year, it still isn't always your best choice. Transferring large record volumes via modem or email can be time-consuming or imperfect unless both parties have the correct software and wide-bandwidth hardware (e.g., T1 lines). There has been tremendous improvement in phone line transfer, but it's still not perfect for every situation. Use your own judgment.

*   *   *

The Final Word...

Good data work will help you comply with USPS and Canada Post addressing standards and minimize your postal costs. Postage is usually the single highest cost component of a direct mail project. Qualify for letter carrier presort rates by using only approved address verification/correction and presorting software.

Contributors:

- *Ken Boone, Boone Consulting, Baltimore, Maryland*
- *Sylvia Konkel, EU Services, Rockville, Maryland*
  www.euservices.com
- *John Leonard, SMR/Tytrek, Toronto, Ontario*
  www.smrtytrek.com
- *John Snyder, HBP, Hagerstown, Maryland*
  www.hbp.com

54 Inkjet Imaging

Inkjet imaging is ubiquitous. It's used by virtually every industry including publishing, direct mail, pharmaceutical, and financial. We see it on the food we buy, the pills we take, our payroll checks, and so much more.

What You Will Learn

- Inkjet printing flexibility
- In-line production
- Postal barcoding

The important distinction between offset printing and inkjet printing is that the latter is a non-impact process and is highly portable. Inkjet printing units can either be standalone or mounted on bindery equipment such as folders, stitchers, and perfect binders. Because it is a non-impact process, inkjet printing works regardless of whether the substrate is flat, folded, or bound. A few years ago, one inkjet company was promoting itself by inkjet imaging on the yolk of a sunny-side-up fried egg.

Another important characteristic of inkjet printing is that it is computer-driven. The latest computer chips have dramatically increased data-processing speed, enabling extraordinary product throughput. Increased memory capacity allows unique images to be placed on every product going through the equipment. This is why inkjet printing is so popular among direct mailers.

An Example

Suppose a national cataloger wants catalogs going to San Francisco to have a ten-dollar discount, those going to Alabama to have a twenty-dollar discount, and those being mailed to Baltimore to be given a two-for-one special offer. With inkjet printing, the codes are automatically interpreted, and the right offer is printed on each piece.

Inkjet Printing and Folders

Mounting inkjet printing equipment on folders allows the printing of barcodes and variable messages on parent sheets prior to folding—a task that cannot be done by a mail house. For example, if you have a double-addressed brochure, such as one with a mailing address on the outside and a pre-filled-out perforated business reply card (BRC) on the inside, every piece will be produced with a perfect match. Direct mailers know that pre-filled-out response vehicles increase promotional effectiveness.

One of our clients conducted research on reply mechanisms and found that 80% of the people who returned cards either incompletely or illegibly filled out their name and address. These discoveries drove this client to recommend the inkjet imaging of addresses and barcodes on both the mailing panel and the reply card.

Inkjet imaging in-line on folding equipment also facilitates lot changes. In the past, printers had to stop the press at certain points in the run to remove coding data from the plate. This was expensive and time-consuming. The inkjet and folder combination allows companies with appropriate equipment to gang-run (print together in one impression) material as many as five across and five down on a sheet, each with different serial numbers and version codes. The proper placement of the area to be inkjetted needs to be considered early in the design phase because inkjet printing has to go in the same direction as the material passes through the equipment. Your finisher can help you with placement of the inkjet image area to make sure it's correct for the folding sequence.

Postal Barcoding

Like any other barcode, those designed for the mail stream use a binary identification system that's based on numerical series and parallel bars. Optical character recognition (OCR) equipment scans the width of the bars and the sequence of numbers and converts the data into electrical signals. Barcodes can be inkjet or offset printed when data are not variable, as in the case of return addressing. Because bulk mail rates increase unless certain requirements are met, the more that direct mailing can be automatically processed by the USPS, the larger the discount.

Accurate and correctly placed designated areas on mailing pieces can translate to substantial savings in mailing costs. Spot gluing, another process that can be performed on folding equipment, can also result in discounts.

✳   ✳   ✳

The Final Word...

While many of us may snub inkjet printing as an unworthy stepchild of the craft of printing, there's no denying that those of us who work with direct marketers are better off since its invention. And the quality is getting better and better.

Contributor:

- *Marty Anson, Bindagraphics, Inc., Baltimore, Maryland*
  www.bindagraphics.com

55 Digital Printing

Although digital printing is not a "plug-and-play" technology, digital printing technology has matured to the point where it's ready for prime-time use. Well-conceived and well-organized systems must be in place to take full advantage of the benefits of digital print technology. Before you take the digital printing plunge, there are several aspects of this exciting technology with which you'll want to become familiar.

What You Will Learn

- The growing market for digital printing
- Digital printing applications
- Finishing considerations

Finishers and mail service providers need to know what's happening in this rapidly emerging marketplace. As of early 2004, The Printing Industries of America Economics and Research Department estimates the market value of digital printing to be about $11 billion. Others estimate it to be as high as $33 billion with a projected 15% annual rate of growth. Considering the total U.S. demand for printed products has been in the $150 billion range throughout the early 2000s, no matter how you tally it, digital printing is a force to be reckoned with.

First Things First: Applications

Today's digital printing technology can be used for a variety of different applications. Some of these applications are similar to offset printing, while others are entirely different. Knowing the difference can help you determine how much of your existing operations—and customers—are suitable for the technology:

- *Static printing.* These are simply short-run color printing applications, such as 150 copies of a 32-page booklet with a four-color cover. Although none of the content changes, static printing applications take advantage of the speed of digital printing to offer quick turnarounds and high-quality production of projects that may otherwise be offset printed.

- *Variable-data printing.* This is perhaps the most common—and most talked-about—digital printing application. Variable-data printing involves the placement of variable content elements that allow for varying degrees of customization on a printed piece. There are several different levels of variable-data printing, ranging from the simple change of a name and salutation to pieces comprised completely of data-driven content, including charts and graphics.

- *Hybrid printing.* Hybrid products combine static and variable content elements, such as a personalized cover applied to an offset-produced text book block. Another possibility is to print shells, such as direct mailers, on an offset press and then customize them on a digital printer. One of the main advantages to hybrid print production is the ability to create a high volume of customized products at a lower cost.

How Do You Sell It?

While early adopters have had no problem finding applications that benefit from digital printing technology, determining the best way to sell it has proven much more difficult. When compared on an "apples to apples" basis, at least for now, digital printing has a much higher unit cost than offset printing. While the complexity of most digital printing applications renders such a comparison inaccurate, a print purchasing agent may determine that the higher cost is unjustified.

To successfully sell digital printing, printers and their finishing partners need to target the key business influencers in a targeted organization. Many digital printing applications are a collaboration of several disciplines and departments: computer programmers, designers, marketers, finishers, binders, and mailers, etc. The goal of such collaboration is to create an application that's much more relevant to the recipient or end user. That increased relevance is designed to increase the response rate or average order size, depending on the application.

As a result, your clients aren't selling a print job. They're selling a solution that provides better bang for what would otherwise be their customer's printing buck. Rather than focus on the per-unit printing cost, you're focusing on the total cost of the sale. That will give you a much better chance of selling the solution and the technology that makes it possible.

The Production Blueprint

Digital printing requires a different infrastructure and a different level of coordination than offset printing. For example, when an offset-printed project needs to be mailed, the customer might not send the printer their mailing database until the project proofing stage. Occasionally, the job may already be on press when the database is transferred.

For a project that includes variable-data printing, the database must arrive in the digital printer's hands much earlier in the process. The content from that database will need to be matched with the artwork and copy that will appear on the piece to be sure everything fits together properly. Such a workflow may require a different order entry process and production control procedures than what many offset printers currently have in place.

Even spoilage—something that's easy to calculate for an offset printed job—requires a different set of procedures. Let's say you're using variable-data printing to produce direct mail pieces that are fully customized for each recipient. If there are two finishing operations that will be performed subsequent to the printing—folding and gluing, for example—you'll need to establish a control system that allows you to easily replace the spoiled pieces while maintaining the proper sequence and mail sort order. Remember, each person in the database must receive a mail piece that's customized for them.

*   *   *

The Final Word…

These are just a few of the concerns that must be considered before embarking on the journey toward supporting the emerging market for finishing of digitally printed products. The incredible flexibility of the technology allows for a nearly limitless range of uses. Every day potential customers are dreaming up exciting new ways to take advantage of digital printing. If you're prepared to meet those challenges, you'll be well on your way to finding success!

Contributors:

- *Sylvia Konkel, EU Services, Rockville, Maryland*
  www.euservices.com

- *Chuck Manthey, Sentinel Printing Company, St. Cloud, Minnesota*
  www.sentinelprinting.com

- *Bruce Sanderson, Springfield Printing Corporation, Springfield, Vermont*
  www.springfieldprinting.com

- *John Snyder, HBP, Hagerstown, Maryland*
  www.hbp.com

56 Continuous-Laser Printing

Today's versatile high-speed continuous-laser printing is the right choice for many direct mail projects. For large-volume jobs, continuous-laser printing can help you decrease both production costs and turnaround times without sacrificing any of the beauty you now expect from laser printing technology.

What You Will Learn

- Appropriate quantities
- Image resolution
- Production tips

High-speed continuous-laser printing is used primarily for large-volume, high-quality mailings. Typical applications include letters, order forms, subscriptions, statements, invoices, reports, Cheshire labels, self-mailers, application forms, and more. The most common format is a personalized letter and matching reply form with preprinted fields, such as name, company, address, account number, salutation, and so forth.

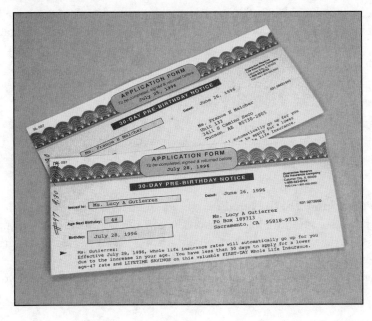

Examples of continuous-laser printing.

Job Quantity

For small quantities, continuous-form paper (a series of connected sheets that feed sequentially through a printing device) costs more than cut sheets, but as projects get larger this differential in cost disappears. Most jobs have a breakeven point at which continuous-laser printing becomes more cost- and time-efficient. Breakeven rules of thumb can be misleading and may cause bad decisions. Each large-volume project should be examined on a case-by-case basis. Once a job has passed its breakeven point, its low per-unit cost can really save a lot of money. During production, continuous-laser printing is about twice as fast as sheetfed laser printing, which means large jobs get in the mail stream faster. For example, jobs requiring five days on a sheetfed machine may need only three on continuous equipment.

Flexibility and Quality Considerations

Continuous-laser printers can accommodate many paper stocks, finishes, and sizes. Business forms suppliers have access to colored paper and usually have a large selection in stock. Most continuous machines will accept paper up to 17 in. (431.8 mm) wide (excluding pin-feed holes) on either fan-folded stock or continuous rolls.

Many late-generation continuous-laser printing systems print at an enhanced 300 dpi; however, not too long ago, 240 dpi was the standard. While 300 dpi beautifully accommodates most fonts and line art, if either halftones or small point sizes (under 6 pt.) are present, then a slower, but still high-speed, 600-dpi sheetfed laser printer may be your best option. All in all, for the majority of high-volume jobs, continuous-laser printing deserves serious consideration.

Registration between laser ink and preprinted offset copy is very good in continuous-laser printing because of precise pin alignment. Bitmapped images and variable text strings can be placed anywhere on a sheet. Many fonts are available and text strings can be rotated 360°. The paper handling and ink positioning capabilities of late-model continuous-laser printers can accommodate almost any personalized design.

Good Planning Prevents Mistakes

Most errors associated with continuous-laser printing can be prevented easily. Good communication between you and your data, laser, and lettershop partners will assure successful projects. To succeed, try to avoid some of the following common production problems:

- ***Don't cut into offset-printed images such as logos, borders, and type.*** Bursting leaves perforation marks on the top and bottom of each form. Most lettershops now use cutters instead of bursting machines and return final pieces with clean edges. Design your product with at least ⅛-in. (3.2-mm) trim margin from the perforations. Although it's rarely a problem, if you're concerned about maintaining tight border registration, be safe and talk with your postpress partner early. Advance planning ensures properly positioned images and is a good time investment. If your finisher is cutting into copy, your only practical alternative is to revert to bursting.

- **Allow for take-out trim margins between different-colored applications.** If a letter has a white background and the companion application on the same form is blue, the slightest slitting variation means that a sliver of the wrong color will show on one of the two pieces. To avoid this problem, allow an ⅛-in. (3.2-mm) bleed margin for each piece, giving you a total ¼-in. (6.4-mm) gap for take-out trim. If you do this on standard 17-in. (431.8-mm) paper, then your final product width will be 8⅜ in. (212.7 mm) instead of 8½ in. (215.9 mm).

- **Use laser-safe ink.** When offset printing on continuous paper, use laser-safe (wax-free) ink. The high heat of laser printers melts wax and can result in messy printing. Although most forms printers know this, err on the side of caution and always specify "laser-safe." When using reflex blue or metallic inks, run a sample of the ink on the right stock through a "hot" laser printer— one that's just run a job—prior to printing. Likewise, test spot varnish and all other paper coatings first. A preproduction meeting among you, your forms printer, and your continuous-laser printing partner is always a good time investment.

- **Don't forget about your samples.** Place sample data at the beginning of each job. On many occasions, companies receive sample requests after jobs are completed. In addition to redoing all the data work, if the laser printer and bindery equipment has been reset, then makereadies need to be redone as well. This inefficiency is a terrible waste of your time and money. Advance planning also assures you of obtaining samples prior to the job's mailing.

- **Poor sequential mailing layouts can cause disasters.** If your mailing is sequential (e.g., letter carrier presort or numerically numbered), clearly communicate to your data house whether the form is to be folded north/south (above/below) or east/west (right/left). If this isn't specified, then you may end up with a production mess that only additional postage or expensive handwork can solve. Maintain the integrity of your letter carrier presort to ensure that you get the benefits of bulk mail postage rates.

- **The inside panel of three-panel pieces shouldn't be the same size.** When planning a three-panel job, if one panel folds into the other two during product conversion, then it must be smaller.

- **Carefully position your large solid-image areas.** Position large-area laser ink solids away from fan folds. For example, a 6×6-in. (152.4×152.4-mm) solid black area may look fine if positioned near the center of the page, but as it nears a fan fold, it may become grainy. If heavy laser ink coverage must be next to folds, consider using sheetfed lasers instead.

※   ※   ※

The Final Word...

Ensure that your laser printing project is a success by choosing continuous-laser printing when appropriate and involve your production partners early in the planning stages. Complex personalized marketing pieces with questionnaires, self-mailers with order forms, and other copy-intensive projects are all practical in the continuous-laser printing world. Projects with right-angle roll folds, slit-to-nest forms, and refolded four- and two-pagers, among others, present you with a rich landscape from which to select your design. But show them to your bindery first.

Contributor:

- *John Leonard, SMR/Tytrek, Toronto, Ontario*
  www.smrtytrek.com

57 Odd Mail Shapes

Direct marketers are always looking for new ways to make their mail pieces stand out. Although odd-shaped pieces do stand out, those produced in unusual shapes and odd dimensions have been notoriously expensive to mail. On August 10, 2003, the USPS created a new classification called Customized MarketMail (CMM), which frees mailers to experiment with nontraditional dimensions. The new category should help direct marketers create unique designs that won't break the budget.

What You Will Learn

- New postal classification
- Dimensional design flexibility
- Future growth?

The main benefit of CMM is that it enables designers get away from the standard rectangle to create more unusual and appealing designs that are economical to mail. Pieces can be almost any shape or dimension. Are you promoting a new auto insurance product or the grand opening of a car dealership? A mail piece in the shape of a car would really stand out in the mailboxes of your recipients. That's the whole idea.

There are some limitations to CMM, however: Since all pieces must be delivered to each destination delivery unit (DDU) specified in the database, CMM is probably

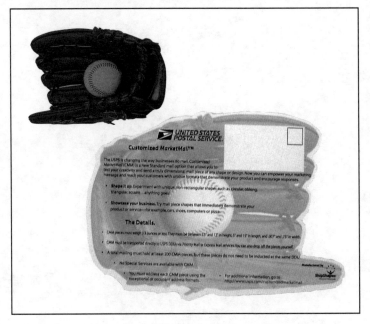

Example of USPS-approved CMM mail piece.

not an attractive option for regional mailings or others with a far-reaching database. The cost of production is also greater for CMM than other mail designs, which may put it out of reach for some budget-conscious direct mailers. Forwarding, address correction, and other list services also are not applicable on CMM pieces.

Despite these restrictions, CMM can be a boon to many businesses. While the requirement that mail be sent directly to DDUs for handling would not suit some applications, for example, it would have little effect on a drop destined for delivery within a large metro area, such as Washington, D.C. Higher anticipated responses also should mitigate the higher production costs of CMM.

*   *   *

The Final Word...

Will CMM revolutionize the direct mail industry? It's too early to tell, but the signs are generally positive, at least for some applications. If direct marketers utilize CMM to their advantage, perhaps the USPS could expand the scope of the program to make it more economical for all who wish to use it.

Contributors:

- *Sylvia Konkel, EU Services, Rockville, Maryland*
  www.euservices.com

- *Bob Windler, Diecrafters, Inc., Chicago, Illinois*
  www.diecrafters.com

58 Return Address Labels

Return address labels are an attractive promotional option, especially for nonprofits. If you've ever received a batch of return address labels, chances are good that they arrived in your mailbox courtesy of a charitable organization. Return address labels not only come in handy, they reinforce your familiarity with the organization that sent them. Many charitable and other nonprofit organizations have issued return address labels for years because, quite simply, they always pay for themselves through the donations they generate.

What You Will Learn

- Raise money by giving away labels
- Layout options
- Production choices

Improved return address label production technology has made this powerful form of brand awareness more economical and attractive than ever. Personalized return address labels have come a long way, from simple and single-color to foil-stamped and full-color. What used to be just a plain white label with your name in black ink now contains logos or pictures, fancy borders, even intricately diecut shapes.

Labels can be printed using either flexographic or lithographic processes, although flexo-printed labels are usually the more economical choice. Foil stamping makes labels stand out. It's commonly used on holiday or other theme-related return address labels that are distributed as part of a unified direct mail package. It's been the experience of our clients that packages containing foil-stamped return address labels generate increased response rates compared with non-foil-stamped labels.

Diecutting also is used to transform labels from the traditional rectangle into an endless variety of different shapes. However, the cost to manufacture custom dies to create those shapes can be prohibitive; it's typically more cost effective to use a pre-existing label template that uses pre-made dies. Most full-service mail services providers have dozens of layout templates to choose from, representing label shape possibilities from American flags to the outline of an open mailbox.

There are a lot of die configurations available, and the layout of your label sheets should be driven by the most economical use of the dies. Two-up, three-up, and side-by-side layouts are possible, depending on the press being used.

The wealth of production options allows for a wide range of printing and die-cutting combinations. As with any other direct mail package, experiment with a few different designs to find the combination that garners the most response. For example, you may want to start with a basic label design and add one element, such as a foil-stamped border, to see which one your customers prefer. Label layouts also can include information return cards and stickers. The more versatile the sheet, the more useful and effective a promotional tool it is likely to be for both you and the recipient.

A good rule of thumb for preconditioning label data is to include four lines of no more than thirty characters each on each label. This may vary slightly, depending on specific design, dimensions, and font size. Without current, accurate data, however, even the most beautifully designed and printed labels are useless.

*   *   *

The Final Word...

Ultimately, it's all about the data. A great-looking label won't be of much use if it isn't filled with accurate data. Unlike the type of data on the rest of your mail piece, return address label personalization isn't terribly complex, but it must be completely accurate. A recipient might be inclined to forgive a slight misspelling or a truncated street address on the front of an envelope, but if the labels aren't to his or her liking, they will be trashed, along with your company's reputation.

Contributors:

- *Ken Boone, Boone Consulting, Baltimore, Maryland*
- *Sylvia Konkel, EU Services, Rockville, Maryland*
  www.euservices.com

59 Preplanned Quick-Mail Packets

Given the technology currently available to direct mail service providers, the need to sacrifice personalization in the name of rapid deployment is dwindling. By utilizing a "rapid response" or "quick mail" package, your existing data can be organized and deployed to generate a mail campaign that's easy to disseminate and personal enough to get noticed. Rapid-response packages are good for testing different offers and tracking response rates and a great way to test different template designs and content to see what works and what doesn't.

What You Will Learn

- Save time and reduce costs with partially prepackaged mail templates.
- Reach customers quickly when an urgent issue arises
- Bridge the gap between "standard" mailings and fully customized packages

---

What happens when your client needs to elicit a rapid response to a sudden "hot-button" issue from your target audience? All of that variation is superfluous, right? After all, how complex can a mail campaign really get if your window to place timely information in the hands of recipients is only a few days?

When you must help your customer reach their recipients as quickly as possible, a predesigned template (*a k a* "urgent-gram") can save a lot of time by enabling your campaign to hit the streets in as few as two or three days.

The key to such rapid production is the use of partially prepackaged direct mail templates. These predesigned templates allow the bulk of production to be performed quickly and within standard design specifications. Packages can contain several individual pieces, such as reply envelopes and color inserts, each one containing customizable fields.

Rapid response mail packages can reduce the time it takes a project to hit the mail stream from weeks to days. Depending on size and complexity, an entire campaign with an "urgent" message can be customized and deployed in as little as three days. The current inkjet printing technology at the disposal of direct mail service providers allows data segments, logos, and images up to 600-dpi resolution to be placed on each piece. Dozens of these variable-data segments can be mixed and matched in designated fields.

For direct mail campaigns that need to be created and deployed at a moment's notice, these rapid-response packages are ideal. They're a cost-effective way to get recipients to take action on any extremely time-sensitive subject, and they incorporate all of the data you already possess about your recipients, enabling you to create highly customized pieces. Remember, templates may be highly customizable in terms of data, but they are less so when it comes to creativity. With turnaround time essential to the success of the project, the templates need to be kept reasonably simple to facilitate production. Stock selection and color are limited, and extras such as diecuts and foil stamps should be avoided.

When You Have More Data Than Time

Many companies and organizations see the opportunity to place timely information in the hands of potential customers or constituents all of the time. Unfortunately, they may not utilize direct mail campaigns to their full potential when the deadline is tight. For example, campaign finance reform lobbyists had a desperate need to get information to their constituents when the Enron and WorldCom scandals made instant headlines. The issue was not a priority immediately beforehand, and the window of opportunity for a lobbyist group to influence lawmakers on the issue was very small.

A "standard" direct mail campaign would get the message across, plain and simple. But a lobbyist group has a wide range of constituents it needs to reach and a great deal of personalized data about them. If they want to use this data and still get the mail campaign out in time for recipients to take action, they need a production solution that can handle all of their needs.

These packages offer several advantages that bridge the gap between "standard," non-personalized mailings and completely customized direct mail campaigns. The prepackaged elements allow for a quick determination of both postage costs and project pricing. Selecting from a variety of existing templates with a streamlined look and feel alerts recipients to the time-sensitive nature of the information contained therein.

An important key to getting the most out of rapid-response packages, of course, is finding a mail services provider with state-of-the-art high-quality inkjet printing, expert database management, and variable-data capabilities.

*   *   *

The Final Word...

Although quick-mail packages are typically used for situations that call for immediate action, such as pleas for disaster relief, prepackaged templates can provide a cost-effective way to execute a direct mail campaign with almost any purpose. One of our clients has several customers who use quick-mail packages to alert customers to time-sensitive special offers for particular products or for an urgent campaign message.

Contributor:

- *Sylvia Konkel, EU Services, Rockville, Maryland*
  www.euservices.com

60 Commingling

Are you trying to squeeze out more direct mail cost savings? Is there a faster way to get your mail to its destination? The answer is "yes" and it involves today's new "commingling" technology.

What You Will Learn

- Commingling definition
- Cost and time savings
- Drop shipping

For the right types of jobs, commingling paired with drop shipping significantly reduces postal costs, gets mail into homes and businesses faster, and provides better test marketing results.

What Is Commingling?

Commingling is the process of merging multiple ZIP-code strings into a single mail stream. When the right types of jobs are combined, significant postal discounts can be attained. The United States Postal Service (USPS) requires 150 pieces per ZIP code as the minimum quantity to achieve desirable five-digit postal discount rates. Commingling shorter runs together improves the chances that more ZIP codes reach this 150-piece threshold. Although "synergy" is an overused buzzword, it accurately describes the commingling process.

Savings

As of the last USPS postal rate increase (on June 30, 2002, as of this writing), the difference between three-digit and five-digit rates is $13/M on for-profit mail and $15/M on nonprofit mail. This is significant because even after factoring in the cost of commingling, it is as if you're getting envelopes for free.

The largest cost component of most direct mail campaigns is postage. Since postage represents up to 30% or even more of total production costs, chipping away at this large number makes a lot of sense. Depending on what a direct mail services provider charges for commingling, customers can reduce their postage and drop shipping costs by up to $30/M after all commingling and drop shipping charges have been factored in.

For Profit			
Per Piece	**Before Commingling**	**After Commingling**	**Savings**
Basic	21.2¢	19.0¢	$22/M
3-digit	20.3¢	19.0¢	$13/M
5-digit	19.0¢	19.0¢	—

Nonprofit			
Per Piece	**Before Commingling**	**After Commingling**	**Savings**
Basic	13.6¢	11.4¢	$22/M
3-digit	12.9¢	11.4¢	$15/M
5-digit	11.4¢	11.4¢	—

Postal rates as of June 30, 2002.

Who Can Benefit?

Companies that segment very large mailings into different cells should consider commingling technology. The financial services and nonprofit sectors frequently can reduce overall production costs and shorten delivery times while increasing market-testing accuracy. During the era of large "shotgun" mailings, postal discounts were easy to achieve. Today's highly targeted "rifle" mailings have increased response rates, but have also reduced the percentage of mail that qualifies for five-digit postal discounts.

Perhaps a credit card company wants to offer sports-oriented cards. If only one "all-sports" credit card is promoted, there may be enough targeted prospects in most ZIP codes to qualify for the five-digit rate. However, if recipients are segmented into

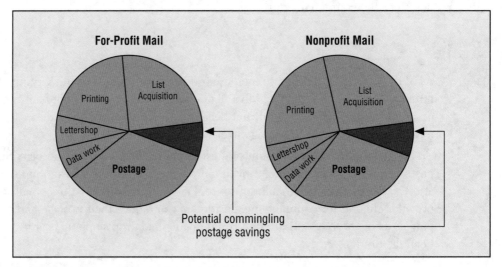

Typical direct mail production costs.

sports enthusiast categories such as tennis, softball, bowling, skiing, and golf, postal costs will increase as more mail is pushed into the higher three-digit rate. Commingling allows them to keep segmentation benefits while maintaining lower postal rates.

Assume you have a for-profit mailing segmented into three cells. If ZIP code 99999 has 150 pieces (50 in each lot), all mail in this ZIP code will be charged at the three-digit rate. However, if the three lots are commingled into the same tray, then all 150 pieces qualify for the lower five-digit rate, saving $1.95 in postage ($2.25 if nonprofit). If you have a million-piece for-profit mailing of which 75% benefits from commingling, then the net savings passed on to you after all commingling costs could be over $6,000.

Evaluation and Production

If properly done, commingling will remain transparent to the client. The first step of any project should be running a presort on the data file to predict the savings associated with commingling, because some jobs simply won't realize any benefit. For example, if you have a million-piece mailing and 95% of it already qualifies for the USPS five-digit rate, the cost of commingling outweighs the savings.

Once in production, presorting projects is important. If your million-piece mailing's presort determines that 20% of the job qualifies for the five-digit rate without commingling, this portion should be processed first so that commingling costs aren't applied to two hundred thousand pieces. Next, the remaining eight hundred thousand should be data-processed and staged in the warehouse by lot and ZIP code order. Then, Job A should be loaded onto the commingling machine in ZIP code sequence followed by Jobs B, C, etc.

Prior to running a commingling job, statistics of each lot need to be downloaded into the commingling machine's computer. If there is a mismatch between expected and actual mail quantities for any reason (i.e., spoilage in the letter shop), commingling systems will track this information.

Test Marketing

Since multiple cells of a job arrive at destination SCFs (section center facilities) in the same trays at the same time, test-marketing results are more accurate. For example, if four different-color envelopes and three messages are being tested, mail from all twelve cells going to ZIP code 99999 will be simultaneously processed. A traditional multiple-cell mailing not only costs more, but it is more susceptible to skewed testing results because of variable delivery dates.

Other Considerations

Before deciding to commingle your next job, consider a few factors. Commingling requires additional coordination time, especially if one company's job is piggybacked onto another's mail. Even though large mailing companies process millions of pieces of mail a month, they still need about three to five extra production days for most commingling jobs. Multiple-cell mailings can be dropped on a specific day as long as different cells of the same job are married together. Mailings that need to be commingled with other jobs usually are given a three- to five-day drop range.

Once the commingling process has begun, it's virtually impossible to stop. First, commingling jobs are data-processed differently and, second, mailing rates for all jobs are interdependent on each other. Since stopping a job from entering the mail stream can only be done by hand, doing so is highly impractical—without even considering the lost postal savings anticipated for the other lots. If there is any realistic chance that a mailing will be halted, commingling isn't for you.

Also, if a commingling job needs to piggyback onto another, there has to be work in your mailer's pipeline. To use an analogy, it is hard to hitchhike when the road is empty.

Drop Shipping: The Other Part of the Equation

Commingling combined with drop shipping increases customer savings. If your project is deposited at a local post office, it will be processed through:

- The local post office
- The local section center facility (SCF)
- The destination bulk mail center (BMC)
- Possibly a destination auxiliary service facility (ASF)
- A destination SCF

Choosing a large-volume mailer that runs trucks of commingled mail to SCFs throughout the country means that your mail will avoid the serendipity of USPS mail processing. Since mail is delayed anywhere from 3 to 72 hours at each USPS facility, drop shipping to destination SCFs should realize a net time gain of three to five days on average. Even though your mailing may require an extra couple of days at your commingling service provider, it should still arrive faster than ever.

*   *   *

The Final Word...

It is not uncommon for large commingling customers to net postage savings of more than $500,000 in a year. For clients like these, commingling is as close to a no-brainer as we get in the graphic arts industry.

Contributor:

- *Ken Boone, Boone Consulting, Baltimore, Maryland*

61 Drop Shipping

Organizations that need their large-volume mail to arrive faster, more predictably, and at a lower cost should consider drop-ship programs. Drop shipping eliminates many United States Postal Service (USPS) processing stages at a cost that is lower than the accompanying postal savings. If the program is well executed, essentially your direct mailer pays you to handle your mail!

What You Will Learn

- Postal discounts
- Faster delivery
- Up-front data analysis

Many companies that send large-volume mailings have been achieving great drop-shipping results for years.

What Is Drop Shipping?

The USPS offers significant discounts in exchange for delivering mail directly to "destination" postal facilities. Long ago, the USPS decided to embrace the concept of work sharing, which means that postal customers can achieve discounts for reducing USPS processing time. Companies that presort, use automation-compatible imaging (bar coding), and transport mail as close to the final destination as possible (i.e., drop ship) achieve the largest postal discounts.

Most direct mailing companies prepare the mail as best as they can and deliver it to a local, or "origin," USPS facility. Mailing companies that take advantage of drop-ship discounts will bypass their origin post office, section center facility (SCF), and bulk mail center (BMC) by delivering mail directly to destination SCFs and BMCs throughout the country, saving a lot of postage costs.

Postal Discounts

As of June 2002, for-profit mail delivered directly to destination BMCs or SCFs achieves a postal discount of $26/M, which is a 62.5% increase from 1999! In addition, mailing companies that offer both commingling and drop-ship services save direct mailers even more money.

Low mailing costs are very important for most organizations. Although the gap has narrowed since 1999, on a percentage basis, drop-ship programs still benefit nonprofit organizations the most. Although for-profit mail qualifying for "five-digit" postal rates delivered directly to destination SCFs achieves a very substantial 13.7% discount, nonprofit mailings get 18.4% (see chart).

	Nonprofit	For-profit
Drop-ship discount to destination BMCs	$20.0/M	$26.0/M
Three-digit postal rate	$0.129/ea.	$0.203/ea.
Drop-ship savings	15.5%	12.8%
Five-digit postal rate	$0.114/ea.	$0.190/ea.
Drop-ship savings	17.5%	13.7%
Drop-ship discount to destination SCFs	$21.00/M	$26.00/M
Three-digit postal rate	$0.129/ea.	$0.203/ea.
Drop-ship savings	$16.3%	12.8%
Five-digit postal rate	$0.114/ea.	$0.190/ea.
Drop-ship savings	$18.4%	13.7%

Drop-shipping savings. (Rates as of June 2002)

To maximize postal savings, direct mailing companies need to run full tractor-trailer loads of mail, and this often requires combining drop-shipped mail from several mail runs. Mailing companies without a critical mass of direct mail volume are forced either to run less-than-truckload (LTL) trailers or have them leave too infrequently—neither of which is good for customers. If too many LTL trailers are used, freight costs will exceed postal discounts and the only winners will be trucking companies.

There's More to Drop Shipping Than Cost Savings

Less USPS handling means mail gets to its destination faster and more predictably. Bypassing the local post office, local SCF, local BMC, and destination BMCs means that there is a lot less chance for mail to be delayed. On average, drop shipping will save between three and seventy-two hours per bypassed USPS postal facility. For example, if four facilities are bypassed, up to eleven days of processing time variance will be eliminated.

Drop shipping allows direct mailers to segment certain portions of the country, which means they have better control of "in-home" dates. For example, if you want a homogeneous drop date for your mailing, drop shipping allows you to schedule all mail so it arrives at destination SCFs and BMCs throughout the country at or near the same time. Although no one can control when destination USPS facilities actually process the mail, less postal handling means that the range of home delivery dates will be narrowed. On the other hand, if you are concerned about overloading your response center capacity, you may want to stagger your in-home dates. Drop shipping allows control of when mail is delivered to destination postal facilities so response centers aren't flooded by an avalanche of simultaneous responses.

In addition, drop shipping offers better test marketing control and tracking ability. Since truck manifests clearly show mail routes, determining when a piece of mail is delivered to destination postal facilities is easy and accurate. Drop shipping allows mail to become "modular" so all trays and pallets are fully traceable: each piece of mail belongs to a tray, each tray belongs to a pallet, and each pallet belongs to a truck. This level of tracing isn't possible without drop shipping.

Outsourcing Direct Mailing Services

If you, like many finishing companies, choose to outsource drop shipping services, ask your direct mailer to perform a data-file analysis to determine how much your client's job will benefit. Some projects just aren't a good fit for drop shipping and an up-front analysis can prevent a lot of wasted effort.

Your mailing company should process your data to achieve maximum drop shipping and postal savings. Large mailing companies that send out regularly scheduled trucks throughout the country can "overlay" the transportation schedules of work already in house over the data of a proposed job and accurately calculate drop-ship savings. Once production on a job has begun, staging it in a drop-ship order that matches jobs already in-house will maximize postal discounts for all involved customers. For example, if your mailing has only ten thousand pieces going to Boston, piggybacking it onto another truck with the same destination may prevent LTL shipments for several companies.

For-profit customer	Client 1	Client 2
Pieces mailed	6,000,000	500,000
Pieces drop shipped to destination SCFs	4,000,000	325,000
Savings/1,000 pieces @ 2002 postal rates	$26	$26
Savings per each mailing	$104,000	$8,450
Pieces drop shipped to destination BMCs	2,000,000	175,000
Savings/1,000 pieces @ 2002 postal rates	$26	$26
Savings per each mailing	$52,000	$4,550
Total postal saving	$156,000	$13,000
Mailing and shipping costs	$63,000	$4,000
Total net savings to customer	$93,000	$9,000
Net savings per 1,000 pieces	$15.50	$18.00

Examples of drop-shipping savings.

Mailing Companies "Pay" You to Process Your Mail

Often, mailing processing costs are far less than the accompanying postal savings. This means direct mail companies essentially "pay" their customers to process mail. Take a look at the following two actual examples of direct mail customers. Client #1 runs four large mailing jobs each year and nets annual postal savings of more than

$350,000 on these jobs alone. Client #2 mails smaller regional jobs and typically saves about $9,000 every month that it mails. (Note: Client #2 saved more on a per-1,000-piece basis because its mail is sent only to a limited geographic area: the East Coast). These are real examples of organizations that greatly benefit from drop shipping. In short, drop-ship savings can be a tremendous competitive advantage if properly planned and executed.

*   *   *

The Final Word...

Drop-shipping programs are not for every company. Some organizations insist that their mail must enter the USPS postal stream on a particular day, regardless of impact on in-home delivery dates. Those who need the security of a postal receipt showing that mail was delivered to a postal facility on a particular day shouldn't use drop-ship services. However, for faster delivery, more production control, and maximum postal savings, it pays to explore the benefits of large-volume drop shipping.

Contributors:

• *Ken Boone, Boone Consulting, Baltimore, Maryland*

62 Fulfillment

While fulfillment has different meanings in different industries, graphic arts companies commonly use it to mean the storing and distribution of products directly to end users—after the initial job has been printed and mailed.

What You Will Learn

- Tracking inventory
- Computerized systems
- Coordination with mailing

Fulfillment seems simple, but attention to detail and quality inventory systems are critical to success. In fact, fulfillment is much more than storing and shipping because there are many technical aspects to full-service fulfillment.

Inventory Management

An efficient inventory tracking system is an important component of a comprehensive fulfillment program. It is not unusual for a fulfillment operation to store dozens, even hundreds, of different items (SKUs in the retail world) such as bound catalogs, CD-ROM discs, audio tapes, inserts, flyers, packaging sleeves, registration cards, shipping cartons, and so forth. Often processed daily, orders must be fulfilled on an individual basis as they arrive, some requiring all of the materials, others only a few. A good fulfillment operation needs a well-organized storage and retrieval system that monitors quantities, replenishes stock when necessary, and allows fast and easy access to ensure delivery deadlines are met.

Electronic Communication

Another important fulfillment-related capability is efficient electronic communication. After the initial job has been printed, bound, and mailed, postpress companies are frequently asked to deal directly with the client for subsequent mailings. Email, modem, and online electronic communication methods enable easy, accurate, and instantaneous data transfer. As orders are received, electronic transmission allows rapid fulfillment of the product.

When fulfillment companies receive fulfillment orders, they should retrieve the items from the warehouse and automatically subtract them from the client's inventory totals. Automated processing and record keeping allow real-time answers to inventory questions. Having access to precise inventory information can translate into big savings for publishers because they can order exact quantities of needed product, thereby reducing inventory waste.

Inkjet Labeling in Conjunction with Fulfillment

Most fulfillment houses have addressing equipment designed for labeling outbound material with adhesive labels. Due to their size limitations, labels restrict the amount of information that can be printed on them. On the other hand, inkjet printing equipment allows more space and flexibility for printing marketing messages directly onto fulfilled mail. It eliminates the cost of labels and provides clients with the opportunity to tailor other marketing offers to their most qualified prospects—namely, customers who have already purchased their product or service.

Some fulfillment companies offer computerized inkjet printing on mailing lines. Packages are automatically positioned on the conveyor belt and inkjet imaged with the address, as well as any other information, text, or image, as they pass under the inkjet printer.

Mailing Services

A good fulfillment operation should also include comprehensive distribution services. Today, computers drive most equipment, keeping production costs down by streamlining and automating work that formerly required hand processing. Finishers that have combined fulfillment and mailing operations offer other benefits. They can help clients take full advantage of the many United States Postal Service (USPS) discounts. For instance, fulfillment companies that are certified by the USPS for in-plant load and direct shipment deliveries can save customers, such as large catalog publishers, tens and even hundreds of thousands of dollars in postage fees.

Full-service finishers that perform fulfillment and mailing services often provide other adjunct services, such as media replication and machine insertion into packaging, catalogs, or periodicals. They can be invaluable assets to printers who are bidding on work requiring fulfillment. Expect your full-service finisher to join you and your customer in early client meetings to design a fulfillment strategy that satisfies unique customer needs. By relying on your finisher's expertise, printers won't waste time getting up to speed on the technical details of fulfillment and mailing.

Printers should evaluate the cost benefit and ease of integrating a finisher into their existing operations before making a decision to offer vertically integrated fulfillment services. Printers have found that the benefits of using finishers with fulfillment capabilities outweigh the outsourcing costs.

*   *   *

The Final Word...

Increasingly, clients look toward their printers to provide a full range of print-related services—including fulfillment and mailing—to compress production times and reap the benefits inherent in sole-sourcing.

Contributor:

- *Marty Anson, Bindagraphics, Inc., Baltimore, Maryland*
  www.bindagraphics.com

Section V
Graphic Arts Management

63 Postpress Quality Assurance

Every bindery has produced jobs that it is embarrassed to admit came in the front door, let alone went out the back—and yet the customer was delighted. Similarly, every bindery has produced what it thought would be award-winning work, but for some reason, the customer was disappointed. What can we conclude? Just this: Quality is whatever the customer needs it to be.

What You Will Learn

- Paper trails are important
- Production time pulls
- Policy examples

On a job-by-job basis, binderies should make every effort to discover how customers define quality and adapt their internal standards to meet customer expectations. To accomplish this, at the very least, binderies need detailed purchase orders with written instructions and preproduction samples, proofs, or samples of prior jobs.

Get Correct Information

Quality assurance begins by obtaining the right information about what needs to be done, how it should be done, and what the applicable quality standards are. All job parameters should be precisely and completely defined. Binderies use the term **preflighting** to denote the process of obtaining and reviewing reliable and detailed information about every aspect of a job before manufacturing operations begin. Without proper information, the scheduler can't plan the job and department leaders won't know what is required.

The old adage that the only dumb question is the one left unasked is as true today as it ever was. Even a simple project like folding an 8½×11-in. sheet in half can be fraught with danger. Should the copy be out or in? Employees should be required to ask questions and get clear instructions before production, even if they're 99% sure that "the copy's out." Rule-up sheets, customer samples, proofs, and any other required information should be collected before production. Preflight all jobs so your customers can be alerted to possible production glitches while there is plenty of time to react.

Prevent miscommunication by speaking in terms of measurements, not standards. For example, avoid saying "standard three-hole drill." Specify "three-hole drill, 4¼-in. center to center, ⁵⁄₁₆-in. diameter hole," because these terms are clearer. Imprecise language leads to wrong assumptions, which can turn profitable companies into unprofitable ones.

Setup

When a bindery has compiled all the information necessary to begin a job, an internal job order must be written up in clear, straightforward language that every operator and supervisor understands. After the job order is approved, but before production begins, a series of approvals and signoffs should be collected.

Maintaining acceptable quality for a wide range of products in a job shop environment is difficult but not impossible. Carefully planned and implemented quality assurance systems are mandatory. More errors are caught when operators develop "ownership" of their job performance and when additional sets of trained eyes look at each job.

Common Issues

When any of the following events occur, make sure that every affected person within your organization knows what happened and their impact on them:

- *Job order changes.* Although this hardly needs to be said, when job specifications change, make sure that everyone knows about them.
- *Employee failure to read or understand a job order.* When an employee makes a mistake and misunderstands instructions, a quality assurance system based on checks and balances should kick in and prevent small mistakes from turning into disasters.
- *Incorrect information.* Good binderies try to double-check everything and inform their customers about their concerns. Binderies should strive to be the "eyes and ears" for their customers while their jobs are "guests" at the plant.
- *Production counts.* Finished work must be counted accurately to ensure that customer quantity requirements are met.

A good motto is, "If it's not written down, it didn't happen." In other words, if someone can't document that they did something, then by default they didn't do it. All employees need to understand this so negative fingerpointing rarely occurs. The paper trail should begin with an instruction sheet that is filled out for every job and provides clear makeready, production, and sample directions. Items like "watch for hickeys" or "pull dog-ears" need to be clearly communicated.

Next, create a unique makeready checklist sheet for every finishing operation. For example, a company in the Midwest has a perfect-binding form with nineteen checkboxes. The cutting form has sixteen check items, and stitching has seventeen.

The first item on all checklists requires setup people to read the instruction sheet. The last item verifies that the job adheres to instruction sheet packing directions. A pre-approved operator or setup person needs to OK the makeready sample. Then, a department supervisor also OKs the job. Some processes, such as high-speed poly-bagging, require a third sign-off because it's easy for people to confuse how poly-bag projects are plowed, overlapped, and inserted.

Whenever this company begins production on a job, the first product off the machine is pulled and every page is examined. Time pulls and visual inspections continue at regular intervals and are approved, time/date stamped, logged, and saved. The interval is never more than an hour and can be as frequent as every ten, or even five, minutes. Part of the control procedure is to check component counts versus final count requirements. If production is short on a job component, the customer will be notified early and the fruitless "who pays for the extra makeready?" conversation is eliminated.

All production waste is saved and bins aren't emptied until a count has been made. Production pulls are kept for ninety days unless the customer requests a longer period of time. Included with customer samples is a self-addressed and prepaid job evaluation postcard.

Production

A company's quality assurance system should include procedural instructions for every machine in the plant. Here are some actual examples:

Example 1
- *Policy:* Carefully follow sample pull examination schedules.
- *Benefit:* Production spoilage is low, and when something is wrong, it's usually easy to isolate the problem.
- *Example:* A web perf disappeared in the middle of a 250,000-piece perfect-binding job. The operator caught the problem early, identified the culprit signature, stopped the job, fixed it offline, and continued to manufacture a properly functioning product.

Example 2
- *Policy:* Prior to manually loading feeders on virtually every machine in the plant, each lift is fanned through and quickly inspected.
- *Benefit:* Several times a month printing quality problems, such as jumping print or incorrectly backed up sheets, are discovered and the customer is notified. Some companies will only call our client when they've had press problems because they know their goal is to function as their "eyes and ears" while their job is outsourced.
- *Example:* A cutting operator producing a small-quantity job fanned through a lift and noticed that 75% of the sheets were flipped. They were promptly

turned around and the cut was properly made. This small catch prevented the job from being shipped short.

Example 3

- **Policy:** Produce a complete sample of every mechanically bound job by hand prior to production. Collate all the signatures, tabs, flysheets, and so forth, then trim, punch, and bind.

- **Benefit:** Copy-punching problems have virtually been eliminated. These pre-production samples frequently uncover improperly stripped signatures. With this policy, customers don't have to be called and told, "The whole book is four-knife trimmed and we're punching into type. What do you want to do?" Instead, customers are called before collation and the problem is explained before any of the job has been converted. This means that one signature can be reprinted, rather than the whole book.

- **Example:** A 25,000-piece Wire-O book included a lot of maps but had a margin problem. The customer was able to reprint one signature at less than 25% of the cost of any other solution…and still make the deadline.

Example 4

- **Policy:** Instruction sheets must be reviewed prior to sample OKs.

- **Benefit:** Job details aren't left to memory or chance.

- **Example:** A 7,000,000-piece magazine insert job was being cut. The customer's samples were to be cut to a different size. Even after many days of repetitious production, the cutting operator followed policy, re-read the instruction sheet, and correctly cut the sample lot.

Example 5

- **Policy:** Instruction sheets must be reviewed during production runs.

- **Benefit:** All customer directions are followed.

- **Example:** A 100,000-piece, 5½×8½-in. (215.9×279.4-mm), 96-page perfect-bound book was near the end of its run. The instruction sheet specified that 500 Wire-O books were needed. For production efficiency, the "best case" plan was to cut the spine off of perfect-bound books although it hadn't yet been determined that there was enough margin to avoid punching into copy. The instruction sheet required converting a perfect-bound book into a Wire-O book in the middle of the perfect-binding run. Because the sample did indeed punch into copy, our client withheld enough stock to run the Wire-O job separately, with no grinding or gluing, to ensure an adequate punching margin.

Example 6

- **Policy:** Each production person who handles a job must place their own unique 1×1-in. (25.4×25.4-mm) numerical identification tag on every packed lift.

- **Benefit:** A company can seamlessly integrate themselves with their customers while maintaining the ability to trace completed work.

- **Example:** A bindery once produced half of a 6,000,000-piece stitching job, with the rest being produced elsewhere. The customer noticed a production problem, and both postpress services companies were called in to do an inspection. Because the product was packed in identical boxes, the only unique identifier was a 1×1-in. identification tag used by the first company. Since the problem was traced to the other company's work, the customer only had to inspect the boxes without tags.

* * *

The Final Word...

Graphic arts companies need more than dedication and skills to produce top-quality products. Effective quality assurance requires systems that ensure consistent results. When organizations function as their customers' "eyes and ears," minor problems are stopped dead in their tracks and are prevented from becoming major. In the highly competitive graphic arts industry, labor costs, raw material costs, the bottom line, and client goodwill are on the firing line every time a job is produced. Consequently, an effective quality assurance program is absolutely vital.

Contributors:

- *Mark Beard, Finishbinders, Inc., Des Moines, Iowa*
  www.finishbinders.com

- *Peter Pape, The Riverside Group, Rochester, New York*
  www.riversidegroup.com

- *Jack Rickard, Rickard Bindery, Chicago, Illinois*
  www.rickardbindery.com

64 Simplicity Is a Virtue

In our detail-oriented industry, it's easy to get wrapped up in needless complexity when it's often the simple approach that is the most effective way to get things done. Simple work processes and direct communication make busy peoples' business lives easier.

What You Will Learn

- Consolidate information for simplified planning
- Use lot and code numbers for easy verification
- Carefully consider plant layouts to simplify workflows

Remember the "telephone game" we used to play as children? You know: one person whispers a phrase into the ear of the next person, who repeats it to the next person, and so on, until the last person hears the message and repeats it for everyone else. Do you remember how simple phrases mysteriously changed? As information passes from ear to ear, it gets distorted. A statement like, "This fall, the Red Sox will win the World Series" may end up as, "Don't fall on red rocks and ripe berries."

Information Gathering

Why do some companies still insist we play a grown-up version of the telephone game during the estimating process? Here's how estimate information is gathered at some companies: Sales reps get estimates from customers, then pass them to CSRs, who in turn give them to estimators. If an estimator needs clarification or more information, the request travels the reverse path: from estimator to CSR to sales rep to customer. Then it goes from customer to sales rep to CSR and back to the estimator. That's a lot of personnel deployed to handle simple questions like, "Does it three-hole punch?" or "What is the fold sequence?"

Wouldn't it be simpler if an estimator picked up the phone and asked the customer the relevant questions without going through extraneous intermediaries? Some sales representatives want to control all forms of customer contact, but is this cumbersome "mother hen" approach practical or beneficial? Most of us can point to certain customers who need handholding, but is this formal communication flow necessary in all cases?

Lots and Code Numbers

Marketing can be a wonderful thing. Operating in the information age means we can test various marketing offers, promotional words, color schemes, demographics, and virtually any other job component. All this marketing flexibility has very real and sometimes complicated consequences for the bindery. A lot of cutting-edge bindery work features coded "lots." If these lots aren't identified by clearly visible codes on the piece, the chances of production errors dramatically increase.

Variable information is difficult to locate if it is buried deep within a piece. To ensure that the right material is used at the right time, machine operators need to be able to identify and understand the codes quickly. If these codes are placed in convenient places on a sheet, comparisons are easily made and the verification process is simple. Operators should not have to open the product and verify coding before proceeding.

It's been said that the postpress industry doesn't employ rocket scientists. This is true. No one your authors know has mastered quantum anything. Our industry employs people with good mechanical aptitude, manual dexterity, and attention to detail. If your project is so complicated that Ph.D.s are needed to understand it, you run a high risk of experiencing production problems. On the other hand, if it is carefully planned and clear and simple communication is used, your job will be a success.

An Example: "Dutch-Cut" Layouts

Simplicity is important when planning press sheet impositions. If your project needs to have "Dutch" cuts (multiple forms placed in unusual sheet positions), reduce your cutting time by aligning common trim positions. For example, if you have a 16-page signature and a 6-page signature imposed on the same press sheet, lay them out so that they share a common trim. You should position the forms such that a single cut will trim the edge off of both forms with one stroke. This simple decision will save your cutter at least two cuts.

Dutch cuts save paper, but your finisher needs to manage forms with different grain directions carefully. Problems will be avoided if your bindery separates and clearly marks the lots by grain direction. If not, they will be mixed up and the grain direction will shift during production, resulting in wildly varying fold positions. If the lots are clearly marked, they can be completely separated and run sequentially. If setup adjustments are necessary between lots, only one change will be needed. Good Dutch-cut planning needn't slow production down at all.

Plant Layout

Some graphic arts plants seem devoid of workflow planning altogether. Companies that place machinery wherever it happens to be convenient at a given time will pay the price on the future bottom line. Simple plant layouts are often the most efficient. A good rule of thumb is to try to move printed material as little as possible. Place the machines with the most tonnage passing through them as close to your loading dock as possible. Do yourself a favor: Plan for a simple workflow. It will make things easier for your people and help you get the work out more quickly.

*   *   *

The Final Word...

Work is hard enough: Don't make it harder. Is there any process you can simplify?

Contributor:

- *Kevin Rickard, Rickard Bindery, Chicago, Illinois*
  www.rickardbindery.com

65 Spoilage

Graphic arts companies must make a profit and remain price competitive. Good spoilage planning helps companies do both. Every significant printing job incurs some spoilage. Since spoilage rates aren't consistent, it's impossible to predict exactly how many sheets will be wasted during any given production run.

What You Will Learn

- Production spoilage causes
- Spoilage during folding
- Spoilage during direct mail

Many things cause bindery spoilage, and many others are just thought to cause bindery spoilage. It helps to know the difference.

Paper characteristics such as thickness, curl, brittleness, grade, and coatings are very important. In general, thin sheets are more easily damaged than thicker ones. For example, when planning saddle-stitched jobs, 4-page signatures should be given twice the spoilage allowance of 16-pagers if the paper is the same weight. Exposure to too much heat can make paper and ink brittle, resulting in excessive cracking and increased spoilage. As the job runs, accumulated press powder and varnish buildup will gradually change the grip of the fold rollers, changing the fold position. Humidity will make paper limp, but excessive dryness can cause static. Either condition can prevent the sheets from moving squarely into plate sections, again increasing spoilage. Here, we discuss these and other conditions in greater detail.

In the bindery, varnish can be both friend and foe. On the one hand, it generally doubles the amount of spoilage during folding; on the other, it certainly reduces marking problems. Varnish buildup eventually changes the coefficient of friction of the fold rollers. Inexperienced operators tend to change fold settings instead of cleaning the rollers. In most cases, cleaning will cause the fold position to return to its original setting.

Shipping

A lot of so-called "bindery" spoilage actually occurs during transportation from the pressroom to the bindery. When shipping printed material between facilities, some damage is inevitable. Not surprisingly, the amount of damage is directly related to the care given during shipping preparation and the skill levels of those involved. Sometimes packing choices come down to the lesser of two evils. Improperly applied banding wire can cut into and damage sheets. Stretch-wrapping without corner boards will bend the corners of the sheets, causing downstream machine-feeding problems. The key to minimizing transit damage is to contain the product carefully and tightly so it won't vibrate during transit or slip off the pallet.

Many wood pallets and tops are made from new, or "green," wood with high moisture content. Without a barrier, moisture will migrate from the wood to the paper. This moisture migration can destroy up to ½ in. of otherwise perfectly good printed material.

Folding Spoilage

Folding is a common area for unplanned spoilage. Here are a few things to watch for:

Improper folding layouts. When laying out any product with decreasing panel size, make sure you shorten each succeeding fold should by about ³⁄₃₂ in. (on normal text-weight stock). This will reduce production spoilage caused by "bend-overs."

Right-angle folds. Spoilage on folders increases as the number of right-angle folds increases. Each directional change gives paper another opportunity to misalign along a side guide or to have a corner caught. Once a jam occurs, sheets continue to pile up behind the jam until the operator stops the machine. Clearly, this wastes a lot of paper.

Recycled paper. Recycled paper can be difficult to work with. The fibers in recycled sheets are inconsistent and short, causing a host of problems, not the least of which is frequent machine jamming. Saddle-stitching production rates usually aren't adversely affected by recycled stock, but operators must constantly check that the backbone is strong enough to hold the stitches firmly. When folding recycled paper at right angles, special attention should be paid to score depth. If the scores are too deep, the paper will split. If they are too shallow, the fold won't occur in the intended position, producing "dog-ears." Since the nature of recycled fiber paper is so inconsistent, operators must find a way to deal effectively with the frustrating fact that the same score setting on two different sheets may yield split paper on the one hand and dog-ears on the other. When allowing for folding spoilage, you should plan on wasting twice as many sheets whenever recycled stock is involved.

Mixed stock. Mixing brands, grades, or even different lots of the same paper will increase spoilage. If a pressman runs out of stock and substitutes a similar sheet, expect different performance levels in the bindery. Paper lot changes should be clearly marked on skids and kept separate as the job transfers between departments. For example, if a cutting operator finishes cutting a job and mixes different papers without identifying which is which, a folding operator will have no idea why a fold position suddenly moved and why the crossover, which was perfect ten sheets ago, is now ⅛ in. out of alignment. If the operator doesn't waste a lot of sheets making the necessary adjustments, he is at least likely to waste a lot of time. Worse, if an unmarked skid from the first lot remains to be used, the machine will have to be readjusted to the original settings. In general, whenever different stock is used on a job, allow for 1½% additional spoilage.

Cut it out. Who should do the cutting: the bindery or the printer? In general, yields will be higher if the bindery cuts the product to final size. Whenever work in process is packed and shipped, some sheets will have damaged corners, curls, and little rips. If your bindery cuts the product after shipping, however, a lot of the damage can be trimmed off during the final cuts, eliminating a lot of "bindery" spoilage.

Personalized products. Personalized jobs requiring 100% successful bindery conversion present special spoilage problems. Let's assume you have a 10,000-piece personalized job and the bindery successfully converts 9,800 of them. From the saved waste, a list of the unsuccessful 200 names can be regenerated. Then, three consecutive lots of the destroyed pieces should be re-personalized, such that every record has three chances of being properly converted. During the second run of 600 pieces (200×3), it is highly unlikely that the exact same sequentially positioned documents would be spoiled on three successive passes, thus making "100% mailings" both doable and manageable.

Overs/unders. Most print customers will accept some flexibility in final count because they understand that graphic arts production involves many variables. Industry standards permit 10% overruns and 10% underruns for most jobs. As the following example illustrates, it is to your customers' economic benefit to accept the industry standard.

If a customer orders 100,000 pieces and won't allow any "unders," prudent estimators will plan to net 110,000 good pieces to eliminate the risk of going back to press at their own expense in the event of an "under" situation. Every manufacturing stage at which spoilage is expected should assign a reasonable expectation of product loss. A 100,000-piece job with no unders allowed will be priced at 110,000 pieces, effectively inflating the price by 10%. Why not just order 110,000 pieces and get an additional 10,000 pieces at no additional charge? (Hint: You should.)

Direct Mail Considerations

In direct mail projects, the question, "How many should I produce?" is one that often goes unanswered until the last second. The resulting decision shouldn't be made in haste, particularly if you want to be sure every name in your database receives your communication. A typical mail campaign will pass through several production steps before it's ready for distribution: printing, perforating, diecutting, folding, lasering, tabbing, stamping, inserting, and more. There's no way to predict exactly how many pieces of stock might be spoiled during the various personalization and mailing production processes. Several quick formulas are available that can assist you in calculating a basic ballpark allowance for processing needs. Making these quick calculations helps to alleviate those costly and annoying stock shortages and reprints.

For direct mail campaigns, spoilage amounts should be computed separately for personalization (lasering), if applicable, and mail processing (folding, inserting, etc).

The spoilage totals for each process then should be combined to determine the total amount of stock needed. The following tables break down industry standard spoilage guidelines for each process:

List Quantity	Spoilage
Less than 999	10%
1,000–2,499	7%
2,500–4,999	5%
5,000–9,999	3%
10,000–24,999	2%
25,000–49,999	1%
50,000–99,999	1%
100,000–above	0.5%

List Quantity	Spoilage
Less than 999	25%
1,000–2,499	15%
2,500–4,999	10%
5,000–9,999	5%
10,000–24,999	4%
25,000–49,999	3%
50,000–99,999	2.5%
100,000–above	2%

*Mail processing spoilage guidelines. **Note:** These are guidelines only; every shop will be different.*

*Data processing spoilage guidelines. **Note:** These are guidelines only; every shop will be different.*

For example, a personalized self-mailer that's being sent to 20,000 names should have processing spoilage calculated as follows:

Mail Processing: $20,000 \times 2\% = 400$ expected spoilage

Data Processing: $20,000 \times 4\% = 800$ expected spoilage

This results in a total expected spoilage of 1,200 pieces during the personalization and mailing processes, based on a total anticipated mailing quantity of 20,000 names. Please note that these calculations are for data and mail processing spoilage only. There are separate industry standards for printing over- and underruns, as well as manufacturing tolerances for custom-produced items such as special window envelopes.

*   *   *

The Final Word...

How can spoilage rates be predicted when it's well known that the same job, run twenty times, will have twenty different yields? There is no substitute for bindery experience and technical competence in this area. Every job, including direct mail projects, needs to be individually analyzed for spoilage exposure.

Contributors:

- *Sylvia Konkel, EU Services, Rockville, Maryland*
  www.euservices.com

- *Jack Rickard, Rickard Bindery, Chicago, Illinois*
  www.rickardbindery.com

66 ISO 9000 Certification

Progressive companies strive to define and measure the elusive concepts of "quality" and "service." Like the old story of a group of blind men who have wildly different concepts of what an elephant is, each person has different views about quality and service.

While fads come and go in the graphic arts industry, some issues continue to be prominently discussed. For example, how does a company maintain profitability? How can a company attract new customers while satisfying current ones? What can a company do to improve products and services? Finally, how does a company beat the competition? Good business leaders look for systems and processes that can help answer these tough questions. ISO 9000 is one solution manufacturers from many industries have turned to for answers to these issues.

What You Will Learn

- ISO 9000 defined
- Productivity benefits
- Customer benefits

What Is ISO 9000?

The ISO 9000 philosophy can be summarized in four steps: (1) say what you do, (2) do what you say, (3) be able to prove it, and (4) improve it. ISO 9000 is a rigorous, thorough system of quality assurance standards for manufacturing and service organizations. These standards were first widely adopted by businesses in the European Economic Community and are now being accepted and implemented by many North American companies. Intended to help businesses improve internal processes through the implementation of effective quality management systems, these standards also give customers a method of comparing competing vendors. For some companies, ISO 9000 has also served as a useful foundation for Total Quality Management (TQM) and other quality-improvement programs.

At the cornerstone of ISO 9000 is a comprehensive audit and documentation method that covers objectives, production processes, quality policies, job descriptions, organizational charts, customer requirements, quality control procedures, and problem-solving tools. Ideally, all this documentation results in clearly stated quality control instructions that are implemented company-wide. Documentation can take the form of manuals, flow charts, and diagrams.

ISO 9000 Benefits

Companies that adopt ISO 9000 standards offer their customers a reliable, widely accepted yardstick against which to measure performance or quality. Internally, the formalization and standardization of processes helps employees become more productive. As companies clearly document their operating procedures and methodically audit them, the likelihood of employee ambiguity and misunderstanding dramatically diminishes. This helps decrease frustration and allows people to do their jobs more effectively and efficiently.

Some large printers have hoisted the ISO 9000 banner because their customers require suppliers to be ISO 9000 certified. As more companies enter international markets, certification, or lack thereof, has become an issue. Even if a printer doesn't have any foreign clients, its customers may, and this exerts pressure on printers to become ISO 9000 certified.

The best reasons printers should consider adopting ISO 9000 standards are to meet customer expectations, improve manufacturing processes, reduce waste, and increase profit margins. Also, certification provides a competitive advantage when seeking new business and forming strategic partnerships. As an added bonus, companies discover that ISO 9000 certification helps their marketing efforts.

A Different Vantage Point

ISO 9000, however, has its critics because it focuses on processes and does not guarantee the quality of the finished product. Detractors have suggested that quality would be measured better through actual product improvements than detailed documentation. One author has pointed out that it's possible to comply with ISO 9000 standards and still have inferior products. While this may be possible, it doesn't mean there's anything

Bindagraphics, the first ISO 9000-certified bindery.

wrong with ISO 9000 itself; rather, the system was never meant to be the answer to all quality issues and business concerns. ISO 9000's true benefit is that it provides a framework for a comprehensive, long-term quality-improvement program.

Why Should a Bindery Become ISO 9000 Certified?

Postpress finishing companies are at the end of the production chain. For that reason, they must respond to the quality expectations of not only customers, but also to their customers' customers. The ISO 9000 certification process has forced a formalization of systems and operating procedures that has improved the quality of services while achieving better productivity. It focuses on eliminating redundancy and inefficient processes that lead to production mistakes and inconsistencies.

In general, the errors of a company lay not with its employees but with its production system. For example, some procedures may never be carried out the same way twice or executed in the most efficient manner. The lack of standardized methods can leave a company vulnerable to errors, oversights, and miscommunication. The ISO 9000 process forces consistent procedural standards, which in turn replaces improvisation with clarity and order. The result is a system that emphasizes a preventive, rather than a reactive, approach to solving potential production problems.

*   *   *

The Final Word...

No matter how talented a company's workforce is, without standardized procedures and continuous improvement even the best people cannot deliver consistently outstanding results. ISO 9000 doesn't claim to point companies in the right direction; rather, it makes day-to-day operations go more smoothly and efficiently.

Contributor:

• *Marty Anson, Bindagraphics, Inc., Baltimore, Maryland*
  www.bindagraphics.com

67 Managing Business Growth and Expansion

Companies can grow the right way or the wrong way. Making commitments, spreading growth across many customers, and maintaining profitability is the right way. Poorly servicing small customers that helped build your business, being disproportionately dependent on your larger customers, and letting profitability slide in the name of growth is the wrong way.

What You Will Learn

- Cash flow/working capital
- Purchasing equipment
- Staffing issues

Growing graphic arts companies should do what their customers need them to do, almost regardless of effort. Prospective employees just looking to punch a clock shouldn't be offered work, no matter how desirable their skills are. Ownership should make it clear to new recruits that there are long-term benefits to being part of a growing team. At the same time, short-term sacrifices are necessary. If people aren't willing to accept that the customer is "king," they shouldn't be on board. In a tough labor market, it's not easy finding exceptional people, but they do exist. When growing companies are full of customer-oriented employees, productivity soars, customers are happy, more work comes in, and people earn more money.

During growth, it's the little things that can drive you nuts. A once-roomy building can suddenly feel cramped. The lunch room, bathrooms, and locker areas can become too small. Seemingly overnight, a rapidly growing company can outgrow its telephone system, parking lot, job staging area, or air conditioning system. Expenses become "$2,000 here, $5,000 there, and $10,000 somewhere else." The aggregate of these small expenses, combined with large equipment investments and increased working capital demands, all add up to strained cash flow.

Get the Cash

Cash flow is the lifeblood of any company, and it is even more important in a rapidly growing business. Poor cash flow has brought some companies to the brink of disaster even though their growth was profitable. It can and does happen. Help yourself by involving your bank in major decisions. If increased market share is a strategic goal, good communication prevents anxiety on both sides of the banker's desk.

Cash-flow management can be difficult during labor-intensive business expansion. Your people are paid on an inflexible net five-day basis compared to net thirty days for raw materials like paper, ink, glue, and wire. Employee benefits and taxes for all practical purposes also accrue immediately.

Effect of New Equipment on Working Capital

When purchasing machinery, determine your labor cost as a percentage of your total revenue and appropriately increase your working capital. A rule of thumb is to set aside at least 15%—and preferably more—of a machine's purchase price to satisfy working capital requirements. (For more on working capital requirements, see Chapter 68 on vertical integration.)

Facilities Expansion = Murphy's Law

Before expanding your facility, learn the building business. New equipment purchases often result in building expansions, which can be stressful to manage—after all, you're a graphic arts professional, not a contractor. Be sure to time equipment installations conservatively based on the construction schedule. Even if construction work begins on schedule, the undesirable situation of a new machine arriving before the roof and concrete foundation are finished can become reality if a contractor misses a deadline. The resulting delays in both installation and construction schedules that result from everyone having to work around each other can strain cash flow unnecessarily.

Staffing Issues

High growth requires keeping many good people in an employment pipeline. Even in a depressed economy such as the current one, your company may be lucky to get reliable employees when you need them. In addition to traditional advertising, try internal job postings and an incentive-based employee referral program.

The key success factor is proper management attention. For example, if a new shift is added and the company's owner and top managers work the new hours for at least a month, the shift will succeed. This may be rough on your top people, but it's a very effective way to show the new shift workers that they're a vital part of the company.

Management Philosophy

A growing company's management team must work well together and focus on profit. Rapid expansion can easily dilute management attention, and this has been the downfall of many rapid growth companies. A rapidly growing company should encourage its people to take calculated risks and make the best decisions they can so that employees don't have to rely on their president for answers. Unless employees are empowered, the energy and brainpower of top management will limit the success of the company. It's difficult for hands-on owners and managers to step back and guide the growth process, but it is necessary.

Supplier relationships are very important, too. Business relationships are never enhanced when suppliers use vendors as unwitting financing sources. Rapidly growing companies should carefully manage their cash flow so that their vendors can be paid in a timely fashion. In turn, growth companies should ask for, and receive, excellent service.

*   *   *

The Final Word...

At some point, rapidly growing graphic arts companies face glass revenue ceilings for a period of time—sometimes months or perhaps years. Owners that learn to rely on their top managers, develop self-duplicating systems, and let go of day-to-day crisis management greatly help their companies. It's tough standing on the sidelines and watching your people make mistakes, but maintaining rapid and profitable growth depends upon it.

Contributors:

- *Mark Beard, Finishbinders, Inc., Des Moines, Iowa*
  www.finishbinders.com

- *Jeff Klein, Spiral of Ohio, Inc., Cleveland, Ohio*
  www.spiralohio.com

- *Ed Miller, K&W Finishing, Inc., Baltimore, Maryland*
  www.kwfinishing.com

68 Vertical Integration

Outsourcing is the way the world does business. More and more companies are sticking to their core competency areas and outsourcing the rest. The graphic arts industry as a whole has been slow to embrace the outsourcing model. Not any longer.

What You Will Learn

- Sizing your investment
- Risk assessment
- Working capital issues

A typical graphic arts job touches all these bases: design, photography, copy, layout, plates, press, bindery, and mail. A leading industry association has long been advising printing companies to diversify into as many of these areas as possible so that the "value-added" percentage of their business increases. If this outdated business model sounds familiar, it is. Value-added concepts have been rammed down our throats for decades.

Printing companies that cling to "value-added" selling philosophies unnecessarily restrict their salespeople to the limited range of bindery services that they happen to produce in-house. These outdated business models encourage print sales representatives to focus on selling what they happen to be able to produce without regard to their customer's needs.

To Buy or Not to Buy Equipment

Graphic arts companies frequently wrestle with equipment-buying decisions. Careful consideration should be given before action is taken whenever vertical integration is involved. By adhering to a few simple principles and answering some key questions, you will be able to decide if vertical integration is appropriate for your company.

Vertical integration occurs when companies add products or services that are fundamentally different than their core competencies. For example, if an automobile company were to manufacture its own car headlights, we would say they have vertically integrated because lighting is not a core competency. However, an automobile company that introduces a new line of cars targeted toward a different audience has not vertically integrated. Similarly, graphic arts companies that offer postpress equipment have vertically integrated, but those that add different printing presses have not. These definitions are important because the further a company strays from its core competencies, the more diluted its market impact becomes.

In our competitive marketplace, printers frequently are tempted to add ancillary postpress services. The lure of perceived scheduling control, value-added manufacturing, and increased profits cause some managers to consider adding bindery functions. Yes, there are situations when buying machinery outside of a company's core competency area is the right decision, but often "sure bets" negatively drain cash and managerial resources for years.

If your customer has made the decision to offer in-house postpress services, help them properly size the operation for maximum payback and minimum hassle. Because bindery operations will never be a printer's core business, help them make their bindery investment the right size to ensure profits and to minimize future headaches.

How Big Should a Bindery Investment Be?

If your printer is determined to get into bindery, have them identify their slowest period of the year and size their bindery to convert a maximum 80% of their expected volume at this low point. This will help them in four ways. First, it will be a hedge against overly optimistic sales forecasts. Second, their equipment will be run at or near a 100% utilization rate. Third, they will be able to farm out work that doesn't suit them well, while retaining the most desirable jobs. And fourth, their trade relationships will remain strong.

Their sales representatives probably complain about orders they could have written if only they had certain pieces of finishing equipment. They've probably been asked by top management if they are willing to commit to keeping new machinery consistently busy. As you know, the most common answer is "no," and herein lies the impasse.

Risk Assessment

How much risk should a printer be willing to accept to keep more work in-house? A major difference between printing and finishing is that most of a product's final value is already in the product when it arrives at the bindery. If a job goes sour on press, paper is wasted, but if a bindery job is ruined, the repercussions are much greater. On a typical printing job, perhaps 30% of a job's value is at risk on press. However, for a typical binding job, 90% or more of a job's value is at risk. If your goal is to make a 10% return on bindery operations and you're handling a job worth ten times your bindery conversion revenue, for every $100 of risk exposure, you have a potential profit of $1. In short, the risk/return ratio in bindery is fundamentally different and much lower than what you're used to in printing.

Management Attention

Will ancillary services significantly divert a printer's attention and resources away from their core competencies? If you think of putting ink on paper as primarily being chemistry, prepress as being bits and bytes, and bindery as being mechanical, how far should the printer stray from their core business involving a completely different skill set? Cutting-edge printers with core competencies in the latest prepress and pressroom technologies may have employees already spread too thinly. Can they absorb another significantly different operation? Will they be able to devote the proper amount of managerial attention needed to harvest their investment?

Working Capital

Postpress cash flow issues are very different from those in printing. Printing tends to be very capital-intensive, while finishing is very labor-intensive. For example, a $1,000,000 printing press may require the same labor cost per manufacturing hour as a $200,000 piece of postpress equipment. In general, binderies need 75 cents of additional working capital for each dollar of equipment cost to cover direct labor expenses and normal collection of receivables. So based on the above example, most binderies would need a total of $350,000 of available cash to successfully purchase a $200,000 machine.

Also, when companies bring capabilities in-house, they essentially change their payable terms from net-thirty days to net-five. This is because labor must be paid once a week, which is five days on average. If your customer has extra cash, this may not be a problem. However, if they have little extra cash, they will be limiting their future flexibility, compromising core business responsiveness, and reducing their ability to satisfy their customers' needs.

Sometimes printers who are less familiar with labor-intensive bindery machinery make bindery expansion decisions that unexpectedly strain their cash flow. Printers who have dealt with bindery issues realize that some "no-brainer" bindery equipment purchases really are marginal after working capital considerations are factored into the cost.

Profit

What types of profits are most printers hoping to generate? Some companies view in-house bindery services as loss leaders. While this strategy sometimes works in the consumer products industry, it rarely does in the relationship-oriented graphic arts business. If a company won't make money on equipment operations, it shouldn't buy the equipment in the first place. In a job shop environment, it isn't worth it.

Selecting Equipment

Printing equipment tends to be versatile. If you purchase a press to handle certain types of work, and that work disappears, you likely will be able to use the press for a variety of other jobs. However, if you buy a stitcher and your big stitching job changes to perfect binding, how do you fill up your stitcher? Bindery equipment by its very nature is specialized and may not offer the flexibility you require. Are you certain that your demand for stitching will outlive your clients' current needs? Or is diecutting a better long-term bet, even though today it appears to be stitching? Unless you have exceptionally deep pockets, you will need to prioritize.

In addition, will your new postpress equipment operators have enough work to keep them busy over the long run? If you're not sure, will you feel pressure to integrate these new employees into existing operations for which they are not well-suited?

The Biggest Question of All

Let's sum up this chapter by repeating the biggest question of all. Doesn't sticking to your core competencies and outsourcing all the rest make sense? Much of the American business community thinks so.

*   *   *

The Final Word...

When analyzing vertical integration opportunities, such as bindery equipment, reduce your future stress and do your homework by considering three factors. First, always keep the best interests of your customer in mind. Second, maintain an appropriate risk level for your situation. Third, make a profit within a reasonable time frame. If you adhere to these principles, you will make the right choice, help your bottom line, and thrive in today's tricky business environment.

Contributors:

- *Jack Rickard, Rickard Bindery, Chicago, Illinois*
  www.rickardbindery.com

- *Frank Shear, Seaboard Bindery, Woburn, Massachusetts*
  www.seaboardbindery.com

- *Bob Windler, Diecrafters, Inc., Chicago, Illinois*
  www.diecrafters.com

69 Outsourcing

Have your customers turned away jobs because a postpress services vendor couldn't help them meet a tight deadline? If they could improve their outsourcing turnaround times, wouldn't they get more work through their plant? Here are some easily implemented and important steps they can take that will allow their finishing and binding partners to help them complete more work faster…and with fewer headaches.

What You Will Learn

- When to call for advice
- Supporting materials
- Reducing transit costs

Help your customers be proactive and speed up their outsourcing turnaround times. It's amazing how many jobs could have been turned around faster and cheaper, if only certain steps had been taken. They can save time and money by including you at the job planning stage. Make sure they clearly describe their product's end use.

For example, assume it's a laminating job that needs to withstand heavy use but also requires a rock bottom price and a quick turnaround. The first step is to explain their needs to you. In this situation, as a good laminator services supplier, you should advise them to increase the weight of the paper and reduce the laminate thickness.

Sending More Than a Purchase Order

For large jobs, have your clients make an extra set of proofs, bulking dummies, and rule-ups for the postpress vendor and deliver it as soon as possible—especially if they need to order materials such as wire, laminate, or glue. When customers don't give trade finishers and binderies much advance notice, they needlessly pay for rush production and shipping charges. However, if your supplier orders materials early enough, your cost savings may be significant. For example, special-order slit laminate material can dramatically reduce production cost, but requires advance notice.

In addition to requesting purchase orders (POs), proofs, and rule-up sheets, supply a sales order form to your customers. These forms should be an internal document that specifies all the information you need to efficiently and effectively produce their job. Giving customers this information allows you to completely plan their job for production in your shop. Filling out this form will reduce telephone tag, protect you in the case of miscommunication, and give you a greater sense of comfort once the job is produced and out of sight.

When postpress cost is a large percentage of total job size, always make sure that your client has included acceptable overs and unders on their PO. For small-run jobs, they might not think much of printing more overs than they really need, but if they don't specify when you should stop production, they usually will be charged for more product than they can bill. Obviously, this is a needless waste of money and production time.

Reduce Courier and Overnight Shipping Costs

Many graphic arts companies use courier and overnight services like water. Smaller jobs rushed by courier often can be sent via UPS instead, without missing any final deadlines. Put this extra money back in your customers' pockets, and watch them choose you over your competition over and over.

*   *   *

The Final Word...

Turn your capabilities into a strategic outsourcing advantage for your customers. Good communication is the first step. When you enthusiastically say, "yes, we can," you will win more jobs, turn them around on time, be more profitable, and have more fun in the process. Most of the examples in this chapter have been oriented around laminating, but these principles also work for binding and finishing in general.

Contributors:

- *Brian Hills, Nationwide Laminating, Lorton, Virginia*
  www.nationwidelaminating.com

- *Jack Rickard, Rickard Bindery, Chicago, Illinois*
  www.rickardbindery.com

- *Frank Shear, Seaboard Bindery, Woburn, Massachusetts*
  www.seaboardbindery.com

- *Bob Windler, Diecrafters, Inc., Chicago, Illinois*
  www.diecrafters.com

70 Finding and Keeping Good Employees

No matter what the balance sheet looks like, a company isn't worth much without its people. Finding good employees and developing a work environment that fosters happiness, motivation, and loyalty is critically important for long-term business success.

What You Will Learn

- Avoiding expensive want ads
- Two-way communication
- Employee teams

Every company needs good employees. Because many parts of the country have almost full-employment labor markets, finding, hiring, and retaining quality people is difficult. Low inflation makes the problem even tougher because competitive companies realistically are prevented from offering wages higher than the going market rate. Most of our clients have fought these employment battles on all fronts.

Companies that are successful at hiring frequently compete for employees by offering a superior work environment that emphasizes fairness, open communication, and advancement possibilities. Although top managers are the leaders of the business community, they should never forget that everyone is equal in the realm of human dignity. This means that respect is of the utmost importance. At good companies, any employee, in any position, can talk to any manager about virtually anything.

Finding Good People

In tight labor markets, many companies find that traditional employment advertising in major newspapers is expensive and largely ineffective. However, by looking for advertising opportunities in smaller papers with more focused distribution, you may save up to 90% of your advertising costs. We have a client that has experimented with off-hour, fifteen-second radio spots and has found the results to be encouraging. Radio advertising has the added benefit of appealing to existing customers, some of whom call to say, "Great radio ad!"

The best results for many companies are from employee referrals. Consider developing a formalized system that rewards the referrer when a referred applicant is hired and again when ninety days of acceptable employment is reached. To get skilled employees, such as lead operators, maintenance professionals, department heads, and shift supervisors, networking and referrals may be your best bet. Throughout the years, we've seen companies gradually stop running ads for skilled positions because of consistently poor results.

Once in the door, candidates should be screened for mechanical aptitude and appropriate job skills, then given an "attitude interview." Here, determine if the candidate is motivated, eager, and a team player. While candidates possessing both skills and a good attitude are certainly preferred, prioritize attitude over skills because skills can be taught while attitude can't.

Check all references and never hire anyone on the basis of one interview. To better gauge if a candidate really wants to work at your company, schedule a date and time for him or her to call you. If for any reason, the candidate doesn't follow these callback instructions, don't offer a job. If someone is unreliable during the interview process, why should subsequent performance as an employee be any different?

First Days on the Job

New employees should receive a formal orientation program. Prevent first-day jitters and take them through your plant, introduce your company's services to them, show them your operating and safety procedures, and introduce them to their coworkers. For the next few days, assign "buddies" to help them adjust to their new work environment. During their ninety-day trial period, carefully watch for performance or attendance problems. If any are detected, clearly explain the problem, extend the probationary period if necessary, and offer guidance to correct the behavior deficiency.

Employee Retention

Have you ever heard of the mushroom theory of management? "Keep 'em in the dark, cover 'em with fertilizer, and after two years, can 'em." Obviously, good employers don't do this. Is it possible for a graphic arts company to communicate well with its customers but not its employees? Probably not.

Business is built on good communication. Develop communication vehicles that efficiently move information all around your company. Extensively use bulletin boards, employee newsletters, and clearly written memos. People are happier and stay employed longer when their concerns are heard, valued, and acted upon. Work hard to know the concerns of your employees.

Bug Box

To facilitate communication between employees and management, one of our clients has a bug box (a suggestion box covered with printed bugs) centrally located in its plant. Employees are encouraged to write down whatever "bugs" them. The only rule for submissions is that they enclose a proposed solution.

One bug box contribution revealed that there was a problem in a bathroom that caused people to lose time waiting for water to heat up. Management followed the suggested recommendation of installing another water heater, which subsequently allowed people to save time and return to work faster. Another person informed the company that its outdoor lighting wasn't bright enough at night. Again, following the recommendation, more lights were installed, which improved safety. Not all suggestions can be implemented, but this bug box helps people know management values and respects good ideas.

No matter what you use as an employee idea solicitation vehicle, once a few suggestions are implemented and employees begin to believe that management is serious about listening, good ideas will begin to regularly flow. Consider publishing all suggestions and management responses in an employee newsletter. Soon two-way information flow will become a part of your company's culture.

Employee Teams

To tap the resources of your people and to facilitate idea ownership, encourage employees to join a "team" that meets to solve a specific problem. Conspicuously post the minutes of each meeting in your plant and make sure that significant contributors get public recognition. Teams should regularly meet until their goals are achieved. Team involvement can become a status symbol, making volunteer spots on the team a premium.

A perfect-binding team at one of our clients was assigned the task of getting a new perfect binder running quickly and efficiently. Within days of its formation, the team had the new binder running a very large job at full speed—with impeccable quality. These excellent results would not have been achieved without this team's valuable input.

Once people know their suggestions won't disappear into a proverbial management "black hole," great results should be achieved. At this company, some employees have even told their supervisors that their job satisfaction was higher after participating on a team than ever before.

Fun Environment

When an employee has a birthday, do something for them. A small cake or even a birthday card makes people feel special. When people achieve significant milestones, such as ten- or twenty-year employment anniversaries, stop production in their area and somehow acknowledge them in the presence of their coworkers. For a few precious moments, the rewarded employee is the center of everyone's attention. In addition, consider offering framed awards for both perfect attendance and exceptional performance and hang them on the lunchroom's walls. These programs don't cost much and clearly communicate that employees are valued.

Evaluations

Evaluate all employees on a regular basis. One company starts its evaluation process by having employees fill out self-evaluation forms. Next, a three-person management team reviews each form and adds comments. A manager then conducts a private meeting with the employee for a formal review. Areas of praise and concern are clearly communicated and the employee signs off on the evaluation form. Finally, the employee is encouraged to give feedback about his or her likes and dislikes of working. In a very real sense, this evaluation process is a two-way assessment.

*   *   *

The Final Word...

It's tough to achieve a good record of attracting excellent employees and keeping turnover rates low. In today's environment, where work is such a large and important part of everyone's life, try to create a "home-away-from-home" atmosphere. If people enjoy their job, everyone will be handsomely rewarded.

Contributors:

- *Mark Beard, Finishbinders, Inc., Des Moines, Iowa*
  www.finishbinders.com

Glossary

accordion fold. Two or more folds parallel to each other with adjacent folds in opposite directions, resembling the bellows of an accordion. Alternative term: *fanfold.*

adhesive binding. Applying a glue or another, usually hot-melt, substance along the backbone edges of assembled, printed sheets. The book or magazine cover is applied directly on top of the tacky adhesive. Alternative term: *perfect binding.*

adhesive bleed. Adhesive that seeps from pressure-sensitive stock before or after processing the finished product. The condition is caused by cold flow or clamp pressure. Alternative terms: *adhesive ooze; adhesive strike-through.*

apron. A blank space at the edge of a foldout that permits the sheet to be folded and tipped in during the finishing process without marring the copy.

archival paper. A long-lasting, nonacidic paper used increasingly to print books and other important records and documents.

assembling. Collecting individual sheets or signatures in a complete set with pages in proper sequence and alignment. Assembling takes place prior to binding. Alternative terms: *collating; gathering; inserting.*

back margin. The distance between the fold edge and the edge of the body of the type (text matter) next to the fold. Alternative terms: *binding margin; gutter margin.*

back matter. Material printed at the end of the book, including the appendix, addenda, glossary, index, and bibliography. Alternative term: *end matter.*

back spinner. The roller used to remove excess glue from the backbone in order to meter glue thickness on a perfect binder.

backbone. The portion of a bound book that connects the front and back covers. Alternative term: *spine.*

backing. See rounding and backing.

backlining. The piece of paper, muslin, or other material that reinforces the backs of books after rounding and backing.

bar code. A binary coding system using a numerical series and bars of varying thicknesses or positions that can be read by optical character recognition (OCR) equipment. Bar codes are used in printing and binding as tracking devices for jobs and sections of jobs in production.

basis weight. The weight in pounds of a ream (500 sheets) of paper cut to its basic size in inches.

bed. On a guillotine paper cutter, the flat metal surface on which the cutting is performed.

Bible paper. A very thin, lightweight, bright, strong, opaque paper made from rag and mineral fiber pulp.

bind. To join the pages of a book together with thread, wire, adhesive, crash (a coarse fabric), or other methods, or enclose them in a cover.

bind margin. The gutter or inner margin of a book, from the binding edge to the printed area.

binder's board. One of the stiffeners (a high-grade stiff pulp board) often used when making book covers. It is placed under cloth or paper binding materials.

binder's creep. See *creep.*

binder's waste. Spoilage allowance that permits the binder to supply the full count required by the job specifications.

binding. Joining the assembled pages of a printed piece together. Binding takes many forms including saddle-stitching, adhesive binding, mechanical binding, loose-leaf binding, and Smyth sewing.

binding, mechanical. Clasping individual sheets together with plastic, small wire, or metal rings. Two examples are three-ring binding and spiral binding.

binding dummy. Blank pages of the assembled signatures, stitched and trimmed to show the amount of compensation needed for creep.

binding edge. The side of the publication where the signatures are joined together.

bleed. A printing area that extends to the edge of the sheet or page after it is trimmed.

blind folio. A page number counted but not printed in a signature.

body. The printed text of a book not including the endpapers or cover.

book block. A book that has been folded, gathered, and stitched but not cased-in.

book cloth. A starch-filled, plastic-coated or impregnated cotton cloth used to form book covers.

book papers. A term used to describe a group of papers of a higher grade than newsprint, which are used primarily for book and publication printing and a wide variety of commercial printing applications. Book papers, as a class, include coated and uncoated papers in a wide variety of basis weights, colors, and finishes.

buckle folder. A bindery machine in which two rollers push the printed sheet between two metal plates, stopping it and causing it to buckle at the entrance to the folder. A third roller working with one of the original rollers uses the buckle to fold the paper. Buckle folders are best suited for parallel folding.

building-in. Placing cased-in books in a forming and pressing machine that holds them tightly under heat and pressure while the adhesive is drying.

bulking dummy. Blank sheets of the actual stock to be used to print the finished job, folded and gathered to show the thickness of the book.

case. In bookbinding, the hardcovers into which bound signatures are affixed.

case binding. The process that produces a hardcover book. Printed covering material is glued to rigid board material and then affixed to the book with endpapers.

casebound. A book bound with a stiff, hard cover.

casemaker. A machine that produces hardcovers for casebound books.

casing-in. Applying adhesive and combining a sewn and trimmed text with a cover (case).

cleat-laced binding. A method of repairing casebound books by first removing the case and cutting off the spine. Grooves are cut into the spine in a diamond pattern, thread is laced into the grooves, and the book is reattached to the case.

closed head. The uncut top of a signature.

collate. The process of sorting the pages of a publication in the proper order.

collating marks. A distinctive, numbered symbol printed on the folded edge of signatures to denote the correct gathering sequence.

comb, plastic binding. A curved or rake-shaped plastic strip inserted through slots punched along the binding edge of the sheet. It is used to hold the product together mechanically. See also: *mechanical binding.*

combination folder. (1) The in-line finishing component of a publication or book web offset press that uses at least three different folds, such as the jaw, former, and chopper folds, to cut and fold the printed web into signatures that are shipped to a bindery. (2) A binding machine that has both knife and buckle folding mechanisms.

converting. Any manufacturing or finishing operation completed after printing in order to form the printed item into the final product. Bagmaking, coating, waxing, laminating, folding, slitting, gluing, box manufacture, and diecutting are some examples. Converting units may be attached to the end of the press, or the operation may be handled by a special outside facility.

counter-stacker. A bindery device that gathers and piles books, newspapers, or printed signatures in predetermined quantities for storage or shipment.

cover nipper. The area in a perfect binder's cover feeder in which each cover is folded and then pushed around the spine.

covering. The process of pasting endpapers to a hardback book and drying them under pressure. See also: *casing-in; building-in.*

crash. A coarse fabric used to strengthen the joints of casebound books. It is placed over the binding edge of a book before it is cased-in to help hold the book within its cover.

creasing. (1) Pressing score lines into a book cover during binding. (2) Crimping or indenting along the binding edge of sheets or pages so that they will lie flat and bend easily.

creep. The slight but cumulative extension of the edges of each inserted spread or signature beyond the edges of the signature that encloses it. This results in a progressively smaller trim size on the inside pages. Alternative terms: *binder's creep; thrust; pushout.* See also: *shingling; wraparound.*

cross-direction. The position across the grain, or at a right angle to the machine direction. The stock is not as strong and is more susceptible to relative humidity in the cross-direction.

cross-grain. Folding at right angles to the binding edge of a book, or at a right angle to the direction of the grain in the paper stock. Folding the stock against the grain.

cross-perforation. A series of holes or slits pierced at a right angle to the direction of web travel to prevent the signature from bursting during folding.

cut score. A crease formed when the paper stock is partially slit.

demographic edition. A printed job, usually an advertising insert or sections of a magazine, that is targeted toward a specific consumer group within a defined geographic area.

die. (1) A pattern of sharp knives or metal tools used to stamp, cut, or emboss specific shapes, designs, and letters into a substrate. (2) A plate cut, etched, or embossed in intaglio to provide a raised impression on paper.

die, embossing. A heated or cold brass or steel tool that impresses a design in relief into a paper substrate. Unlike a cutting die, the edge is not sharp.

die board. The plywood base into which the steel rule dies are inserted.

die press. (1) A manually operated press that forms steel rules. (2) A machine that cuts the shape of the die into the substrate.

diecut. A printed subject cut to a specific shape with sharp steel rules on a press.

diecutting. Using sharp steel rules to slice paper or board to a specific shape on a printing press or specialized stamping press.

digest size. A publication with a final size of approximately $5\frac{1}{2} \times 7$ in. (139.7×177.8 mm).

double-sixteen. A folder that takes a thirty-two-page form and folds it as two separate or inserted sixteen-page forms.

double-thirty-two. A folder that takes a sixty-four-page form and folds it as two separate or inserted thirty-two-page forms.

dummy. A set of blank pages prepared to show the size, shape, form, and general appearance of a printed piece.

edge gilding. Coating the borders of book pages with gold leaf.

edge gluing. Applying a narrow strip of glue to the gutter of a book during binding.

edge staining. Coloring one or more of the trimmed ends of a book.

edition binding. See *case binding.*

embossing. Using impressed dies to print text or designs in relief on any one of a variety of paper stocks.

end leaf. A strong paper manufactured for the specific requirements of combining and securing the body of a book to its case. One leaf is pasted against the book's front cover and one against the back cover. The remaining four, six, or eight pages (flyleaves), which are made of the same heavy stock, separate the case from the text pages. These leaves may be marbleized or carry other ornamental printed designs. Alternative terms: *end papers; end sheets.*

end matter. The material printed at the end of a book, after the text proper, including appendixes, bibliographies, glossaries, indexes, etc. Alternative terms: *back matter; reference matter.*

film laminating. A finishing process in which a plastic film is bonded by heat and pressure to a printed sheet to enhance protection or appearance.

finishing. All postpress operations, including folding, trimming, assembling sections, and specialized tasks, such as diecutting and foil stamping.

flush cover. A book cover that has been trimmed to the same size as the text pages.

fold. Bending and creasing a sheet of paper as required to form a printed product.

fold marks. Guides on the original copy and printed sheet that indicate where a printed piece will be folded.

fold plates. Two smooth, flat metal sheets that receive the paper that has come through the buckling mechanism on buckle or combination folders during binding and finishing.

folder. The machine that bends and creases printed sheets of paper to particular specifications during binding and finishing. The process itself is called folding.

folder, quad. A machine that folds and delivers four sixteen-page signatures separately or as two thirty-two-page signatures from a single press sheet with sixty-four pages printed across it.

folder dummy. A mockup that shows the placement of page heads, the binding edge, and the gripper and side guide edges, as well as the page sequence and the arrangement of signatures.

folding endurance. The number of double folds a paper will withstand under tension and specified conditions before it breaks at the fold line.

folding to paper. Folding sheets without regard to alignment of headers, footers, and other images throughout the signatures.

folding to print. Folding sheets so that the headers, footers, and other image areas are aligned throughout the signatures.

foldout. An oversize leaf often a map, an illustration, or a table, folded to fit within the trim size of a book and tipped (pasted) in. See also *gatefold*.

folio. (1) In printing, a page number, often placed outside of the running head, at the top (head) of the page. See also: *header*. (2) In a descriptive bibliography, a leaf of a manuscript or early printed book, the two sides designated as "r" (recto or front) and "v" (verso or back). (3) Formerly, a book made from standard-size sheets folded once, each sheet forming two leaves, or four pages.

folio, blind. A folio counted in numbering pages but not printed.

folio, drop. In printing, a page number, often placed at the bottom (foot) of the page outside of the footer. See also: *footer*.

folio lap. See *lip*.

footer. A book's title or chapter title printed at the bottom of a page. A drop folio (page number) may or may not be included. Alternative term: *running foot*.

former. A smooth, triangular-shaped metal plate over which a printed web passes prior to entering the in-line folder. The former folds the moving web in half lengthwise. Alternative term: *former board*.

forwarding. Backing, rounding, shaping, lining up, and head banding, among other operations performed before a casebound book is covered.

french fold. A press sheet in which all of the pages are printed on one side and folded, first vertically and then horizontally, to produce a four-page signature. The blank side is folded inward before the other folds are made.

french stitch. A method of binding a prestitched booklet into a saddle-bound magazine.

front matter. The pages preceding the text of a book, including the title and copyright pages, the preface, foreword, table of contents, list of illustrations, and dedication.

frontispiece. An illustration facing the title page of a book; frequently printed on enamel paper and tipped (glued) in.

gatefold. A four-page insert that is larger than some dimension of the page and opens from each side of the center. See also: *foldout*.

gathering. Assembling a set of signatures sequentially.

gild. To apply gold or other metallic leaf to the trim edges of a book.

glue lap. The area of a printed package or container reserved for adhesive material used to fasten the folded carton.

glue pot. The container that holds the glue on a perfect binder. It contains a heating element to keep hot-melt glue at the proper temperature.

gluing-off. Applying glue to the spine of a book that is to be casebound. Gluing-off is performed after sewing and smashing, but before the book is trimmed.

gluing wheels. Devices that apply a small coating of glue to the binding edge of a sheet. Gluing wheels are sometimes used instead of stitching on small pamphlets.

grain direction. (1) In papermaking, the alignment of the fibers in the direction of web travel. (2) In printing, paper is said to be "grain-long" if the grain direction parallels the long dimension of the sheet. The paper is referred to as "grain-short" if it parallels the short dimension of the sheet.

guillotine cutter. A device with a long, heavy sloping blade that descends to a table or bed and slices through a stack of paper.

gusseting. Waviness or actual creases that form at the top of the inner pages of a closed-head signature.

gutter. In typography or bookbinding, the inside margin between facing pages, or the margin at the binding edge. Alternative terms: *gutter margin; back margin.*

hangout. The amount that the book block protrudes beneath the clamp on a perfect binder.

head. The top of a page, book, or printing form.

head margin. The distance between the top edge of the trimmed page and the top edge of the body of type (text matter) on a page.

head trim. The amount of paper that is cut off above the head margin; usually about ⅛ in. (3 mm).

headband. An ornamental strip of reinforced cotton or silk attached to the top and bottom of the inner back of a bound book.

head-to-head imposition. Arranging pages on a form during stripping so that the top of one page butts against the top of the opposite page.

head-to-tail imposition. Arranging pages on a form during stripping so that the top of one page butts against the bottom of the opposite page.

heat sealing. The converting operation in which two or more surfaces are fused together using specific heat, time, and pressure.

heat tunnel. On shrink wrap equipment, the heat unit that "shrinks" the plastic film around the product being wrapped.

imposition. Assembling the units of a page before printing and placing them on a form so that they will fold correctly.

imposition layout. A guide that indicates folding sequence, number of pages and signatures used, guide and gripper edges, and cutting and scoring lines for a specific job.

imprinting. Reproducing a few lines of type, such as a company name and address, on previously printed sheets.

indexing. In bookbinding, printing or affixing reference tabs along the edge of a book to mark the major divisions or subjects found within.

inkjet printing. A nonimpact printing process in which a stream of electrostatically charged microscopic ink droplets are projected onto a substrate at a high velocity from a pressurized system. Inkjet printing is used to personalize demographic mailings.

in-line finishing. Manufacturing operations such as numbering, addressing, sorting, folding, diecutting, and converting that are performed as part of a continuous operation right after the printing section on a press or on a single piece of equipment as part of the binding process.

insert. (1) A page that is printed separately and then bound into the main publication. (2) An advertising leaflet often on low-grade paper that is placed inside a periodical or newspaper.

insert, free-standing (FSI). A self-contained signature typically added to a newspaper.

jacket. The wrapper placed around a finished casebound book.

jog. To align flat, stacked sheets or signatures to a common edge, either manually or with a vibrating table or hopper. Some in-line finishing systems are equipped with a jogger-stacker that piles and aligns folded signatures as they are delivered.

joint. The flexible portion of a casebound book where the cover meets the spine. It functions as a hinge, permitting the cover to be opened and closed without damage to the spine. Alternative term: *hinge.*

knife. (1) In knife folding machines, the three or four blades at different levels and at right angles to each other that force the paper between the folding rollers. The sheet of paper is pushed from one knife folding mechanism to the other until the desired number of folds has been made. (2) A sharp steel blade that trims excess from sheets and/or cuts them to a specific size. Automatic trimmers and cutters have knives that are programmed to make precise cuts.

lay. The arrangement and position of printed forms on a press sheet.

leaf. (1) A separate, usually blank, sheet of paper in a book. (2) Pigmented stamping material used to decorate book edges.

letter fold. Creasing a sheet several times in the same direction with two or more creases wrapping around the inner leaf.

library binding. A book bound in conformance with the specifications of the American Library Association. The requirements include stitched signatures, sewn-on four-cord thread, strong end papers, muslin-reinforced endpapers, and flannel backlining extended into the boards.

lining. The reinforcing material pasted on the spine of a casebound book before the cover is applied.

lip. In saddle-stitched binding, the extended edge of one side of a signature that is gripped to open the signature to the center spread to facilitate inserting. Alternative terms: *lap; pickup.*

log. Signatures tightly compressed in a stack.

loop stitching. A method of saddle stitching whereby the stitch is formed into a semi-circular loop that sticks out beyond the spine of the publication. These loops slip over the rings of a three-ring binder, serving as an alternative to hole punching.

loose-leaf binding. A process in which individual sheets can be inserted and removed at will from a section of a larger document often held in a three-ring binder. Alternative term: *mechanical binding.*

margin. The white space extending from the edge of the printed image to a page's trim edge.

milling head. The device on a perfect binder that chops off the folded spines of the signatures to expose the individual sheets to the glue.

nailhead. A paper-covered book that is thickest at the spine. A book that has an end profile resembling a nail.

nip. A crease line at the joint of a case-bound book. It gives the book uniform bulk and reduces the swelling caused by the sewing thread. See also: *smash.*

nippers. In bookbinding, the flat irons on a "building-in" machine or casing-in line. When heated, nippers clamp the book joint, joining the case and the book at the base.

nipping. In binding, squeezing and clamping books or signatures after sewing or stitching to remove excess air and reduce the swell caused by stitching. Hard papers are nipped and soft pages are smashed. See also: *smash.*

notch binding. Small serrations cut in the spine of a perfect-bound book and filled with glue. This method eliminates the need to mill material off the spine of the book.

octavo. A sheet folded to form eight leaves or sixteen pages, or a book prepared from sheets so folded. The page size varies with the sheet dimensions, but this binding term is sometimes used to designate a page that is approximately 8×5 in. (203×127 mm). Alternative terms: *8vo; 8°.*

offline converting. Coating, cutting, folding, embossing, stamping, or otherwise altering newly printed sheets or rolls of material to form the final printed piece or product on a machine separate from the printing press. Printing plants may have dedicated converting equipment, or they may send the work to companies that specialize in converting. See also: *in-line finishing.*

overleaf. The other side of a page.

oversewing. A method of repairing casebound books in which the book is removed from its case and the spine is cut off. Loose pages are side-sewn in small groups, which are then tied together to form the new binding. In the final step, the book block is glued-off and returned to its case. An oversewn book does not open flat.

padding. Applying a flexible adhesive to one edge of a stack of clamped loose sheets to create a "pad" of sheets when the glue dries.

page. One side of a sheet or leaf of paper.

page flex. The stretching and strain that the pages of a bound book can withstand before coming loose from the binding.

page-pull test. A test that measures the force required to pull a page from the backbone of an adhesive-bound book.

paperback. An adhesive-bound book with a flexible paper cover. Alternative terms: *paper-bound; softcover.*

pebbling. Embossing paper after it has been printed to give it a rippled effect.

perfect binding. The use of glue to hold the pages of a book or magazine together. Alternative term: *adhesive binding.*

perforating. Punching a row of small holes or incisions into or through a sheet of paper to permit part of it to be detached; to guide in folding; to allow air to escape from signatures; or to prevent wrinkling when folding heavy papers.

pop-up. A sheet that is diecut, creased, and folded in two directions. It is flattened for delivery and, when opened, expands to form a three-dimensional image.

post binder. A looseleaf binding method in which straight rods instead of rings are used to hold the pages together. The binder can be expanded as the bulk of the contents increases. The front and back covers are separate pieces.

postpress. Term used to describe all activities that take place after presswork, specifically binding and finishing.

quarter binding. A method of casebinding in which two different materials are used for the front and back covers and the spine of a book; e.g., cloth or leather for the spine, and paper for the front and back covers.

quarto. (1) A sheet folded into four leaves or eight pages. (2) A booklet, or the pages of a book, formed by folding the sheets into four leaves, with a final size usually measuring about 12×9½ in. (304.8×241.3 mm). Alternative terms: *4to; 4°.*

rebind. To reassemble a book in its original form with its original case.

recto. The right-hand page of an open book, usually an odd-numbered page; sometimes the first or cover page. See also: *verso.*

roughening head. The cutting head on a perfect binder that prepares the backbone fibers for exposure to the glue.

rounding and backing. Shaping a book to fits its cover. Rounding gives books a convex spine and a concave fore-edge. Backing makes the spine wider than the thickness of the rest of the book to provide a shoulder against which the cardboard front and back covers rest. It also provides the hinge crease for the joints of the book. See also: *nip; smash.*

saddle stitch. Binding multiple sheets by opening the signatures in the center and gathering and stitching them with a wire through the fold line. The folded sheets rest on supports called saddles as they are transported through the stitcher. Booklets, brochures, and pamphlets are most often bound this way. Alternative terms: *saddle wire; wire stitch.*

saddle-sewn. Binding multiple sheets on a saddle stitcher with a thread instead of a wire.

self-cover. A cover composed of the same paper used for the inside text pages.

sewing. In bookbinding, fastening printed signatures together with needle and thread or cord.

shingling. Condition that results when the edges of the outside pages in a saddle-stitched book project out, nearer to the center. Alternative terms: *thrust; pushout.* See also: *creep.*

shrink wrap. Using heat to affix a thin plastic material around printed and bound products to prepare them for shipment.

side-sewing. A method of binding in which the entire book is sewn as a single unit, instead of as individual sections. Side-sewn books will not lie flat when open.

side-stitch. A method of binding in which the folded signatures or cut sheets are stitched along and through the side close to the gutter margin. The pages cannot be opened fully to lie flat.

signature. One or more printed sheets folded to form a section of a book or pamphlet.

smash. The heavy pressure used to compress a book so that it will have less bulk. See also: *nip; nipping.*

Smyth sewing. Bookbinding by sewing thread through the backfold of a signature and from signature to signature. This links the signatures together, while permitting the opened book to lay flat.

spine-see binding. A form of mechanical binding in which a continuous wire (corkscrew or spring coil) is run through round holes punched in the binding edge of the sheets. These bindings can be exposed, semiconcealed, or concealed.

spiral binding. A mechanical binding method in which a continuous wire coil is run through a series of closely spaced holes near the gutter margin of loose sheets.

spiral raceway. The section on a gathering machine in which the book block is stood on its spine for subsequent feeding into the perfect binder.

stacker. A device attached to the delivery conveyor of a web press that collects, compresses, and bundles printed signatures.

stacker, compensating/counter. A device that alternates the layering of a stack of printed products by turning them 180° to offset the uneven thickness between face and spine.

stamping. Using a die and often colored foil or gold leaf to press a design into a book cover, a sheet of paper, or another substrate. The die may be used alone (in blind stamping) if no color or other ornamentation is necessary. Special presses fitted with heating devices can stamp designs into book covers.

stitch. Binding printed matter by piercing the pages and securing them together with wire or thread.

sword. The part of a saddle stitcher feeder on which signatures are dropped for subsequent pickup by the chain pin. Alternative term: *bayonet.*

tip-in. Using an adhesive to attach a leaf, illustration, or foldout to a book.

tooling. Impressing book covers with a blind, gold leaf, or color design formed by a heated stamp or die.

trim. The excess area of a printed form or page in which instructions, register marks, and quality control devices are printed. The trim is cut off before binding.

trim marks. Guide marks on the original copy and the printed sheet to indicate where the sheet will be cut.

trim size. The final dimensions of a page.

trimmer, collecting. A machine that gathers two books, one on top of the other, and then trims them.

trimmer, three-knife. A cutting machine with three knives, two parallel and one at a right angle, used to trim the three unbound sides of a book or booklet in one pass. It operates automatically, usually at the end of a saddle stitcher, perfect binder, or casebinding system.

trim-out. The area between two books that is removed when a job bound two-up is cut apart by the fourth and fifth knife of a trimmer.

two-on binding. Term used to describe two books trimmed one on top of the other.

two-up binding. Binding two units at a time, then cutting them apart and trimming them.

work-and-tumble. An imposition (layout) in which the front and back of a form is printed from a single plate. After the first run through the press, the stock pile is inverted so that the back edge becomes the gripper edge for the second printing. Work-and-tumble differs from work-and-turn in that the gripper edge changes, often leading to misregister unless the stock has been accurately squared. Alternative terms: *work-and-flop; work-and-roll.*

work-and-turn. A common printing imposition or layout in which all the images on both sides of a press sheet are placed in such a way that when the sheet is turned over and the same gripper edge is used, one half of the sheet automatically backs up the previously printed half. When the sheet is cut in half parallel to the guide edge, two identical sheets are produced. Work-and-turn impositions are preferred over work-and-tumble impositions for accuracy because the same gripper edge and the same side of the press sheet are used to guide the sheet twice through the press.

work-and-twist. An imposition format in which a single film flat is used to produce two different images on a plate. After the first exposure, the flat is turned 180° to produce the second exposure.

wraparound. (1) A folio or insert placed around a signature before stitching and binding. (2) An increased gutter allowance for the outside pages of larger (thirty-two-, forty-eight-, and sixty-four-page) signatures to compensate for creep.

zip sorting. The process by which mail is separated according to destination and grouped into bundles. This is often completed during postpress.

Index

About the Authors

T.J. Tedesco is the president of Grow Sales, Inc. He has a Bachelor of Arts in English from Grinnell College and a Master of Business Administration in marketing and finance from Northeastern University, where he was class valedictorian. He is a well-known speaker in the graphic arts industry and is a regular columnist for *High Volume Printing*. In addition, he has had numerous articles published in dozens of other well-known graphic arts publications.

Prior to founding Grow Sales, Inc., T.J. was the director of marketing for a large graphic arts company and a product manager for a consumer products company. He also has sold graphic arts machinery, printing, and binding services. He started his career in finance with a Fortune 100 company. T.J. lives in Rockville, Maryland, and has all his teeth even though he still plays adult league hockey and baseball. He can be reached at 301-294-9900 or tj@growsales.com.

Dave Clossey is lead consultant for Grow Sales, Inc. He has a Bachelor of Arts in English from Goucher College and is pursuing a Master of Arts in publications design from The University of Baltimore. He has been a featured speaker at various graphic arts industry functions. Prior to joining Grow Sales, Inc., Dave was an editor at Cygnus Business Media.

Dave lives in Baltimore, Maryland, with his wife Lisa and can be reached at 301-294-9900 or dave@growsales.com. Dave was crazy enough to have played four years of college lacrosse…as goalie.

Jean-Marie Hershey is an accomplished writer and editor, as well as the director of Write Hand Communications, a graphic arts/public relations consultancy. She is a Phi Beta Kappa graduate of Skidmore College and holds a Master of Arts in literature from the University of Chicago and a Master of Fine Arts from Vermont College of Norwich University. The author of numerous published works of literary fiction, she is a former college teacher, as well as the cofounder and publicist of a jazz nightclub. She lives with her family near Roanoke, Virginia, and can be reached at 540-297-3556 or jmh@writehandcom.com.

About Grow Sales, Inc.

Since 1996, Grow Sales, Inc. has helped dozens of North American graphic arts companies achieve success. Grow Sales, Inc. offers an integrated, sustainable approach to generating business that involves merging marketing, public relations, web/graphic design, and executive coaching disciplines and has yielded solid results.

Grow Sales, Inc. was founded with three client objectives in mind:

- Win top-of-mind positioning
- Move the battlefield away from price
- Create irresistible relationships

For more information about Grow Sales, Inc., visit www.growsales.com or call 301-294-9900.

About PIA/GATF

The Graphic Arts Technical Foundation (GATF) and the Printing Industries of America, Inc. (PIA), along with its affiliates, deliver products and services that enhance the growth, efficiency, and profitability of its members and the industry through advocacy, education, research, and technical information.

The 1999 consolidation of PIA and GATF brought together two powerful partners: the world's largest graphic arts trade association representing an industry with more than 1 million employees and $156 billion in sales and a nonprofit, technical, scientific, and educational organization dedicated to the advancement of the graphic communications industries worldwide.

Founded in 1924, the Foundation's staff of researchers, educators, and technical specialists help members in more than 80 countries maintain their competitive edge by increasing productivity, print quality, process control, and environmental compliance and by implementing new techniques and technologies. Through conferences, Internet symposia, workshops, consulting, technical support, laboratory services, and publications, GATF strives to advance a global graphic communications community.

In continuous operation since 1887, PIA promotes programs, services, and an environment that helps its members operate profitably. Many of PIA's members are commercial printers, allied graphic arts firms such as electronic imaging companies, equipment manufacturers, and suppliers. To serve the unique needs of specific segments of the print and graphic communications industries, PIA developed special industry groups, sections, and councils. Each provides members with current information on their specific segment, helping them to meet the business challenges of a constantly changing environment. Special industry groups include the Web Offset Association (WOA), Graphic Arts Marketing Information Service (GAMIS), Label Printing Industries of America (LPIA), and Binding Industries of America International (BIA). The sections include Printing Industry Financial Executives (PIFE), Sales & Marketing Executives (S&ME), *EPS—the Digital Workflow Group (EPS)*, Digital Printing Council (DPC), and the E-Business Council (EBC).

The PIA/GATF*Press* publishes books on nearly every aspect of the field; training curricula; audiovisuals (CD-ROMs and videocassettes); and research and technology reports. It also publishes *GATFWorld,* a bimonthly magazine providing articles on industry technologies, trends, and practices, and PIA's *Management Portfolio,* a bimonthly magazine that provides information on business management practices for printers; economic trends, benchmarks, and forecasts; legislative and regulatory affairs; human and industrial relations issues; sales, marketing, and customer service techniques; and management resources.

For more information about PIA/GATF, special industry groups, sections, products, and services, visit *www.gain.net.*

About BIA

The Binding Industries Association represents graphic finishers, loose-leaf manufacturers, and suppliers to these industries throughout the United States, Canada, and Europe. Founded in 1955, BIA functions as a Special Industry Group of PIA/GATF. BIA helps its members with technical problems, offers information and evaluation on manufacturing equipment, provides credit and collection information, and assists with personnel problems, among other services.

Membership benefits in BIA include the following:

- *The Binding Edge,* published bimonthly, is BIA's official publication.
- *The Binder's Bulletin* is a monthly newsletter that keeps members updated on industry change. (A BIA members-only benefit.)
- BIA List Serve provides updates on industry news and networking.
- Member News (available online) is devoted to news and press releases provided by BIA members.
- Special Bulletins, including email updates on OSHA, NIOSHA, EEOC, environmental issues, survey results and information on other government agencies plus pertinent tax information.

For more information about the Bindery Industries of America, visit *www.gain.net.*

PIA/GATF*Press:* Selected Titles

Colophon

Binding, Finishing, and Mailing: The Final Word was edited, designed, and printed at PIA/GATF, headquartered in Sewickley, Pennsylvania. The authors wrote the manuscript using Microsoft Word and emailed it to PIA/GATF. The edited files were imported into QuarkXPress running on an Apple Power Macintosh G3. The primary typefaces for the interior are New Caledonia and Helvetica Condensed. Line drawings were created in Adobe Illustrator and Macromedia FreeHand, and photographs were scaled and cropped in Adobe Photoshop. Adobe Acrobat PDFs and page proofs produced on a Xerox Regal color copier with Splash RIP were used for author approval.

Upon completion of the editorial/page layout process, the illustrations were transmitted to PIA/GATF's Robert Howard Center for Imaging Excellence, where all images were adjusted for the printing parameters of PIA/GATF's in-house printing department and proofed.

After the book was preflighted using a Power Macintosh, Creo's Prinergy production system was used to impose the pages, and then the book was output to a Creo Trendsetter 3244 platesetter. The interior of the book was printed at PIA/GATF on a 26×40-in., four-color Heidelberg Speedmaster Model 102-4P sheetfed perfecting press, and the cover was printed two-up on a 20×28-in., six-color Komori Lithrone 28 sheetfed press with tower coater. The book was then sent to a trade bindery for case binding.